Plate 1. The Rhine River near Bingen, where Hildegard of Bingen (No. 17) wrote her religious verses and music. (Courtesy of the German Information Center)

LYRICS OF THE MIDDLE AGES

GARLAND REFERENCE LIBRARY
OF THE HUMANITIES
(VOL. 1268)

LYRICS OF THE MIDDLE AGES
AN ANTHOLOGY

Edited by James J. Wilhelm

Garland Publishing, Inc.
New York & London
1990

OTHER MEDIEVAL WORKS BY
THE AUTHOR

THE CRUELEST MONTH: SPRING, NATURE AND LOVE
IN CLASSICAL AND MEDIEVAL LYRICS
SEVEN TROUBADOURS: THE CREATORS OF MODERN VERSE
DANTE AND POUND: THE EPIC OF JUDGMENT
THE POETRY OF ARNAUT DANIEL
THE POETRY OF SORDELLO
IL MIGLIOR FABBRO: THE CULT OF THE DIFFICULT
IN DANIEL, DANTE AND POUND
THE ROMANCE OF ARTHUR, I, II, AND III

Library of Congress Cataloging-in-Publication Data

Lyrics of the Middle Ages : an anthology / edited by James J. Wilhelm
    p.   cm.   —(Garland reference library of the humanities ; v.
1268)
    Includes bibliographical references.
    ISBN 0-8240-3345-0.   —   ISBN 0-8240-7049-6 (pbk.)
    1. Poetry, Medieval.   I. Wilhelm, James J.   II. Series.
PN1601.L97   1990   89-25639
                                                                CIP

Printed on acid-free, 250-year-life paper
Manufactured in the United States of America

For all of my students of Provençal
at Rutgers

CONTENTS

[II] THE *CARMINA BURANA*

[III] PROVENÇAL LYRICS

[IV] ITALIAN LYRICS

[V] NORTH FRENCH LYRICS

[VI] GERMAN LYRICS

[VII] LYRICS OF IBERIA

A. ARABIC LYRICS (Translated by James T. Monroe)

B. HEBREW LYRICS (Translated by Miriam Billig)

C. MOZARABIC *KHARJAS* (Edited and translated by Samuel G. Armistead)

D. GALICIAN-PORTUGUESE LYRICS (Translated by James J. Wilhelm)

E. CASTILIAN LYRICS

F. CATALAN LYRICS (Translated by Nathaniel B. Smith)

[VIII] LYRICS OF GREAT BRITAIN

E. SCOTTISH-ENGLISH BALLADS

[IX] SELECTED ORIGINAL TEXTS

[X] INDICES

ACKNOWLEDGMENTS

Grateful acknowledgment is made to the Regents of the University of California for permission to reprint the translations of James T. Monroe (Nos. 200–206) from his *Hispano-Arabic Poetry: A Student Anthology* (© 1974), as well as to James T. Monroe and Deirdre Lashgari for permission to reprint their translation of No. 207 A and B from *Women Poets of the World* (Macmillan, 1983), ed. J. Bankier, D. Lashgari, and D. Earnshaw; also to the Center for Medieval and Early Renaissance Studies at the State University of New York at Binghamton for permission to reprint Richard M. Loomis's translations (Nos. 259–263) from his *Dafydd ap Gwilym: The Poems*, Vol. 9, in their Medieval and Renaissance Texts and Studies Series.

I would also like to thank the following editors and firms for their permission to print the following original texts in Section IX: Carl Winter Verlag for *Carmina Burana* Nos. 34, 38, and 40 from the edition of A. Hilka and O. Schumann, 1930–1978; Riccardo Ricciardi for No. 129 from *Petrarch*, ed. F. Neri et al.; C. H. Beck Verlag for Nos. 187 and 189 from *Die deutsche Literatur: Mittelalter*, ed. H. de Boor (copyright © 1965 by Oscar Beck); Librairie Honoré Champion for No. 157 from *Poésies de Charles d'Orléans*, ed. P. Champion, 1927; Clarendon Press, Oxford, for No. 112 from *Dante's Lyric Poetry*, ed. K. Foster and P. Boyde, 1967; Barbara Sargent-Baur for No. 168 from her edition of François Villon's *Le Testament et poésies diverses* (Appleton-Century-Crofts, 1967); Oxford University Press for Nos. 4, 20, and 21 from the *Oxford Book of Medieval Latin Verse*, ed. F. J. E. Raby, 1959, as well as for other rights of translation.

I would also like to thank the many editors of the Garland Library of Medieval Literature (see the listing at the end of this book) for permission to publish the following texts in Section IX: Gerald A. Bond for No. 45 from *The Poetry of William VII, Count of Poitiers, IX Duke of Aquitaine* (Vol. 4); George Wolf and Roy Rosenstein for No. 53 by Jaufre Rudel from *The Poetry of Cercamon and Jaufre Rudel* (Vol. 5); William D. Paden for No. 52 by Marcabru(n) from his *Medieval Pastourelle* (Vols. 34, 35); Frede Jensen for No. 91 by Giacomo da Lentini from his *Poetry of the Sicilian School* (Vol. 22) and for No. 236 by King Denis I from his *Earliest Portuguese Lyrics* (Odense University Press, 1978); Robert Edwards for No. 103 from his *Poetry of Guido Guinizelli* (Vol. 27); and Lowry Nelson, Jr., for No. 106 from his *Poetry of Guido Cavalcanti* (Vol. 18).

In addition, I would like to thank the following for permission to reprint my own translations from their volumes: Dell Publishing Co. and Angel

Flores for Nos. 46 and 69 from *Medieval Age*, ed. Flores, Copyright ©
1963; Random House and Angel Flores for Nos. 70, 71, 73, 105, and 119
from *An Anthology of Medieval Lyrics*, ed. Flores, Copyright © 1962; Yale
University Press for No. 55 from my *Cruelest Month*, 1965; and the Pennsylvania State University Press for the following from my *Seven Troubadours*, 1970: Nos. 43, 44, 49, 50, 51, 53, 54, 56–59, 63, 64, 68, 72, 75,
84–86.

In addition, I would like to thank the numerous editors and publishers
who have granted me free permission to translate their texts, which are cited
in the footnotes and introductions to the various chapters that follow.
Without their cooperation and generosity, this book could never have been
published.

PREFACE

When I decided to do a completely new version of my *Medieval Song* anthology of 1971, I consulted with numerous academicians about advisable changes. Most of these agreed that the book should be expanded to include the poetry of the Iberian Peninsula and some Celtic works. Since I do not have competence in most of these areas, I asked the following people to contribute their translations: James T. Monroe for Hispano-Arabic; Miriam Billig for Hispano-Hebrew; Samuel G. Armistead for Mozarabic *kharjas*; Nathaniel B. Smith for Catalan; Joseph Eska for Irish; and Richard M. Loomis for Welsh. I owe them all my deepest thanks, and have noted their contributions within.

In addition, I consulted with the following either for specific linguistic advice or for comments about the general structure of the book: Jan Ziolkowski, Frede Jensen, Philip B. Miller, George Wolf, Caroline D. Eckhardt, Valerie Lagorio, Michel-André Bossy, Thomas L. Wright, Roberta Bedor, Joseph Consoli, and Jon M. Tolman. Dale Demy read the manuscript with her usual skill and care, as did my editor, Gary Kuris.

From the start, it was my intention to focus more on Romance lyrics and to diminish the space given to hymns, but, as one can see from the Index of Selected Genres at the end, the hymn is not meagerly represented. I also decided to increase the writings of women, augmenting the number from only two in the first volume to nine (see the asterisked items in the Index of Authors). More attention is also paid here to such developments as *trobar clus* (hermetic composition), as in Poems 61 to 63 and 76 to 78. Photographs have been added, not as mere window dressing, but to show the locales native to some of the poets.

As in the preceding volume, some original texts are contained in Section IX. References to music can be found in many of the notes with some discographic information in an area that is controversial and constantly changing.

Rutgers University   J. J. W.

Lyrics of the Middle Ages

[I] LATIN HYMNS AND LYRICS FROM 850 TO 1300

Although the main purpose of this anthology is to present the vernacular secular lyric, one cannot ignore Latin literature in the Middle Ages and the influence of the hymn. Any starting point is somewhat arbitrary, but the year 850 has been selected because by that time Europe had experienced the Carolingian Revival under King Charlemagne, and a new spirit of humanism was operating under the mystical Christianity that had dominated thought for centuries.

The anthology begins with Gottschalk, whose moving poem to a young novice prefigures the love poetry that had been silent since the end of the Roman Empire, but which would break forth with renewed energy in the eleventh and twelfth centuries. A poem often called the first love poem of the modern world, *O admirabile Veneris idolum* (No. 4), follows hard on Gottschalk's work. With the *Cambridge Songs*, collected in the eleventh century (Nos. 9 to 11), we feel a new sense of romance stirring into being— with debts to the Roman poet Ovid and the Song of Songs in the Bible.

As both Erich Auerbach and Northrop Frye have shown, the new romanticism shares much of the same spirit as religion, and religious literature itself becomes humanized. The dignified Virgin of No. 8 becomes the emotional mother of No. 21, as the metaphysical Passion adapts itself to the individual passion. The struggle between an affirming self and an idealized Other can be seen especially in the Lament of the Nun (No. 15), and in the homosexual poetry (No. 13). Even the beautiful Hymn to Nature (No. 18) by Alan of Lille is inspired because the author fears the workings of egotistical sexuality.

The poems in this section clearly establish many of the basic genres of the Middle Ages: the dramatic Trope (No. 6), the Dawn Song (No. 7), the Pastourelle (No. 14), the Debate Poem (No. 19), and the Threnody or Planctus (No. 20). In almost every case, one can see the Latin preceding the vernacular developments or existing side by side with them. Latin went on after the year 1300, but by this time most of the works had become secular and were more Renaissance in spirit than medieval.

Unless otherwise indicated, the selections in this section were translated from the *Oxford Book of Medieval Latin Verse*, edited by F. J. E. Raby (Oxford U. P., 1959). For the connection between religion and romance, see Northrop Frye's *Anatomy of Criticism* (Princeton U. P., 1957); Erich Auerbach's "Gloria passionis" in *Literary Language and Its Public . . .* (Eng. trans., Pantheon, 1965, pp. 33 ff.); and Peter Dronke, *Medieval Latin and the Rise of European Love-Lyric*, 2 vols. (Oxford U. P., 2nd ed., 1968). For bibliographic information, *Initia carminum latinorum*, ed. D. Schaller and E. Könsgen (Göttingen, 1977).

GOTTSCHALK

---

[1] *Ut quid jubes, pusiole*

1. Why do you order, little laddie,
    Why command me, little son,
        Telling me to sing a sweet song
        When I'm exiled far away
            Out at sea?   5
    Why do you order me to sing?

2. Better for me, poor little young one,
    To do some weeping, little boy-child;
        I'm for descant, not for chanting
        The kind of song that you demand,   10
            My sweet dear one.
    Why do you order me to sing?

3. You know I'd rather, little lad,
    Have you join me, brother of mine,
        Weeping with a ready heart,   15
        Sharing now my heavy mind
            In lamentations.
    Why do you order me to sing?

4. Well you know, divine novitiate,
    You know, heavenly protégé,   20
        I have been here long in exile
        Many nights and many days
            Always suffering.
    Why do you order me to sing? . . .

7. Yet since you desire it so strongly,   25
    Finest companion for a man,
        I shall sing to the Son and Father
        And of the Spirit that always runs
            Out of them both.
    This I'll sing voluntarily.   30

1. Or Godescalc (*ca.* 805–869). German monk whose aristocratic Saxon father placed him in the Monastery of Fulda at a young age. He tried unsuccessfully to get out, but was refused. Later at Orbais he wrote an inflammatory treatise in which he pronounced pre-Calvinistic views of man's predestination. Bitterly attacked by Hrabanus Maurus and John Scotus Erigena (who committed the opposite heresy of denying ultimate judgments). Apparently died after long imprisonment, when this Complaint was written to a young monk who had asked him for a song. Every one of the lines rhymes with *-e*. I have omitted the rather digressive fifth and sixth stanzas, which compare the captivity of the Jews with the poet's exile. Raby uses as incipit *O cur jubes, pusiole*, No. 92.

8. Blesséd art thou, holy Master,
    Father, Son, and Paraclete,
    God of might, of majesty,
        Just Divinity.
    This I *will* sing willingly.   35

SEDULIUS SCOTTUS

---

[2] *Nunc viridant segetes, nunc florent germine campi*

1. Now the grain is green, now field-grass is in flower;
   Now the vines are heavy; now's the best of the year;
   Now colored birds soothe the heavens with their songs;
   Now sea, now earth, now stars in the sky are laughing.

2. But not one drop disturbs me with sad-making swill,   5
   Since Mead and Beer and the gifts of Bacchus I lack.
   Alas! how I miss the multiple substance of flesh
   Which is born on the tender earth, in the dew-filled air.

3. I'm a writer (confession!), a musician, Orpheus Junior.
   I'm a treadmill ox. I wish you whatever you will.   10
   I'm your soldier of God armed with the weapons of Wisdom.
   For me, O Muse, beg the good Bishop for alms.

[3] *Aut lego vel scribo, doceo scrutorve sophiam*

I read or write; I teach or I study wisdom.
   I obey the Heaven-throned One both night and day.
I eat, I imbibe, and rhyming invoke the Muses;
   Asleep I snore; awake to my God I pray.
My mind, conscious of its crimes, mourns sinful mortality: 5
   Have mercy, O Christ and Mary, on miserable me.

2. Sedulius Scottus, Scotus (*fl.* 848–874). Irishman summoned to the continent by Emperor Charles the Bald in 848. He settled for a time with Bishop Hartgar of Liège, to whom this Begging Poem is directed. No. 3 is a Confessional Poem.

ANONYMOUS LOVE SONG

[4*] *O admirabile Veneris idolum*

1. O admirable image of Venus,
    Of whose material nothing is frivolous:
    May the Ruler protect thee who set stars and poles
    And fashioned the waters and made the earth whole;
    May the cunning of thievery never come near to thee   5
    And Clotho, who bears the distaff, look on thee tenderly.

2. "Please save this young man" without hypocrisy
    I cry to Lachesis, sister of Atropos,
    With fervent heart not to cut him away.
    May you have Neptune and Lady Thetis   10
    As guides as you sail on the River Adige.
    Where, I ask, are you fleeing, since I love you?
    What shall I do when I in misery can't see you?

3. Hard-shelled matter created mankind
    From Mother Earth's bones as stones were tossed down;   15
    This one boy-child was born out of these,
    Since he pays no attention to tears and sighs.
    As long as I'm desolate, my rival will be happy,
    While I bellow like a hind whose young stag runs away.

    4. (Circa 900). Contained in a Verona manuscript and in the *Cambridge Songs*, Nos. 9–11, with neums to indicate music: consult RCA Victor LM 6015(2). The same tune was used for *O Roma nobilis*, which follows. Long considered the first love song of the modern world. Graecisms abound, showing a learned author, probably male. Clotho is one of the three Fates who measure life, with Lachesis the spinner and Atropos the thread-cutter.
    *See Section IX for original text.

ANONYMOUS HYMN TO ROME

[5] *O Roma nobilis, orbis et domina*

1. O noble Rome, most wonderful mistress
   Of all cities in all of the world,
   Running crimson with the red blood of martyrs,
   Resplendent with the white lilies of virgins,
   We wish you good health in all things   5
   And we bless you—hail through the ages!

2. Peter, you supreme key-giver to the heavens,
   Hear our vows as we pray constantly
   When you sit supreme as judge of the twelve tribes;
   Becoming placable, judge them leniently   10
   And as we beg you now at this time,
   Cast your vote for us mercifully.

3. O Paul, accept these prayers of ours—
   You whose hard work crushed the philosophers;
   Now the steward of the heavenly palace,   15
   Serve up courses of the divine gift,
   So that whatever Holy Wisdom replenished you with,
   You may now fill us entirely with your teachings.

ANONYMOUS TROPE

[6] *Quem quaeritis in sepulchro*

ANGEL:
Whom are you seeking in the tomb, O Christ-worshipers?

THREE WOMEN:
Jesus the Nazarene crucified, O dweller in heaven.

5. (Circa 900). Long considered a Pilgrim Song, but without proof. This and No. 4, sharing the same tune, are North Italian in origin. Both show in their monorhymed stanzas a rhythmic beat that was vying with Latin quantitative meter.

6. Dramatic dialogue from the Easter Mass (late 800s). Consult RCA Victor LM 6015(2), which contains the music and text; for a shortened version, Raby, *Oxford Book*, No. 99, which pluralizes the Angels. See Karl Young, *The Drama of the Medieval Church* (Oxford, 1933), I, 201 ff.

ANGEL:
He is not here; he has risen, just as he foretold.
Go now, announce that he has arisen, and say—

THREE WOMEN:
Alleluia, he has risen, our God, today,   5
A lion strong, Christ Son of God;
Give thanks to God, exclaiming *eia!*

ANGEL:
Come and see the place where your Lord was put.
Alleluia, alleluia. Go quick and tell the disciples
Your Master has arisen. Alleluia, alleluia.   10

THREE WOMEN:
Our Lord has risen from the tomb
Who hanged for us upon the Cross.
            Alleluia.

BILINGUAL DAWN SONG

[7*] *Phoebi claro nondum orto iubare*

1. When the clear radiance of Phoebus has not yet risen,
   Aurora covers the earth with her faint light;
   A watchman shouts to the lazy ones: "Arise!"
       Dawn over the humid sea draws on the sun;
       The vigil's over! Watch the shadows brighten!   5

2. Look at the treacherous enemies as they burst out
   To ambush the unwary as they laze,
   Although the herald's cry urges them to rise.
       Dawn over the humid sea draws on the sun;
       The vigil's over! Watch the shadows brighten!   10

   7. (900s). Latin Dawn Song, with refrain in Provençal, one of the earliest specimens of the
language. Found only in Vatican Regina 1462, which is largely a legal dictionary, it blends
Christian and classical rhetoric, recalling St. Ambrose's *Aeterne rerum conditor* and Ovid's
dawn songs in his *Amores* (I.6, 13). The Dipper in 13 could be the Bear or the Plough.
   *Original text in Section IX, taken from E. Monaci, *Facsimili di Antichi Manoscritti* (1892),
p. 57.

3. The North Wind from Arcturus now is loosed,
   As stars now are hiding their heavenly rays;
   The Dipper is dropping closer toward the sunrise.
   Dawn over the humid sea draws on the sun;
   The vigil's over! Watch the shadows brighten! 15

ANONYMOUS HYMN TO THE VIRGIN

---

[8] *Alma redemptoris mater, quae pervia caeli*

Blessèd mother of the Redeemer, who remains for us
The open gateway to Heaven and the star of the sea,
Help those falling who care to rise,
You who, with Nature gaping, gave birth to your own holy parent,
Virgin before and after, receiving that Ave 5
From the mouth of Gabriel: take pity on us sinners!

THREE CAMBRIDGE SONGS

---

[9] *Vestiunt silve tenera ramorum*

1. The woods are dressing their branches
   With tender spray, weighted with fruit buds.
   High overhead the pigeons are crooning
       Tunes for us all.

2. The turtledove's groaning; the thrush sings lushly; 5
   The age-old cry of the blackbird twangs again;

8. (1000s?). Antiphon (hymn sung in responsive parts) showing the growth of Mariolatry. Medieval writers liked to note that AVE (hail) is EVA spelled backwards, as Mary redeemed the original sinner. Tape: Philips 420879-2.

9. A collection made about 1050 of poems written earlier, some in the 900s. Contained in a manuscript in Cambridge, England, that was once housed in the Monastery of St. Augustine in Canterbury, possibly deriving from German sources. The collection contains selections from Horace and Vergil, laments for deceased monarchs, hymns, a *fabliau* (obscene narrative), and the text of No. 4. Edited by Walther Bulst (Winter, 1950). The last stanza may have been added by another hand.

The sparrow's not quiet, but high under the elm leaf
  Strikes with a chuckle.

3. Here now the nightingale's happy in green-leaf,
   While with syllables long on the night breeze   10
   The kite in his ceremonious quaver
       Sets air aquiver.

4. The eagle soars to the stars, as through fields
   The lark looses many a trill of a song,
   Oft plunging down, striking a different key,   15
       Before touching ground.

5. Swift swallows force out raspings in unison;
   Jackdaw jaws; the quail's wail echoes;
   Thus all of the birds together are offering
       Everywhere summer songs.   20

6. But none of these creatures is like the bee,
   Who embodies the ideal of chastity—
   Only Mary, who carried Christ in her womb
       Untouched by man.

[10] *Iam, dulcis amica, venito*

MAN:
1. Now, my sweet girl friend, come—
   I love you like my very own heart.
   Come inside my cubicle door,
   Where I have ornaments galore.

2. There you'll find some couches spread,   5
   Tapestries hung up overhead,
   Flowers sprinkled everywhere
   With fragrant herbs to spice the air.

3. A table laid out you will find,
   Weighted with food of every kind;   10
   There the sparkling wine will pour
   And whatever, dear, you adore.

4. There you'll hear chamber music soft,
   And flutes will raise their shrills aloft,
   A learned girl, a little boy   15
   Will offer songs that you'll enjoy.

10. Dialogue Poem, often called "Invitation to the Beloved." Severely effaced by a monk
who considered it sacrilegious. Restored by E. P. Vuolo, *Cultura Neolatina*, *10* (1950), 5–25.
Much indebted to the Song of Songs. The rhyme scheme is roughly *aabb*, but imperfect. A
melody survives.

3. O how blesséd I would be
   If, by finding someone else,   10
   As is the custom these days,
   I could slough off this current love!

4. But I'll succeed, I do believe,
   And I'm yielding myself as your prey;   15
   I'm the spoils, and you the spoiler,
   And I gladly surrender to such a thief.

5. Even the Ruler of the gods above
   Was once a kidnaper of young men;
   If he were here, he would surely snatch
   Your beautiful form to his heavenly bed.   20

6. In his great palace up on high,
   You could render him double duty:
   At night in bed, pouring drinks by day
   You could wholly please our great Jove.

WALTER OF CHÂTILLON

---

[14] *Declinante frigore*

1. As the winter cold was waning
   And the face of the land grew colored,
   The earth began to pay us back
   For our long loan with interest.
   Rising up during that season   5
   At an hour when night had just passed,
   I took a place beneath a tree.

2. Under that broad-spreading elm
   There flowed a talkative brook;

14. French: Gauthier de Châtillon (*ca.* 1135–1184). Born at Lille, but took his name from a French town where he taught. He wrote his epic *Alexandreis* in Reims and died in Amiens. Glycerium (line 20) is a name from Roman comedies. This Pastourelle owes much to Ovid: see William D. Paden, *The Medieval Pastourelle*, 2 vols. (Garland, 1987), I, No. 12, who translates the last line "Flattery will get you anywhere!" (*predicatus vincitur*). I attempt a subject-predicate pun (Walter was a grammarian, after all). Some emend *predicatus* to *pedicatus* and translate: "Pederasty is overcome."

5. He'll pluck a plectrum on his cithara;
   A lyre will strike a melody with her.
   Serving men then will offer up
   Winebowls brimming to painted cups.   20

GIRL(?):
6. But all this carousing is not my care;
   It's the talking later I hold dear.
   It's not the richness of the material,
   Dear familiarity is all I will.

MAN:
7. Come now, my chosen sister, the best   25
   Delight for me, before all the rest,
   Shining light to his pupil of mine,
   Greater part of this soul divine!

GIRL:
8. I walked alone through forest spaces,
   Delighting in those hidden places;   30
   How often I fled the vulgar classes,
   Trying to avoid the common masses.

MAN:
9. Snow and ice are no more to be seen.
   Flowers and grass are growing green.
   Philomela high up takes her part: 35
   Love burns in the cavern of my heart.

10. O dearest one, please don't delay!
    Be eager—yes, love me right away!
    Without you I just can't fend;
    We must carry our love to the end.   40

11. Why keep deferring, my elect one,
    Things that later will have to be done?
    Do quickly everything you have to do.
    Me—I'm ready anytime for you!

[11] *Levis exsurgit Zephirus*

1. Now Zephyr's rising lightly
   While Sun comes on more brightly;
   Now Earth is opening up her lap
   And everything's aflow with sap.

2. Scarlet Spring comes walking out   5
   With gaudy clothes wrapped about,

11. Complaint to Spring. Escaped mutilation perhaps because of its melancholy tone and allegorical possibilities. Written in Ambrosian stanzas with the regular rhyme *aabb*.

Sprinkling land with many flowers,
Hanging fronds on woodland bowers.

3. Four-footed beasts prepare their lairs
While nests are formed for those in air; 10
On every branch among the wood
The fowls are singing: joy is good.

4. But what my ears explain to me
And what my eyes force me to see—
Alas!—in the midst of this happiness 15
Fill me instead with sorrowfulness.

5. For here I'm sitting all alone,
Considering life, as white as stone.
And the minute that I lift my head
Every sound and sight is fled. 20

6. You at least, for the sake of the Spring,
Go out and walk, considering
The fronds and flowers and the grain—
This soul of mine is sick with pain.

PETER ABELARD

[12] *O quanta qualia sunt illa Sabbata*

1. How mighty, how manifold those holy Sabbaths
Which forever are held in the curia on high!
What rest for the weary, what prize for the valiant,
When God will be everywhere through everybody!

2. That heavenly city is truly Jerusalem, 5
Whose peace is forever, whose pleasure's supreme,
Where desire never goes beyond its object
And reward is not despised as short of its goal.

12. Pierre Abélard (1079–1142). Famous French philosopher and teacher whose tragic love affair with Heloise is well known. This Hymn to the Eternal Sabbath, meant to be sung at Saturday Vespers, was written at her request for use in the Abbey of the Paraclete, which was built by Abelard but handed over to Heloise to direct as abbess. Composed in rhymed pairs of accentual dactyls grouped into quatrains.

3. Of that King and his kingdom, his marvelous palace,
The peace and repose and the pleasure found there— 10
O tell us, partakers of that heavenly glory,
If tongue can transcribe what things they experienced there.

4. But meanwhile our duty is to lift our spirits
And seek our homeland in all of our prayers:
To go back to Jerusalem, leave Babylonia, 15
And return from our exile at long last.

5. There when all troubles have come to an ending
Let us sing songs of Zion secure and carefree;
Rendering thanks endless for the granting of graces
This blesséd folk offers praise to you, Lord. 20

6. There shall a Sabbath succeed every Sabbath,
The joy of the day-resters last ever-long;
Jubilation unceasing will be there ineffable
Which we and the angels express in our songs.

7. To the Master Almighty be glory eternal, 25
From whom, through whom, in whom all things flow;
The source is the Father and through him the Son,
And in him the Holy Spirit of both.

HILARY THE ENGLISHMAN

[13] *Puer decus, decor floris*

1. Beautiful boy, with the beauty of flowers,
My glittering jewel, I would like you to know
That the radiance of your visage
Was for me a torch of love.

2. As soon as I saw you, immediately 5
Desire struck me—but with despair,
For my Dido is now restraining me
And greatly do I fear her wrath.

13. Latin: Hilarius Anglicus (first half of 12th century). Studied at the Hermitage of the Paraclete under Peter Abelard in 1125. For this and other homosexual poems, see *Medieval Latin Poems of Male Love and Friendship*, trans. Thomas Stehling (Garland, 1984). This poem, which is monorhymed in each stanza, compares the beloved to Dido, Queen of Carthage, who detained Aeneas from his divine mission to found Rome, and Ganymede, the young cupbearer abducted by Jove. Text by N. M. Häring, *Studi Medievali*, 17 (1976), 915–968.

Spring in those fields was offering 10
Shady umbrellas along the streams
That flowed in every place
Casting drops of spray
That hung from the bushes nearby.

3. As the choirings of the birds 15
And the whisperings of the streams
With the babbling of that brook
That ran through that mountainous dale
Lifted away my weariness,
Suddenly I saw Glycerium coming 20
With her bosom all exposed.

4. A glittering head-dress
Of multifaceted craftsmanship
Was dangling from her head,
Trimmed with vair. 25
Her dress, which was dyed
With Tyrian purple,
Was finely embroidered.

5. Her face looked completely untarnished
And her lips were very tender. 30
"Come!" I said. "To me you are
The most desirable of women;
You're my heart and my soul,
A lily whose very image
Nurtures my innermost parts. 35

6. "I always yearn for you;
Scarcely can I control my desire;
Whatever I try to do—
Whether reading or writing—
I shall be crucified (rightly so) 40
Unless you let me enjoy
What I constantly covet."

7. She was broken by these words;
She sat down upon the grass
Under those lacy leaves, 45
Scarcely able to stand any delay,
As she was compelled to be my subject.
Who doesn't know all the rest?
Predicates with praise conquer!

ANONYMOUS LAMENT OF A NUN

[15] *Plangit nonna fletibus*

1. The nun laments with tears
   That can't be told,
   Grieving with sighs,
   Saying to her companions:
   "Alas, poor me!   5
   Nothing could be worse
   Than such a life,
   For although I feel lusty
   And lascivious,

2. "I ring the bell,   10
   I recite my psalms,
   I abandon my welcomed sleep
   Even when I want to sleep—
   Alas, poor me!
   All night long, I keep my vigil   15
   When I don't want to;
   Instead, the thing I'd most like to do
   Is: hug a young man!"

ANONYMOUS SONG FOR THE FEAST OF FOOLS

[16] *Gregis pastor Tityrus*

1. Tityrus, the shepherd of our flock,
   The Lord of Asses,
   Is our bishop.
       Eia, eia, eia!
       The banquet of Tityrus   5
       Is calling us to joy!

15. (1100s). Continues with some indecipherable verses; this theme is common in vernacular verse. See No. 238; cf. No. 98.
16. (1100s). On the Feast of the Circumcision, Jan. 1, the lower clergy in many French cities elected a Lord of Asses, who was given a staff to lead celebrants along with a jackass into the cathedral for a banquet. Tityrus is a pastoral name from Vergil's *Eclogues*.

2. In honor of Tityrus
   Let all bigwigs and jackasses
   Celebrate the Feast of the Staff.
   Eia, eia, eia! . . .   10

3. Let us celebrate our Tityrus
   With melodies and strings,
   With an organ and a drum.
   Eia, eia, eia! . . .

4. Let us worship our Tityrus,   15
   Who invites us with his staff
   To a marvelous banquet.
   Eia, eia, eia!. . .

HILDEGARD OF BINGEN

[17] *De Sancta Maria: O viridissima virga, ave*

O greenest branch, hail! You budded
In the wintry blasts of the inquiries of the holy.
When the time was ripe, you flowered
Into full form; so hail to you, hail!
Because the heat of the sun brought forth from you   5
Vapors with the scent of balsam;
Yes, a beautiful flower sprouted in you
Which spread perfume to all the spice-trees
That were dry, and they all appeared full green!
After this, the heavens spread dew on the grass,   10
And all of the earth was made merry
Because its womb gave forth grain,
While the birds nested upon it;
And so food was produced for men
And abounding joy for all feasters.   15
And so, my gentle Virgin, you lack no joy
From all of the things that Eva once spurned.
Now let us lift our praises to the Highest!

17. Hildegard von Bingen (1098–1179). Benedictine mystic from the Rhineland; in 1136 abbess of a community near Mainz and after 1151 near Bingen. Wrote *Scivias* (Know the Ways; 1141–1151), the music drama *Ordo Virtutum* (The Order of Virtues), and more than 75 songs and lyrics; distinguished for the way that she honors nature and especially greenness. See her *Book of Divine Works with Letters and Songs*, ed. Matthew Fox (Bear, 1987), pp. 376–379 for text and music.

ALAN OF LILLE

[*18*] *O Dei proles, genetrixque rerum*

1. O offspring of God and mother of all things,
   Chain of world-being and stable bond,
   Jewel for the earthbound, mirror for the fallen,
       Light-bearer of the world,

2. Peace, love, virtue, governing, power,   5
   Order, law, the way and the ending, light and source,
   Life, glory, splendor, beauty and form,
       Model for the world,

3. Who, controlling the earth with your reins,
   Binds all things that are held here together   10
   With a peaceful tie, for with a bond of peace
       You wed heaven and earth.

4. You, gathering the pure ideas of Nous (Mind),
   Coin the individual species of things,
   Clothing all matter with form and shaping the cloak   15
       Of form with your finger.

5. The heavens look with favor on you, and the air attends you,
   While the land worships you, and water reveres you;
   Treating you as mistress of the world, everything
       Pays you tribute.   20

6. You link each day to each night in turn,
   Providing the candle of the sun for the daytime
   And at night stilling the clouds with the clear mirror
       Of the moon.

7. You gild the poles with their various stars,   25
   Making the realm of the atmosphere bright and fair,
   Filling the heavens with your jeweled stars
       And your armies of constellations.

18. Or Alain de Lille, Alanus de Insulis (*ca.* 1128–*ca.* 1202), French Scholastic philosopher called "the Universal Doctor"; interested in Aristotelian developments, but his imagination was primarily Neoplatonic, as revealed in this praise of Nature, taken from his *De Planctu Naturae* (*Plaint of Nature*, trans. J. J. Sheridan, Toronto, 1980), a complaint against humankind's violations of the rules of Nature, especially in homosexuality. Also wrote the encyclopedic *Anticlaudian* (trans. J. J. Sheridan, Toronto, 1973).

8. Proteus-like you change the face of the sky
   By adding new figures, donating both breath   30
   And bodies to our region of the air,
         Binding all with laws;

9. At your nod, the world grows young again;
   The forest waves its leafy head of hair,
   And the land grows proud as it puts on its   35
         Tunic of flowers.

10. You release and repress the threats of the sea,
    Truncating the furious rushing of its storm,
    So that the force of the waters can never succeed
          In burying our land.   40

PHILIP THE CHANCELLOR

---

[19] *Quisquis cordis et oculi*

1. Whoever does not sense the strife
   Between the Heart and the Eye
   Is not aware of their incitements
   Or how they act as seedbeds of sin,
   Nor can they know the grounds for danger   5
   Because these two alternate their charges
   So that recklessly and contentiously
   They can hurl back vices on each other.

2. The Heart addresses the Eye like this:
   "You are the beginning of all our evil,   10
   The nourisher and the instigator,
   And I call you the messenger of death;
   You, the doorman of my mansion,
   Do not keep the enemy away from our gates;
   Instead, like a friendly betrayer,   15
   You let the adversary enter.

19. Or Philippe de Paris (d. 1236). Famous for writing a variety of poems. This Debate Between the Heart and the Eye is well known; see *Medieval Debate Poetry: Vernacular Works*, ed. and trans. Michel-André Bossy (Garland, 1987), pp. 48 ff., for a French version and the genre in general.

3. "Can't you be called the window
   Through which death enters the soul?
   Don't you always pursue what you see,
   Like an ox being led to slaughter?   20
   Why don't you just once wash clean
   The filth you acquire with some tears?
   Or why don't you get rid of it totally
   By fermenting an unleavened mind?"

4. The Eye replies to the Heart: 25
   "You complain unjustly about me;
   I am your dutiful servant;
   I carry out whatever you order;
   Don't you always order me
   The way you do to your other members?   30
   I'm not your betrayer; you are.
   I'm just a messenger for wherever you send me.

5. "Why is this opening that is so necessary
   For the body's functions so maligned,
   Since without my obsequiousness   35
   Every single duty would fail?
   If there occurs some creeping-in
   (Since I'm just a glassy window)
   And if I report what I have suffered,
   How can you consider this an injury?   40

6. "I shall add that you are not contaminated
   By any dust that I let in,
   And no evil act can wound you
   Unless you consent to allow it.
   Evil acts proceed from the heart,   45
   And you won't let anything go against your will.
   Your powers will never falter
   Unless you yourself commit the fault."

7. While the two were disputing together,
   They loosed a kiss of peace   50
   As Reason cut off their quarrel
   With some definitive reasoning.
   She decided that they both were guilty
   But not in an equal way,
   For she attributed the cause to the Heart   55
   And the occasion to the Eye.

THOMAS OF CELANO

[20*] *Dies irae, dies illa*

1. Day of vengeance, ah, that day!
   When the world shall burn away,
   As David and the Sibyl say.

2. Ah, the trembling! ah, the fearing
   As the Judge to us is nearing,　　　　　　　　　5
   Our world in pieces strict to lay.

3. Trumpets sprinkling awesome soundings
   In the graveyards and surroundings
   Will drive us all before the throne.

4. Death stands gaping, as does Nature;　　　　　10
   While arises every creature
   Facing the judge to atone.

5. Out will come the written books
   Where our actions yield to looks
   As the world is judged in fame.　　　　　　　15

6. As the Judge to judgment's veering
   All that's latent is appearing,
   Nothing hidden will remain.

7. Ah, poor me! what shall I mutter?
   To what patron shall I stutter?　　　　　　　20
   Since scarcely just men can be sure?

8. Monarch of mighty majesty,
   Who frees the men who should be free,
   Save me, fountain of the pure!

9. Ah, remember, loving Christ,　　　　　　　　25
   I'm the causer of your life—
   Don't abandon me that day!

20. Tommaso di Celano (*ca.* 1200–*ca.* 1255). Attribution of this Hymn for the Funeral Mass sometimes questioned, but it is usually ascribed to this biographer of St. Francis and staunch member of the Franciscan Order. The latter part of the poem seems to have been added in the transition from personal hymn to sequence for the Requiem Mass. Strong monorhymed tercets. See Kees Vellekoop, *Dies ire . . .* (Bilthoven, 1978).

*Original text appears in Section IX, taken from *Analecta Hymnica, 21*, No. 157.

10. Seeking me, you sat all weary;
    Suffered Passion to come near me;
    This labor must not fade away.   30

11. O just judger of perdition,
    Give my soul gift of remission
    Before the issue of the Word!

12. I am groaning like one guilty;
    Redness now has overspilled me—   35
    Spare this kneeling man, O Lord!

13. You made Mary innocent,
    Heard the thief make his lament,
    Allowed me too some hope to earn.

14. All my prayers sound so lowly,   40
    But be kindly and be holy
    Lest in endless ash I burn!

15. Put me with your shriven sheep,
    No company with goats I'll keep,
    Standing ever at your right hand.   45

16. Let all evil be confounded
    And with dire flames surrounded:
    Summon me with the saved to stand.

17. I beg humbly, I beg bending,
    Heart worn like an ember spending: 50
    God, take care about my ending!

ANONYMOUS FRANCISCAN HYMN
TO MARY

[21*] *Stabat mater dolorosa*

1. There stood the Mother deeply sorrowing
   At the Cross-side, tears outpouring,
      As they hanged her Son, her Christ;
   How her heart was gravely groaning,
   Wracked with pain and full of moaning,   5
   As the swords inside her sliced.

2. Ah, the grieving, great affliction
   Heaped on this maid of benediction,
      Mother of the Chosen One;
   Full of suffering, filled with pining   10
   She stood shuddering while divining
      The penalties for her great Son.

3. Where's the man who is not weeping
   As he sees Christ's Mother keeping
      Watch upon such bitterness?   15
   Who's not filled with agitation
   In the Virgin's contemplation
      Of her Son's most dire duress?

4. She sees Jesus stretched on the yoke,
   Paying for the sins of other folk,   20
      Handed over to the whips;
   There she sees her Boy-Child mild
   In the death-grip, alone, defiled,
      As his man-soul from him slips.

5. Eia, Mother, fount of loving,   25
   Let me bear with you the groveling,
      Let me suffer woe with you;
   Let my heart be filled with burning;
   For the Lord Christ set me yearning,
      Make your child love me too.   30

21. The most famous Marian hymn (1200s), formerly attributed to Iacopone da Todi (see Nos. 96, 97). Strong end and interior rhyme throughout, which the translation attempts to approximate. Set to music by Verdi, Rossini, Palestrina, and Pergolesi. Tape of chant: Philips 420879-2.
   *Original text appears in Section IX, taken from *Analecta Hymnica*, 54, No. 201.

6. Holy Mother, please abide me—
   Let the nail-blows pound inside me,
     Let them strike within my heart;
   As I spy those sundering blows
   That your loved one undergoes   35
     Let me also share a part!

7. Let me with you stand there crying,
   Lending comfort at the crucifying
     For as long as I have breath;
   At the Cross-side let me stand   40
   Offering you a kindly hand
     As we keen the dirge of death.

8. Maiden, foremost among maidens,
   Let me not be overladen,
     Let me mourn along with you;   45
   Let the Christ-death be my ration,
   Make me consort to his Passion,
     Let me bear the beatings too!

9. Let me feel the flails aflying,
   Make me drunk in the crucifying   50
     In the blest love of your Son;
   Save me from the Hell-flames' kindling:
   Virgin! save this sinner spindling
     When the Judgment Day has come!

10. Let the Cross attend my breath,   55
    Stay with me until my death
      And the grace of princely prize;
    When this body knows it's dying,
    Let this soul go upward flying
      To the praise of Paradise.   60

ST. THOMAS AQUINAS

[22] *Adoro devote, latens veritas*

1. I adore you devoutly, O hidden truth,
   Lurking inside all these outward forms;
   To you my heart will gladly surrender,
   For in contemplation of you it fails.

2. Taste, sight, and touch when near you falter;   5
   Only the hearing is safely believed.
   I believe what the Son of God has uttered:
   There is nothing truer than the word of truth.

3. On the Cross Jesus' godhead was totally hidden;
   But here the humanity also hides;   10
   I believe in them both, I confess them:
   I cry what the thief penitential cried.

4. Unlike doubting Thomas, I do not see the woundings,
   But still I confess that you are my Lord.
   Make me believe in you always more strongly,   15
   Have stout hope in you and forever adore.

5. You, reminder of the death of our Master,
   Bread that offers true life to mankind,
   Offer my soul some life-stuff out of you.
   Allow it to savor your delicate taste.   20

6. Pity-filled pelican, Jesus, my Master,
   Purge my pollution with your holy blood.
   One single droplet can offer salvation
   And make the whole world free of its crime.

7. Jesus, I see you veiled and in darkness.   25
   When can I have what I strongly desire?
   When can I gaze on your face that's now hidden
   And bask in the glory that comes with this sight?

22. San Tommaso d'Aquino (*ca.* 1225–1274). Foremost member of the Dominican Order, who reconciled Aristotelian philosophy with Catholic theology in his *Summas*. Attribution questioned, but the hymn shows the objective, intellectual spirit of Dominicanism as opposed to the more emotional spirit of Franciscanism. Widely known in a variant version as *Adoro Te devote, latens Deitas*, but see F. J. E. Raby, *Speculum*, 20 (1945), 236–238. Tape of chant: Philips 420879-2.

Plate 2. The Cologne Cathedral on the Rhine River, a site associated with the so-called "Archpoet" (author of No. 24), a friend of Archbishop Rainald of Dassel. (Courtesy of the German Information Center)

[II] THE *CARMINA BURANA*

The *Carmina Burana* are the stepchildren of European literature. They are a collection of poems written down in the latter half of the thirteenth century, although most of them were composed well before that time. The anthology was collected and stored at the Benediktbeuern Monastery in Bavaria, not far from Munich. The latter part of the monastery name supplies the Latin adjective "*Burana*" that describes these *carmina* or songs. For years this manuscript was left uncatalogued, known only to the monks who had access to it; but in the early 1800s when the Bavarian government was secularizing the Beuern complex, the anthology was brought to light.

Actually, many of the poems in the collection had long been known because they were included in other manuscripts found elsewhere. The authors of the *Burana* lyrics were by no means necessarily the monks who transcribed the words. They were clerics or laymen drawn from many parts of Europe. Some of the poems in the collection are written in a macaronic verse that blends Latin with French, Italian, or German, thus showing the varied sources of the writing. Furthermore, although it is romantic to imagine some of the authors as wandering scholars (*vagantes* or Goliards, based on the legendary author Golias), there is every reason to believe that the composers were often quite respectable men with roots who had a lively knowledge of music and rhetoric.

The collection itself is varied in genres. There are sequences and dramatic episodes within it, as well as a sizable section devoted to drinking songs, gambling songs, and love poems. Some of the most famous poems have been set to music by Carl Orff. Indeed, my translations of Poems 23 to 30 follow his selection, and have been rendered into English with his music in mind as a possible background. Those who resent Orff's romantic approach can find a more authentic treatment in the Telefunken Das Alte Werk series, 6.41184, where twenty songs are performed from transcriptions of the original manuscript.

No matter how they are performed musically, the tone of the secular poems is clear. The Hymn to Fortune (No. 23), for example, could have been used as part of the celebration for a Black Mass, in which random Chance replaces the providential workings of God. As an entity, the *Burana* celebrate nature, love, and fortune in a way that runs directly counter to the supernatural doctrines of the Church. The Confession of Golias (No. 24) purports to be a shriving of the soul, but is in actuality an exaltation of the flesh. The speaker revels in his mortality, even daring to mimic the last line of the *Dies irae* ("God, take care about my ending!"), which is twisted in the *Burana* version to express the speaker's "care . . . only for my skin."

Some of the poems, like the Dirge of the Roasted Swan (No. 25) and the Gambling Song (No. 26), are almost grotesque parodies. The brutal end of

the cooked fowl must be viewed as a travesty of martyrdom, just as the cry
of the naked gambler ("Bitter Fate, O why hast thou forsaken me?")
mimics Christ's cry from the Cross. Sometimes, of course, the tone is
gentler, as in the Drinking Song (No. 27), where the whole world seems to
drown in liquid, or in Poem No. 29, where the equation of men with
flowers seems more comic than sacrilegious.

However, lest we try to write off these poems as mere playful skits, we
must consider the haunting *Stetit puella* (No. 28), which parodies the *Stabat
mater* (No. 21). There is also the excerpt *Ave, formosissima* (No. 30), which
masquerades as a tribute to Mary until it breaks forth into a eulogy of the
heroine Blancheflor, Helen of Troy, and Venus. If these poems are comic,
they are also diabolical, no matter how much like schoolbook exercises they
may seem. On the other hand, some of the most outrageous pieces, like the
Hymn to the Belly (No. 31), can obviously be read in a moral way as the
exposition of a glutton's weakness. Similarly, the portrayal of the world
buffeted in wild conflict (No. 32) can demand an acceptance of order. As
the *Burana* themselves remark in a pithy epigram: "in all that is/It is good to
have a mean."

The gradual working toward a mean is apparent in the love lyrics from
34 to 40. The earlier ones tend to view man's life in terms of the flowers, as
the late classical poets did, but they blend Christian assurance and even
assumption with their pagan acceptance of nature. The third stanza of 34 is
a marching song, with the vigor of a Christian hymn. The first three stanzas
of 35 are delicate and graceful; they play with the words "virgin" and
"love" in an ambiguous way, and only in the fourth stanza are the material
motives bluntly stated.

The *Carmina Burana* travesty classical rhetoric as well as Christian. Poem
No. 36 is a violent reworking of Horace's famous *sententiae* "it's sweet to be
foolish in the right place" and "seize the day." Poem No. 37 wreaks havoc
with Vergil's "Love conquers all." In the late medieval poems, these state-
ments are given their most extreme meanings, and the singsong quality of
the verse helps to hammer the points home.

In Poems 38 to 40, however, one is aware of a different sensibility. The
sixth stanza of 38 plays with Ovid's famous remarks about the difficulty of
maintaining one's balance in love; to this dilemma the poet adds the coloring
of Christian suffering in stanzas 3 and 7. As a result, one gets more than a
simple declaration of the necessity of sex; the natural world itself seems
complicated, and perhaps not so far removed from the religious as the
previous poems indicated. The beautiful Hymn to Sleep (No. 39), often
attributed to Abelard (but without convincing proof), strikes a note of calm
seriousness. This tone is sustained in 40, where the poet writes a love song
to his lady employing standard Christian symbolism blended with classical
allusions, all done with taste and assurance. At this point parody is left
behind and one enters the brave new world of medieval secular composition,
where passion has a new dignity (since it has The Passion as its backdrop).
When the beloved is finally described like Mary as a star of the sky, we see
the religious and the secular unite in a way that also occurs in the polished
poetry of the troubadours.

In Poems 23 to 30, where I have the Carl Orff music in mind, I have used
the third edition of J. A. Schmeller (Stuttgart, 1894), which Orff used. In

other cases, I rely on the more authoritative edition of A. Hilka and O. Schumann, 2 vols. (Heidelberg: Carl Winter Universitätsverlag, 1930–1978). Of the many recordings of Orff, see CBS BL-37217. For a tape of versions from the original manuscript, arranged by Thomas Binkley, see Teldec 8.43775 and 8.44012 for Nos. 29, 35, 38. For other translations, see *Love Songs of the Carmina Burana*, trans. E. D. Blodgett and R. A. Swanson (Garland, 1987), and *Vagabond Verse*, trans. E. H. Zeydel (Wayne State, 1966).

ANONYMOUS

[23*] O Fortuna

1. O Fortuna,
   Like the moon, you
Shift in everchanging state—
   Always waxing,
   Then collapsing,   5
Making man's life rife with hate;
   Hard perversely,
   Then with mercy
How you tease our reason's thrust!
   Poor one hour,   10
   Ah, comes power!
Which soon melts like ice's crust.

2. Luck is mighty
   Yet as flighty
As an ever-shifting wheel: 15
   High will stumble,
   Health will crumble
In a flow that will not heal.
   Wearing veils
   Along dark trails   20
Suddenly you loom in view;
   My back's stripped,
   I've lost my chips
With many thanks to wicked you!

23. Hymn to Fortune.

*See Section IX for original text, taken from Schmeller, No. 1; cf. Hilka-Schumann, No. 17.

3. Slipping virtue,   25
   Health that hurts you—
All that's kind now cruelly chokes;
   Fine condition
   Feels perdition
Quickly lunging for its throat: 30
   Just one hour—
   O the power!—
Then come lamentations deep.
   Luck starts crumbling—
   Knights go tumbling—   35
O my brothers, with me—weep!

[24] *Estuans intrinsecus ira vehementi*

1. As my inner self's on fire
      With a raging flame,
   In a blaze of bitter ire
      I address my brain:
   Manufactured out of matter,   5
      Air my element—
   I'm a bough the breezes batter
      With a playful bent.

2. Wise men who heed imprecations
      When their reason talks   10
   Carefully place their foundations
      On the mighty Rock.
   Idiot me! Shall you compare me
      To the river's run?
   A path pursued will never bear me   15
      Back where I've begun.

3. No, I'm swept on ocean foam
      Skipperless and drifting,
   A bird that flies skyways alone,
      Flitting, ever shifting.   20
   Chains will never fetter fast,
      Locks not last long whiles.
   I hunt friends of my own cast
      And bind me to—the vile!

4. Affairs high-serious belabor   25
      Hearts, too little funny.

24. Confession of Golias. Continues for about 14 stanzas as the speaker runs through his
sins in a rather exhaustive way. Attributed to a certain Archpoet (*ca.* 1130–1167), an otherwise
unknown German who was a friend of Rainald of Dassel, the Archbishop of Cologne. Ed.
Schmeller, No. 172.

I love jokes; to me their savor's
   Sweeter far than honey.
Labor bearing Venus' stamp
   Seems suavely empowered;   30
She has never pitched her camp
   In the breasts of cowards.

5. Down life's open road meandering
    In the guise of youth,
  Ever given to philandering,   35
    Never shriven to truth,
  Greedy to try all lustful fare
    More than health to win—
Dead in soul, O God! my care
    Is only for my skin! . . .   40

[25] *Olim lacus colueram*

1. Once I skimmed over inland seas;
  Once my white down was fine to see;
  I lived my swan-life peacefully—
      Poor me! Poor me!
      Now basted blackly   5
      And roasted totally!

2. Turn me, turn me now the sculleries;
  Burn me, burn me the rotisseries;
  Here comes the serving boy to offer me—
      Poor me! Poor me!
      Now basted blackly   10
      And roasted totally! . . .

5. Now on a serving-plate stretched out I lie,
  Thinking in vain of flying through the skies;
  Now gnashing molars start to catch my eye—
      Poor me! Poor me!   15
      Now basted blackly
      And roasted totally!

[26] *Ego sum Abbas Cucaniensis*

I am the Abbot of Cuckoo-Ninny
And my counsel is always with drinkers like me,

25. Dirge of the Roasted Swan; ed. Schmeller, No. 92. *Lacus* in title preferred to *latus*, as in Hilka-Schumann, No. 130. The two omitted stanzas say: "I would prefer to live in the water/ Always under the clear sky/ Than to lie here in hot pepper./ I was whiter than snow,/ prettier than any other bird./ Now I'm blacker than a crow."

26. Gambling Song. *Cucaniensis* can be Cockaigne, a fictional land of luxurious life. *Wafna* is an emergency cry for help.

And I follow the sect of Decius, Lord of the Dice,
And whoever runs after me mornings in taverns
    At nightfall will issue naked   5
    And stripped of his shirt will cry:
    Wafna! Wafna!
    Bitter Chance, O why hast thou forsaken me?
    All the pleasures of this life
    You have stolen away!   10

[27] *In taberna quando sumus*

1. In the tavern when we're toping
   No one sits with death-sighs moping—
   To the gambling we go rushing,
   Sweating from the heavy crushing;
   If you have a lust for mastering   5
   How we pass our time in casting
   (There where Penny summons schooners)
   Listen to these random rumors.

2. This one's slurping, that one's sporting,
   Someone's foolishly cavorting,   10
   But of those who stay for gambling
   Some will exit nudely scrambling,
   Some will put on fine apparel,
   Others sackcloth or a barrel;
   There where death is all forgotten   15
   With Bacchus they toss dice all sodden.

3. First throw says who pays for wine,
   That liquid of the libertine.
   Next to prisoners toasts they're giving,
   Thrice saluting then the living;   20
   Four times for each Christian head,
   Five times for the faithful dead,
   Six for sisters who are bolting;
   Seven's a soldier who's not revolting.

4. Eight's for all the Brothers Perverse;   25
   Nine's for all those monks dispersed;
   Ten is for the sailor at sea;
   Eleven for brawlers constantly;
   Twelve for the truly penitent;
   Thirteen for men on missions sent.   30
   Here's to the Pope! Here's to the King!
   Everyone drink—no end to the thing!

27. Drinking Song. Ed. Schmeller, No. CLXXII.

5. Drinks the mistress, drinks the master;
   Drinks the soldier with the pastor;
   Drinks the Madame with Monsieur;   35
   Drinks the maid-girl with the steward;
   Drinks the slinker, drinks the slack one,
   Drinks the pinkie with the black one;
   Drinks the set man, drinks the bummer;
   Drinks the genius with his dumber.   40

6. Drinks the pauper and the weak one;
   Drinks Old Prelate with the Deacon;
   Drinks the exile, drinks the cipher;
   Drinks teen-ager with long-lifer;
   Drinks the sister, drinks the brother,   45
   Drinks old grandma with your mother;
   This girl's swilling; that churl's plundered—
   Thousands drinking—yes, and hundreds!

7. Six-hundred coins could not remotely
   Fill the bill, for there's no quota   50
   To this drink that knows no measure.
   And though nothing gives more pleasure,
   Still are some who pick and carp,
   Hoping to make our guilt pangs sharp.
   Let those carpers go depraved—   55
   Write their names not with the saved!

[28] Stetit puella

1. There stood the girl
        In the crimson dress—
        At the softest press,
   How that tunic rustled:
                 Eia!   5

2. There stood the girl,
        Rosebud on a vine;
        Face ashine,
   Mouth a reddish bloom.
                 Eia!   10

3. There stood the girl *by a tree*;
   She wrote of love *on a leaf*;
   Then came Venus very quickly—
   Great charity,

---

28. Parody of hymns to Mary (see No. 8). The third stanza mixes German and Latin,
with the German italicized here. It equates "great charity" in Latin (*caritatem magnam*) with
hohe Minne ("high love") in German. Ed. Schmeller, No. 138.

Highest love;   15
She gave herself to her man.

[29] *Tempus est iocundum*

1. Pleasant is the weather—you maidens!
   Now rejoice together—with young men!
       O! O! O!
       I flower from head to toe!
       I'm all on fire   5
       For the girl I desire;
       New's this love I cherish:
       New, new, new by which
           I perish . . .

4. O the better solace—accepted!   10
   O the bitter malice—rejected!
       O! O! O! . . .

7. In cold Winter's fling—man's trusty!
   Comes the sudden breath of Spring—lusty!
       O! O! O! . . .   15

5. Virginity quite jestfully—speeds me;
   And yet simplicity—impedes me.
       O! O! O! . . .

8. Come with joy, my lady—abounding;
   Come, O come, my beauty—I'm floundering!   20
       O! O! O! . . .

[30] *Ave, formosissima*

Hail, most beautiful and good,
   Jewel held most dear by us;
Hail, honor of maidenhood,
   Virgin ever glorious—
Hail, thou light above all lights,   5
   Hail, rose of the world—
   Blancheflor
   And Helen,
           Venus,
           Venus,   10
       Venus noble-souled!

29. Verses so arranged by Orff. Ed. Schmeller, No. 140.
   30. Parody of *Ave, Maria.* This stanza is the opening address of a man to a woman in a longish pastourelle: *Si linguis angelicis,* ed. Hilka-Schumann, No. 77.

[31] *Alte clamat Epicurus*

1. Epicurus cries aloud:
   "A belly full is surer.
   Belly is my own true god—
   Throat is his procurer;
   Kitchen is his sacred shrine   5
   Where are fragrant goods divine.

2. "Behold! this god is awfully good;
   Fasts he does not cherish;
   And before the morning food,
   There's a burp of sherry;   10
   To him tables and big bowls
   Are the truly heavenly goals.

3. "Yes, his flesh is always bulging
   Like a bloated jug of sack:
   Ruby cheeks show his indulging;   15
   Lunch meets dinner back to back;
   When his desire stirs the veins
   It is stronger than a chain."

4. This religious cult expresses
   Devotion in its belched excesses;   20
   Belly folds in agony;
   Beer is battling burgundy;
   Yet life is blessèd with much leisure
   When its center's belly's pleasure.

5. Belly speaks now: "Not one damn   25
   Care I for anything but me;
   I just quietly want to jam
   Plenty of stuff inside of me,
   And then above the chow and wine
   To sleep, to rest in peace divine."   30

[32] *Iste mundus*

1. This old world
   In fury furled
   Sets false joys before our eyes—
   These all spill,
   Run downhill   5
   As the lily quickly lies.

31. Hymn to the Belly. Epicurus is the Greek philosopher whom thinkers of the Middle Ages associated with hedonism and a denial of immortality. Ed. Schmeller, No. CLXXXVI.
32. Poem reflects the *contemptus mundi* or "contempt of the world" tradition. Ed. Schmeller, No. VI.

2. Worldly schemes,
   Life's vain dreams
   Steal away the truer prize;
   They impel   10
   Man to Hell
   Where he fully buried lies.

3. Carnal matters,
   Law that shatters
   Truly full of frivolousness   15
   Falters, fades
   Like a shade
   That has lost its mesh of flesh.

4. All we spy,
   Hold close by   20
   In our fatherland today
   We'll dismiss,
   Slowly miss
   As the oak leaves drift away. . . .

6. Let us batter,   25
   Let us scatter
   All desires of the skin;
   Stand erect
   Among the elect
   And the justest of all men.   30

7. Heavenly pleasure
   We shall treasure
   Through the ages that never end!
                        Amen.

[33] *Non est crimen amor*

Love is not wrong because
       If it were a crime,
God would never have used love
       To bind even the divine.

33. Ed. Hilka-Schumann, No. 121a.

[34*] *Iam iam rident prata*

1. Now, yes now the fields are smiling;
   Now, yes now the girls agree
   In gaiety, while all beguiling
   Earth laughs too in harmony.
   Summer has entered on the stage,   5
   And, decked in flowers,
        Is all the rage.

2. Grove again wears greenish sleeves,
   Bushes with their budlets snap;
   Cruel Winter has taken leave.   10
   Young men full of joy and sap,
   Go be happy in the tendrils!
   Love is now enticing you
        To the girls.

3. Our resolution: let's all fight   15
   Together for our Lady Venus;
   Let's keep sadness out of sight—
   To us real violence is heinous.
   The looks and ah! the ploys,
   Hope and Love will lead us   20
        To our joys.

[35] *Veris dulcis in tempore*

1. In the time of pleasant spring,
   Under a tree that's blossoming
   Juliana with sister standing—
        O sweet love!
   Whoever lacks you in this hour   5
        'S all the poorer.

2. Look! the trees burst into flower,
   Birdies singing with lusty power,
   Virgins warming hour by hour—
        O sweet love!
   Whoever lacks you in this hour   10
        'S all the poorer.

---

34. I read "rident" instead of "virent" in the opening line. For discussion, see my *Cruelest Month* (Yale, 1965), pp. 105 ff.
   *Original text appears in Section IX, following Hilka-Schumann, No. 144.
35. Follows Hilka-Schumann, No. 85.

3. Look! the lily's taken to flowering,
    And ranks of virgins start to sing
    Songs to the highest godlike thing—   15
            O sweet love!
    Whoever lacks you in this hour
            'S all the poorer.

4. If I could catch what I most covet
    In a dark wood—kiss and love it—   20
    There'd be no other joy above it—
          . O sweet love!
    Whoever lacks you in this hour
            'S all the poorer.

[36] *Omittamus studia*

1. Let's put aside our studying:
    Sweet it is to play the fool.
    Let's seize all the sweeter things
    Youth offers in its languid rule.
    There'll be time for pondering   5
    Weighty things when life grows cool.
        Time too swiftly rushes;
            Study crushes;
        Young blood strongly urges
            Love's sweet surges.   10

2. The spring of age away is slipping,
    Winter soon comes rushing on;
    Life feels loss against it chipping
    Until the flesh with care's all gone;
    Heart is hardened; blood just trickles;   15
    One by one goes all that pleases;
    Old Age hails us with his sickle:
    Coming with his family of diseases.
        Time too swiftly rushes . . .

3. Let's imitate the gods above!   20
    That's a maxim well worth heeding.
    Toward us come those nets of love
    To ensnare fair men of breeding.
    Let us pay heed to our prayers!
    That's the code the gods maintain.   25
    Let's go down then to the square
    And watch the virgins entertain.
        Time too swiftly rushes . . .

36. Two lines from stanza 1 omitted from manuscript. The poems of Horace parodied are *Odes* IV.12 and I.11. Hilka-Schumann, No. 75.

4. Ah, there's plenty there for grabbing
   If it's only with the eyes.   30
   Shiny arms the air are stabbing,
   Slender slink those splendid thighs—
   While the girls are leaping, stalking
   With the beat that never dies,
   I stand gaping; in my gawking   35
   Feel my soul outside me rise!
   > *Time too swiftly rushes;*
   > *Study crushes;*
   > *Young blood strongly urges*
   > *Love's sweet surges.*   40

[37] *Ianus annum circinat*

1. Janus circles round the year;
   Spring announces Summer's back;
   Gradually toward Taurus veers
   Phoebus with his hoofbeats near
   Outside Aries' racing-track.   5
   > *Love can anything defeat,*
   > *Love can turn the harsh to sweet.*

2. Let all sadness fast depart;
   Let sweet pleasures consecrate
   The schoolhouse of the Queen of Hearts!   10
   Now's the time for euphony,
   You soldiers who will dedicate
   Your lives to our Lord Dione (Venus).
   > *Love can anything defeat,*
   > *Love can turn the harsh to sweet.*   15

3. When I entered Venus College,
   A graduate of Pallas,
   Among those devotees of knowledge
   There was not one girl as
   Beautiful as one I spied: 20
   O her face was Helen's!
   Venus only with her vied
   In affairs of elegance.
   She was tops in modest pride.
   > *Love can anything defeat,*   25
   > *Love can turn the harsh to sweet.*

37. Lines compressed from text. Refrain mimics Vergil, *Eclogue* X.69. The phrase *Dioneo lari* in stanza 2, translated "Lord Dione," relates to the masculinizing of the woman and is comparable with Provençal *midons* ("Milord"), which is used by troubadours to describe a lady. Hilka-Schumann, No. 56.

4. Different from other women
   Is the one I love uniquely.
   Once this novel flame begins,
   It flares within   30
   And never shows a weakening.
   There's no other girl more noble,
   Ever able,
   Beautiful and lovable;
   None is less mobile,   35
   Less unstable,
   Less ready for cowing,
   Less false in her vowing.
   To be aware she lives in bliss
   Would bring me great delight;   40
   And I'd feel even doubly blessed
   If I could share that plight.
       Love conquers everything!
       Love governs everything!

5. Spare this boy, you boy-god, spare;   45
   Venus, look with loving care;
   Move that fire,
   Stir desire,
   And don't allow my life to die!
   Don't let her deceive us   50
   As Daphne did Phoebus!
   Once a freshman in Wisdom School,
   Venus, Venus, I yield to your rule!
       Love conquers everything!
       Love governs everything!   55

[38*] *Axe Phebus aureo*

1. Phoebus in his golden car
       Lights the firmament,
   And with rosy glows imparts
       His shaftings down to men.
   Cybele in elegance arrayed   5
       With her flowering face
   To Bacchus gives a fresh bouquet,
       While Phoebus beams with grace.

2. With the help of winds that blend
       All throughout the grove,   10
   Little birds their beauties lend
       As they chant of love.

*Original text appears in Section IX, following Hilka-Schumann, No. 71.

Philomel now renews her blame
　　Of Tereus for wrongs,
Joining the blackbird in refrains　　　　　　　15
Adapted for their songs.

3. Now Dione's
Chorus joyously
Zealously answers
Their various chants.　　　　　　　　　　　20
And now Dione
In jest and in agony
Lightens, then tightens
Her worshipers' hearts.

4. Me too she pulls　　　　　　　　　　　　25
　　Away from my sleep.
Me too she rules:
　　"Now vigil keep!"
Cupid's golden shaft
　　I'm forced to bear;　　　　　　　　　　30
Ire-filled fires
　　Through my body tear!

5. Whatever I'm plied
　　I recant.
For what I'm denied　　　　　　　　　　　35
　　I will pant
In a mind severely swayed.
When a thing is ceded me,
　　I waver;
Yet whoever won't heed me　　　　　　　　40
　　I favor;
About me you can truly say:

6. I'm faithful; I'll go to my grave
For her, or else for her I'm saved.
If she wants me, I'm all through.　　　　　　45
If she taunts me, I pursue.
The more I've rejected the lawful,
The more I deflect toward the awful.
The more the unspiced one's allowed me,
The more the unlicensed one cows me.　　　　50

7. O Dione's
Baleful decrees!
Poison to flee
Working inwardly,
Fearsome lechery,　　　　　　　　　　　　55
Full of treachery.

Mistress of might,
Whose torture's a fright,
Your serfs you requite
With bitterness' bite,   60
Full of all slights
And fiery spite!

8. And so in me
      A fear is swelling,
   And down my cheeks   65
      The tears come welling.
   And so my face
      Looks frayed and pale:
   It is: in love I've been
      Betrayed, I fail.   70

[39] *Dum Diane vitrea*

1. When Diana with lamp of glass
   Arises in the evening skies
   Soft and glowing pinkly as
   Her brother's fires around her die,
   Zephyr's gentle breezes often   5
   Force the clouds on high to soften,
   Then steal away;
   Music too can sway
   Human breasts from inner broil,
   Subtly changing   10
   Heart, which ranges
   Nodding toward love's heavy toil.

2. Vesper's slender ray of light
   Gives the pleasing
   Dew that eases   15
   Entrance into dreamland's portals
   For weary mortals.

3. O how blessed is sleep's potion,
   Curing cares and worldly commotion!
   Stealthily stealing through pores of eyes,   20
   Joyous rival to love's enterprise.

4. Morpheus through the mind
   Draws a wind as kind
   As that which wafts a field of ripened grain;

39. Hymn to Sleep. Follows Hilka-Schumann, No. 62. Poem continues for four more
stanzas, which the editors regard as spurious. Diana is the moon.

Murmuring rivers glide through sandy plains;   25
Mill wheels circle slowly round and round—
While we in sleep lie robbed of light and sound.

[40*] *Dira vi amoris teror*

1. By the dire force of love I'm worn,
   By the chariot of Venus borne,
   By a fervent fire I lie choked:
   Blessèd one, remove this forkèd yoke!

2. You're the ember of this lively burning;   5
   Heart's standards feel you inside turning,
   While I recline on this fire too real
   And shut you tight in my heart's seal.

3. This heart is sad that once was joyous
   On that day when it saw you, glorious,   10
   Modest, with charms that never end:
   It took you instantly for its friend.

4. Sighs come pouring out of my breast,
   Racks of sorrow that give me no rest;
   The vigor of love without remission   15
   Presses me into this chained condition.

5. Virgin lily, O send, I pray
   Help to guide me on my way!
   I, an exile on parade,
   Humbly call on you for aid.   20

6. I don't know what to do; I fail
   For the love of you by which I sail;
   Venus' shaftings will soon destroy
   Unless you rush to help this boy.

7. Orphan from the reign of Venus,   25
   Blessed with chastity to clean us,
   Face neat, ornate for all to see,
   Garbed in the robe of Philosophy:

8. To you alone I hymn my praise;
   O don't despise my earthly ways;   30
   Let me, I pray you, hold you high,
   Shining as lodestar of my sky!

*Original text appears in Section IX, following Hilka-Schumann, No. 107.

Plate 3. The Triumphal Arch built by the Romans in Orange, on the Rhone River, a city made famous by Prince Raimbaut of Orange (Nos. 61 to 63). The Arch is mentioned by Azalais of Porcairagues in Poem 66, stanza 6. (Courtesy of the French Government Tourist Office)

[III] PROVENÇAL LYRICS

The Provençal lyric bursts upon the late medieval world like a welcomed ray of spring sunlight. The first known poet is Duke William IX of Aquitaine, grandfather of the famous Eleanor and lord of most of south-western France. In his work we can detect a transformation from cruder poems (Nos. 44 and 45), where women are treated as mere objects for possession, to the more refined but still masculinely dominated love lyric or *canso* (No. 45). William establishes many of the rhetorical patterns which recur in later compositions. He calls his woman *midons* (which I translate "Milord," or sometimes "Milordess," to preserve the wit), treats her like a medieval duke writing the real duke into her charter, and in short establishes that socially oriented world that is often associated with the overused phrase "courtly love." On the other hand, William's tone is often brusque and frankly Ovidian. His imagery runs the gamut from the castle bedroom to the cathedral. He plays with sacred allusions in a way that makes his poems sound every bit as "churchly" in their overtones as courtly.

William's tampering with Christian mysticism can best be seen in his famous Riddle Poem (No. 46), where religious mysteries are transferred to secular paradox. Still, lest we see him merely as a rude parodist, his Hymn on His Own Death (No. 47) shows the bowing of the earthly lord to the Celestial Lord in clear, certain terms. William's stanzas, rhyme schemes, and rhetoric can all be related to Latin rhetoric amd Christian hymnology, especially in his pilfering of the touchstone word "joy."

Cercamon continues the tradition admirably, preserving the Duke's easy colloquial flavor (which I have exaggerated in my translation of No. 48), yet also insisting on the divine madness of love. His supposed pupil Marcabrun voices the reaction to the new love credo that one might have expected in an age of faith. Marcabrun speaks about Good Love and Refined Love, which the troubadours use in their descriptions of their personal affairs, but he identifies Good Love in Poem 49 with Christian charity and Low Loving, its opposite, with lust; in this way he is in accord with St. Augustine, not Duke William. Yet Marcabrun is no bland conservative; his Crusade Song (No. 50) is also a scathing attack on the society of his day. His sensitivity shows especially in his handling of the *pastourelle*, a form that he left his imprint on: No. 51 is still rather crude, like some of the *Carmina Burana*, but 52 is indeed refined. Here a highborn woman voices her love for her man, who is away on crusade, refusing the comfort of the narrator, who tries to interest her in God, although he is actually concerned with seduction. As an entity, the poem expresses through the characters the love of this world in poignant terms, but it also gives voice to the demands of the world beyond.

With Jaufre Rudel we encounter the ethereal and the mystical in a secular context. His famous 53, which speaks of his burning desire for his "far-off

love," has led some people to interpret his poems as expressions of Mani-
chean or Catharist doctrine: they see the far-off lady as a dim ideal of the
Good shining bleakly upon a poet lost in a world of Evil. The poem is not,
however, Catharist, for stanza 6 says clearly that God, not Satan, is the
creator of the world. One can find a sense of idealism contending with tragic
separation in the mystical works of St. Bernard of Clairvaux, Richard of
St. Victor, and elsewhere. The situation is, in fact, basic to the lyric of any
time. The mysterious godfather of stanzas 7 and 8 is probably Adam,
whose sin intensified the gap between ideals and reality that forms the basic
tension in the poem. Jaufre's Riddle Poem (No. 54) is a further extension of
the treatment of human love in a mystical framework. It sounds sacrilegious, but the *Burana* proved that one can be that without being heretical.

Bernart de Ventadorn is now usually considered The Master Singer. A
mixture of tone and gestures is an integral part of Bernart's method, for he
developed the Provençal *canso* into a sophisticated form that was capable of
many sudden turns. In his works, his woman appears as a divine agent like
Mary (that other "good woman"), like a lordly duke (continuing William's
Milord), and often, quite suddenly, like Eve, the dark destroyer of man's
dreams. Yet no matter how she is portrayed, the medium of the poem is
always graceful, witty, and polished. He can toy with mentions of Christ-
mas and Easter in 59 or play with a reversal of seasons in Poem 56, but
Bernart will never be accused of heresy; he expresses that willful acceptance
of madness that is the property of poets, lovers, and saints.

After Bernart, some poets moved into obscurantism, embracing the so-
called *trobar clus* or "closed-invention" style. One of the strongest expo-
nents is Raimbaut of Orange, who in 61 expresses his determination to be
highly individual, yet in a language that is still apprehensible. His poem 62,
however, shows certain stances that might be labeled Satanic. More typical
is Arnaut Daniel, who shows what can be done with this attitude toward
composition. One admires the original Provençal for the experiments with
sound, as Ezra Pound did, and the rebellious spirit behind the works. Other
poets tried to do the simple thing. In 80 and 81, Raimbaut de Vaqueiras
attempts to capture the spirit of folk song, as does Peire Vidal in 74.
Possibly the best love poem of the latter half of the twelfth century is
Bertran de Born's No. 72, where he frankly confesses that his Self-Conceived Lady is a supreme fiction.

As South French society began to crumble under the incursions of the
English and the North French, compounded by the Papacy's calling of the
Albigensian Crusade, the poetry turned from the sweet style of love to
bitter satire, usually expressed in a form called the *sirventes*. Bertran de Born
communicates the anguish of living in a land torn by internal and external
dissension. Peire Cardenal in 84 attacks the Church for its sinful hypocrisy,
which is shown by the Monk of Montaudon (No. 79). Cardenal paints the
general scene in 85, when he writes of a society that has gone mad. Yet lest
we believe that the tradition ended in heresy, we have Cardenal's reasoned
Complaint to God (No. 86) and the beautiful religious Dawn Song of
Folquet of Marseille (No. 83).

In one sense, the change of the whole tradition is mirrored in the Dawn
Song or *alba*. We have the fresh, anonymous, popular alba (No. 41), which
seems to emanate from pagan spring rites and yet suggests the aristocratic

world of the beautiful queen, her young lover, and her jealous husband. We have the balanced creation of Guiraut de Bornelh (No. 67), where the references to the supernatural order are beautifully locked with the human. We have the rather slick, but still effective, piece of Raimbaut of Vaqueiras (No. 80), where one can sense the dilution of the tradition. Finally, the work of Folquet shows a complete turning away from the human in preference for the religious. After the Church and the Albigensian Crusaders conquered in southern France, the poets followed the lead of Folquet (persuaded to no slight degree by the Inquisition that he helped to institute). Southern France thus reversed the trend of other countries by returning to hymns at the close of its golden age. Still, its unique contribution to Western letters was not lost. We must simply look to other countries to find the traditions that were carried on.

Aside from specific editions cited in notes, one can find most of these poems in the two-volume *Anthology of Provençal Troubadours*, ed. R. T. Hill and T. G. Bergin, revised with others (Yale, 1973), and *Lyrics of the Troubadours and Trouvères*, ed. and trans. Frederick Goldin (Doubleday, 1973). For tapes: Nimbus N 5002, Gallo DC 529, ECM 1368 and Harmonia Mundi HMC 90396.

ANONYMOUS DAWN SONG

[41] *En un vergier sotz fuella d'albespi*

1. In a garden under a hawthorn bower
   A lover to his lady's closely drawn
   Until a watchman shouts the morning hour.
   O God! O God! how swift it comes—the dawn!

2. "Dear God, if this night would never fail   5
   And my lover never far from me was gone,
   And the watchman never saw the morning pale—
   But, O my God! how swift it comes—the dawn!

3. "Come, pretty boy, give me a little kiss
   Down in the meadow where birds sing endless song.   10
   Forget my husband! Think—just think of this—
   For, O my God! how swift it comes—the dawn!

4. "Hurry, my boy. The new games end at morn.
   Down to that garden—those birds—that song!

41. Oldest complete Dawn Song in a modern European language. Text in Hill-Bergin *Anthology*, No. 178.

Play, play till the crier blows his horn,   15
For, O my God! how swift it comes—the dawn!

5. "Down in the sweet air over the meadow hovering
    I drank a sweet draught—long, so long—
    Out of the air of my handsome, noble lover."
    O God! O God! how swift it comes—the dawn!   20

6. The lady's pretty. She has many charms.
   Toward her beauty many men are drawn.
   But she lies happy in one pair of arms.
   O God! O God! how swift it comes—the dawn!

ANONYMOUS SPRING DANCE SONG

[42*] *A l'entrada del tens clar—eya*

1. At the start of the shining season—*eya!*
   In order to renew again our joy—*eya!*
   And to irritate all jealous husbands—*eya!*
   Our Queen would like to show
   That she is full of love.   5
     Go away, go away, jealous ones!
     Leave us, yes let us
     Dance together, together.

2. She has proclaimed it everywhere—*eya!*
   Down to the very edge of the sea—*eya!*   10
   That every bachelor and young girl—*eya!*
   Should come together to dance—
   To join us in our dance of joy!
     Go away, go away, jealous ones! . . .

3. The King is coming from another place—*eya!*   15
   To try to break up our dance—*eya!*
   For he is terribly afraid—*eya!*

42. Dansa, Balada. Despite the hymnal refrain of *eya*, strongly pagan in origin, suggesting
Roman or Celtic rites of May or Beltane, and also showing the power of joy, youth and the
feminine earth force. Text: Karl Bartsch, *Chrestomathie provençale*, 6th ed. E. Koschwitz
(Elwert, 1904), p. 122; many other editors use a North French version. For music: Telefunken
Das Alte Werk 6.41126(2); Archiv 14018 APM; Harmonia Mundi HMC 90396.
    *Original text appears in Section IX.

That someone might want to snatch
His April Queen away!
> *Go away, go away, jealous ones! . . .*   20

4. But she will have nothing of this—*eya!*
   For she doesn't need an old man—*eya!*
   No—she likes lusty bachelors—*eya!*
   Who know the art of solacing
   A very savorous lady!
   > *Go away, go away, jealous ones! . . .*   25

5. Whoever should see her dance—*eya!*
   Carrying her body with grace—*eya!*
   Could proclaim in all truth—*eya!*
   That there is no peer in this world   30
   To our Queen of Joy.
   > *Go away, go away, jealous ones!*
   > *Leave us, yes let us*
   > *Dance together, together.*

DUKE WILLIAM IX OF AQUITAINE, COUNT VII OF POITIERS

[43] *Farai un vers, pos mi sonelh*

1. I'll write a poem, then take a nap,
   And then go stand in the sun.
   Some ladies are really misguided;
      I know which ones:
   Those who turn the love of a knight   5
      Into grief.

43. Or Guilhem, Coms de Peiteus (1071–1126). First known secular love poet after the Dark Ages. Owner of more territory than the kings of France in his day. Increased his holdings by marrying Philippa of Toulouse, who later abandoned him for the monastic life. Usurped church lands, for which he was excommunicated. Took a major part in the disastrous Crusades of 1101, barely escaping death in Asia Minor. Led a brief, successful skirmish against the Moors in Spain. Notoriously fond of songs, parties, and women, as the chroniclers fondly point out. Succeeded by his son, William X, father of Eleanor of Aquitaine. Ten or eleven poems survive. This one, a *fabliau*, is one of the few examples of the obscene-story poem in Provençal. See Boccaccio, *Decameron* III.1 for the deaf-mute seducer. For texts and history, see *The Poetry of William VII, Count of Poitiers, IX Duke of Aquitaine*, ed. Gerald A. Bond (Garland, 1982), No. 5.

2. A lady commits a mortal sin
   If she doesn't love a faithful knight;
   And if she loves a monk or a priest,
       She's very wrong;   10
   It's right that we should burn her
       At the stake.

3. In Auvergne, that side of Limousin,
   I was cruising all alone on the sly;
   Then I found the wife of Lord Guari   15
       And Bernard's too.
   All they did was salute me simply
       By St. Leonard.

4. Then one of them said in her dialect,
   "God protect you, sir pilgrim;   20
   You're a man of excellent breeding,
       I do believe;
   We see far too many fools around
       In this world."

5. Now hear what I said in reply: 25
   I didn't say this and I didn't say that,
   Didn't mention a stick, not a tool;
       All I said was:
   "Babariol, Babariol,
       Babarian."   30

6. Then Lady Agnes said to Lady Emma:
   "He's just what we're looking for.
   For the love of God, let's put him up!
       He's a mute.
   He'll never be able to tattle about   35
       What we do."

7. The one covered me up with her mantle
   And led me in to her bedroom fire.
   Listen! It was all pretty nice:
       A fire nice and warm,   40
   And it made me feel good to get heated
       By her coals.

8. They gave me some capons to eat,
   And listen! I had more than a few,
   With no cook or scullion hanging around—   45
       Just us three.
   The bread was white, the wine was choice,
       And the pepper hot.

9. "Sister, I think he's a sly one;
    Dropped his speech just for our account;   50
    Let's bring out that big red tomcat
        Right this minute.
    That'll loosen his tongue in a hurry
        If he's fooling."

10. Lady Agnes went out for the beast;   55
    It was big and had long mustaches.
    The minute I saw him come in,
        I was scared;
    I almost lost all of my courage,
        My nerve.   60

11. After we ate and we had some drinks,
    I shucked off my clothes as they asked.
    And they brought up that cat behind me—
        That evil thing!
    And the one dragged him along my flank   65
        Down to the heels.

12. Then all at once she pulls that cat
    By his tail, and does he scratch!
    They gave me more than a hundred strokes
        In just that time;   70
    But I wouldn't have moved an inch—
        Till brink of death.

13. "Sister," said Agnes to Emma,
    "He's mute, and that's for sure!
    Let's get him ready for his bath   75
        And a nice, long stay."
    I stayed there a good eight days or more
        In their oven.

14. And I screwed them this many times:
    One hundred and eighty-eight.   80
    And I almost fractured my straps
        And my gear.
    And I'll never be able to tell you
        My later pain.

15. No, I'll never be able to tell you   85
    About that pain!

[44] *Companho, farai un vers tot covinen*

1. Friends, I'll write a poem that will do:
   But it'll be full of fun
       And not much sense,
   A grab bag all about love
   And joy and youth.   5

2. A man's a fool if he doesn't get it
   Or deep down inside won't try
       To learn.
   It's very hard to escape from love
   Once you find you like it.   10

3. I've got two pretty good fillies in my corral:
   They're ready for any combat—
       They're tough.
   But I can't keep 'em both together:
   Don't get along.   15

4. If I could tame 'em the way I want,
   I wouldn't have to change
       This setup,
   For I'd be the best-mounted man
   In all this world.   20

5. One's the fastest filly up in the hills,
   And she's been fierce and wild
       A long, long time.
   In fact, she's been so fierce and wild,
   Can't stick her in my pen.   25

6. The other was born here—Confolens way—
   And I never saw a better mare,
       I swear!
   But she won't change her wild, wild ways
   For silver or gold.   30

7. I gave her to her master a feeding colt;
   But I kept myself a share
       In the bargain too:
   If he'll keep her one whole year,
   I will a hundred or more.   35

---

44. Ed. Bond, No. 1. For the extended sexual metaphor of a woman as an automobile instead of a horse, see E. E. Cummings' "She being Brand/—new."

8. Knights, your advice in this affair!
   I was never so troubled by
      Any business before.
   Which of these nags should I keep:
   Miss Agnes? Miss Arsen? 40

9. I've got the castle at Gimel under thumb,
   And over at Nieul I strut
      For all the folks to see.
   Both castles are sworn and pledged by oath:
   They belong to *me!* 45

[45*] *Ab la dolchor del temps novel*

1. In the sweetness of the budding spring
   When woods are leafing, winged things
   Cast their songs in native speech
   By the verse of their own spring chant;
   Ah, then for men it's right that each 5
   Should have the easing that he wants.

2. From where all's goodness, all is beauty,
   Comes no seal, no runner on duty,
   And so my heart can't laugh or rest;
   And I dare not draw on for a task 10
   Till I know if my entire behest
   Will be fulfilled as I have asked.

3. Our love affair will be reborn
   Like a branch upon a hawthorn
   Which, trembling over the trunk, will sway 15
   At nighttime in the hail and rain,
   But come the dawn, the sun's bright rays
   Make leaf and branch all green again.

4. O I still remember that day
   When we signed a truce to our fray, 20
   And she gave me that gift I adore:
   Her loving, with ring in troth.
   God, let me live some more
   To put my hand beneath her cloak!

5. No strange Latin do I need 25
   To part my Good Neighbor from me:

45. Simile in stanza 3 adapted by Dante in *Inferno* II.127 ff. The *senhal* (secret name) Good Neighbor in stanza 5 deliberately mimics Christian charity.
   *Original text appears in Section IX, taken from Bond, No. 10.

For I know how the gossiping spreads
In some quick talk that runs rife.
We don't need to brag how our love's bred:
No, we have the meat and the knife!   30

[46] *Farai un vers de dreit nien*

1. I'll write a verse about sheer nil—
   Not about me or any other guy.
   Of youth and love I've had my fill,
       As of other hack.
   I wrote this ditty with one half-open eye   5
       On my horse's back.

2. I don't know the hour I first saw the light.
   I'm not way up high, yet I'm not in a ditch,
   I'm not all involved, yet I'm not up-tight.
       (That's the way it's willed);   10
   With a fairy's wand I was bewitched
       Atop a high hill.

3. I don't know when I wallow in sleep
   Or when I wake—unless I'm told.
   My heart from my body would like to sneak   15
       To escape heart's care.
   All this for a single ant could be sold—
       By Saint Martial I swear!

4. I'm sick, Lord, I'm afraid of dying.
   And I only understand what I hear.   20
   I need a doctor for my fantasizing,
       But don't know who.
   He'll be a good healer if he sets me clear—
       If not, I'm through.

5. I have a girl friend—don't know who—   25
   For I've never seen her (in faith I swear!).
   She never solaced me, never abused—
       But what the hell!
   A Norman or Frank never once dared
       Enter my *grand hôtel!*   30

6. I never saw her, but love her strong;
   She never did me good or bad;

---

46. Riddle Poem. The cause of the confusion is undoubtedly love; the ending is clearly sexual. Some editors read *soritz* (mouse) in line 17; Bond reads *fromitz*, "ant." St. Martial's cult was centered in Limoges, where it was noted for its music school.

When I don't see her, there's nothing wrong,
    It's an even score,
For a prettier, better one makes me glad,   35
    Who's worth a lot more.

7. I don't know the place where she stays—
   If it's in the hills or on the plain—
   And I can't mention the wrong she relays
     So I'll let it die;   40
   And since it costs too much to remain,
     Away I'll fly.

8. I've made the *vers* about someone or other
   And I'm sending it to a man I've pressed
   To pass it onward through another   45
     Toward Anjou for me;
   And let that one send for her secret chest
     The counterkey.

[47] *Pos de chantar m'es pres talenz*

1. Now that I've singing's bent
   I'll strike a tune for a lament
   Never to be love's obedient
   In Limoges or in Poitou.

2. Now into exile I will go.   5
   In peril, in frightful woe,
   I leave my son to face war's throe
   And the wrongs my neighbors do.

3. O leaving the lordship of Poitou
   Is such a bitter thing to do!   10
   Watch my lands, Foulques d'Anjou—
   And your little cousin too.

4. If Foulques refuses to lift a hand,
   Like the King, grace of my land,
   Evils will come from those bands   15
   Of Gascons and men of Anjou.

47. Threnody (Planh) on His Own Death. Safest date of composition in 1111–1112 or 1119, before the actual death, when his son, William X, succeeded him under very peaceful circumstances. William conducted a long, adulterous love affair in his later years with the wife of Foulques IV (the Rough) of Anjou. "Vair" and "gris" in the last line are expensive furs. This poem was not sung at William's funeral. No music survives for his poems, but a fragment from the *Jeu de Sainte Agnes* contains the melody.

5. Unless my son is wise, shows worth,
   Once I've left this native earth
   Tossing him over will bring them mirth
   Because he's weak and new.   20

6. Mercy I beg of you, dear friend.
   If ever I wronged you, make amends.
   To Jesus enthroned, I pray: defend!—
   In Provençal, in Latin too.

7. O I was a man of prowess and wit,   25
   But now I renounce each single bit;
   I'll go to him who sin remits
   Where men can end renewed.

8. Yes, I was a jaunty lord, and gay.
   But another Lord points another way.   30
   Now these shoulders, burdened, sway
   As my end looms in view.

9. Now I abandon chivalry, pride,
   Everything that I never denied.
   What pleases him I'll abide: 35
   May he hold me ages through!

10. At my funeral, friends, I pray:
    Gather around, shout your praise,
    For I've known many happy days
    Far and near, and in Poitou.   40

11. But now I surrender my joy, my pleasure:
    My vair and gris, my sable treasure.

CERCAMON

[48] *Qant la douch'aura s'amarcis*

1. When the gentle breeze turns bitter
   And the leaf snaps off the bough
   And the birds reverse their twitter,
   Then I have to weep and sigh,
   For Love's got me in her clutches,   5
   And power over her I've not had much.

2. Hell no! from Love I get zero,
   Except for some trouble and pain.
   It would take some hard-working hero
   To get what I've got on my brain,   10
   For nothing stirred up my envy so
   Like the thing from which there's always "No!"

3. A jewel has set me bounding with joy;
   To a finer one I never aspired;
   But when I'm with her I feel so low   15
   I can't even tell her of my desire,
   And when I'm away (it seems to me)
   Sense goes, with sensibility.

4. The prettiest one you ever glimpsed
   Next to her isn't worth a damn;   20
   When the world goes into full eclipse
   She'll be a beacon in the gloom.
   O God! I pray: let me cling to her,
   Or watch her undressing in her room.

5. I hassle and I fret; I'm all up-tight   25
   For her love, asleep or awake.
   The thought of failing causes such fright
   It makes me afraid to make my demand.
   Okay, I'll serve her two years or three—
   This way she'll get the word from me.   30

48. Cercamon (*fl.* 1130–1148). Gascon singer and composer who traveled widely (his name means Search-the-World); the supposed teacher of Marcabrun. His Lament on the Death of William X (1137) is datable. The translation attempts to suggest a certain primitiveness in the verse, which has an *ABABCD* rhyme scheme. (Note: capital letters for rhyme schemes indicate that the very same rhymes are used in every single stanza of the poem.) Only 8 poems survive. See *The Poetry of Cercamon and Jaufre Rudel*, ed. G. Wolf and R. Rosenstein (Garland, 1983), No. 3. For another colloquial translation, see Paul Blackburn, *Proensa* (U. California, 1978), pp. 25–30.

6. I'm not alive or dead or well;
   I don't feel pain, but I've got a lot;
   Her love's a thing I just can't tell:
   Whether I'll get it or how or when.
   But the power of grace is in her all   35
   And that can lift me or make me fall.

7. I like it when she makes me crazy:
   I walk and gape or I stand and stare;
   It's all right if she yaps at me
   And bitches me constantly everywhere.   40
   For after the evil comes the good—
   Or at least it will if she thinks it should.

8. If she doesn't want me, I wish I'd died
   The day I put her high up above.
   O God! she killed deliciously   45
   When she gave me one fond look of love.
   She's cornered me in such a pen
   I can't see another woman again!

9. And so I go all hung up in this joy
   For if I respect and follow her,   50
   She'll make me false or make me fine,
   A conniver or a loyal courtier,
   A common peasant or a noble guy,
   All up-tight or flying high.

10 You can agree or feel affronts—   55
   She can retain me if she wants.

11. Cercamon says: to be debonair,
    Man, about Love you must never despair!

MARCABRU(N)

[49] *L'iverns vai e'l temps s'aizina*

1. Winter goes, and the time is pleasant,
   And the woods again are growing green,
   And flowers peep along the hawthorn,
   As birds go bounding with their joy—
      Ay!   5
   Now all men are gay with love;
   Each one's drawn to his mate—
      Yeah!
   According to his heart's desire.

2. Cold is quaking, drizzle rustles   10
   Against the gentle season's coming;
   Through the groves and thickets
   I hear the contests of those songs—
      Ay!
   And put myself to the trobar task,   15
   For I'll tell you how Love wanders,
      Yeah!
   And, maybe, how he rolls back too.

3. Low Loving spreads, confounding
   Control with gluttonous appetite,   20
   Searching for that sweet dish of meat,
   Ever warmed by those nasty fires—
      Ay!
   Once a man slips in there—
   For real or just for a try—   25
      Yeah!
   Got to leave his skin behind in the pot!

4. Good Love packs a panacea
   To heal his loyal followers;
   But Low Loving spanks his disciples   30
   And sends 'em straight to Hell—
      Ay!

49. Marcabru(n) (*fl.* 1130–1150). According to the questionable *vidas* (biographies) in the songbooks, a Gascon orphan tended by Aldrics of Vilar and taught by Cercamon. First had the name Pamperdut (Lost Bread or Lost Britches), but later acquired his current name, which means Dark Spot. Perfected the *sirventes*, a non-amatory poem that is often satiric: example here. Supposedly murdered by some lords of Guyenne because of his wicked tongue. Some 45 poems survive. Here, sense obscure in stanzas 5 and 8. The lord in stanza 9 is probably Ebles II (the Singer) of Ventadorn. "Refined Love" in line 47 is *amor fina*; its opposite in line 19 is *Amars*. Edited by J. M. L. Dejeanne (Bibliothèque méridionale, *12*, 1909).

As long as the geld lasts here,
The poor fool thinks he's loved,
   Yeah!   35
But once the geld's gone, botch-up!

5. Low Loving lays a marvelous trap,
Luring the dupe into his lime
From the top down to his toes:
All messed up! Shall I? No?   40
   Ay!
Want a blonde, brunette, or black?
And will I do it? Or won't I?
   Yeah!
This way a fool gets a skinny rump.   45

6. A lady who loves her farmhand
Just doesn't know Refined Love.
No, she's got the bitch's instinct
Like the greyhound for the cur.
   Ay!   50
Out come those savage, mongrel rich
Who won't give you parties or pay—
   Yeah!
So swears Marcabrun!

7. The farmhand sneaks into the kitchen   55
To warm up some fire among the twigs
And lap up some of the fresh bouquet
From the cask of Milady Goodfount—
   Ay!
I know how he stays and loafs there,   60
Separating the grain from the chaff—
   Yeah!
Impeasantizing his master.

8. Who has Good Love as neighbor
And lives within his bondage   65
Sees Honor and Worth inclining
And Value—not any danger—
   Ay!
Does so much with honest words,
He need never fear the wrath—   70
   Yeah!
Of that lecher-livin' Sir Aigline.

9. I'll never pledge my troth
With Lord Eblés' pack of poets,
For too often there good sense   75
Falters, contrary to reason—
   Ay!

I said, I say, and always will:
High and Low Love have different cries—
    Yeah!
And whoever blames Good Love's an ass.
80

[50] *Pax in nomine Domini!*

1. *Pax in nomine Domini!*
   Marcabrun made the words and the song:
      Hear what he says.
   The most gracious Lord of Heaven
   Out of his sweetness has fashioned
   For our use here a washing tub,
   Unlike any other (except the one
   Overseas in the vale of Josephat).
   But to this one I summon you.
5

2. And it's rightful that we should bathe
   Our bodies from night till morn—
      I assure you.
   Everyone has his chance to scrub.
   And until he's healthy and hale,
   He ought to go straight to the tub,
   For there's our true therapy.
   And if we pass first to death,
   We'll fall to lowly lodging.
10
15

3. Small-Souledness and Lack-of-Faith
   Part Youth from his good companion.
      Ach, what grief!
   That most men prefer to go where
   The winnings belong to Hell!
   If we don't run quick to that big washtub
   Before our mouths and eyes are closed,
   Not a one's so puffed with pride
   That he won't face death's stronger match.
20
25

4. For the Lord who knows all that is
   And all that will be, and all that was
      Has promised us
   Honor in the name of the Emperor.
   And the beauty to come—do you know?—
   For those who will go to the tub:
30

---

50. Crusade Song with strong *sirventes* flavor. Written for the Second Crusade, about 1147. The Count in line 70 is probably Duke William X of Aquitaine, who died 10 years earlier at Compostela in Spain; his brother Raymond was Prince of Antioch (67). For music: Elektra EKL 31; CEPEDIC CEP 104; Harmonia Mundi HM 441; Hispavox HH (S) 6. Opening Latin line means: "Peace in the name of Our Lord!"

More than the star of morning joy,
If only they'll avenge the wrongs   35
To God, here and in Damascus.

5. In the line of Cain's descendants,
From that first villainous man,
      Come many heirs
Who won't bear their honor to God.   40
We'll see now who's his loyal friend.
For by virtue of the washing tub
We'll all own Jesus equally.
And let's throw back the loot
That accrues from luck and fortune.   45

6. And all those horny wineheads,
Dinner-snatchers and brand-blowers,
      Highway-crouchers
Can lurk behind in the lazy house:
God wants the brave and the fair   50
To step up to his washing tub;
And those will keep his mansions safe
And find the Adversary strong
And, 'gainst their shame, I chase them out!

7. In Spain, over here, Marquis Ramon   55
And those from the Temple of Solomon
      Suffer the weight
And the pain of the Paynim pride.
And so Youth gets a vile report.
And the cry for this washing tub   60
Rolls over the richest overlords
Who're feeble, failing, bereft of nerve,
For they don't value Joy nor Fun.

8. The Franks are all degenerates
If they say no to the task of God   65
      That I commend.
Ah, Antioch! Virtue and Valor
Are mourned in Guyenne and Poitou!
God our Lord, to your washing tub
Bring the Count's soul in peace;   70
And here guard Poitiers and Niort,
O Lord who issued from the tomb!

[51] *L'autrier jost'una sebissa*

1. The other day along a hedgerow
   I found a half-breed shepherdess
   Who was rich with joy and sense,
   Seeming the daughter of a farmer,
   Wearing a hood and cape and gown,   5
   And a blouse of very rough stuff,
   With shoes and stockings of wool.

2. I approached her across the meadow:
   "Little girl," said I, "pretty thing,
   I'm worried the wind may sting you."   10
   —"Lord," said the little farm girl,
   "Thanks be to God and my nanny too,
   Little care I if the wind should blow
   Because I'm lighthearted and hale."

3. "Little girl," said I, "charming thing,   15
   I've torn myself away from the road
   To lend you some companionship,
   For a little farm girl like you
   Shouldn't go around pasturing beasts
   Without some equal fellowship   20
   In country like this, all by yourself."

4. "Sir," said she, "whatever I am,
   At least I know folly from sense.
   This equal fellowship of yours,
   Milord," said the little farm girl,   25
   "You can put where it rightly belongs,
   For whoever thinks she's got it
   In her grip's got only a pose."

5. "Little girl with noble manners,
   That man must have been a knight   30
   Who engendered you in your mother,
   And she was a courtly farm girl.
   The more I look, the prettier you are,
   And the joy of you makes me glitter.
   If only you'd be a bit humane!"   35

6. "Sir, my line and my heritage
   I see reverting directly back
   To the sickle and to the plow,

51. Comic Pastourelle where courtly attitudes are misdirected toward a serious peasant
girl. Strong rhyme: *aaabaab*. For music: Harmonia Mundi HM 398A, 566; Elektra EKL 31;
Studio Monastères SM 33=48; ECM 1368. Text by William D. Paden, *Medieval Pastourelle*
(Garland, 1987), II, No. 8.

Milord," said the little farm girl,
"But some men pretend to be knights   40
Who by right should be toiling away
In fields for six days a week."

7. "Little girl," said I, "a kindly fairy
   Cast a spell when you were born,
   One of radiant enchantment   45
   Far beyond any other farm girl's;
   And this charm would even double now
   If I could see you just one time
   Below me, with me on top!"

8. "Sire, you've praised me so much   50
   You've made me completely annoyed.
   Since you've raised my value so,
   Milord," said the little farm girl,
   "Now you'll draw this reward
   As my good-bye: 'Gape, fool, gape!   55
   And stand there staring till mid of day!'"

9. "Little girl, a savage heart and fierce
   A man can tame with a little handling.
   I'm well aware, at this time,
   That with a little farm girl like you   60
   A man can have some fine company
   In good, warmhearted friendship,
   As long as one doesn't dupe the other!"

10. "Sir, a man screwed-up and mad
    Will swear, pledge, put up stakes;   65
    And so you'd bring me homage, eh?
    Milord," said the little farm girl.
    "But I, for a piddling entrance fee,
    Don't want to change my name
    From a virgin into a slut."   70

11. "Little girl, let every creature
    Revert directly to his nature;
    Let's use pure words,"
    Said I, "my little peasant girl,
    In the bower over by the meadow;   75
    There you'll feel much safer
    When we do the sweet, sweet thing!"

12. "Sire, yes! but according to rightness:
    A fool pursues his own folly,
    A noble man a noble outcome,   80
    And a farmhand with his farm girl;

Good sense is ruptured in that place
Where a man doesn't look for measure—
So say the ancient folk."

13. "Little girl, I never saw a figure   85
    More mischievous than yours,
    And I never met a heart more vile."

14. "Lord, the owl sends you this prophecy:
    One man gapes at a painting
    While the other prays for his manna."   90

[52*] *A la fontana del vergier*

1. In the orchard at a stream
   Where grass is green along the sand
   Under the shade of a budding tree
   With flowers white for company
   And the usual spring refrains,   5
   I found alone, with no friend there,
   A girl who did not want my care.

2. She was a maiden lovely to see,
   Daughter of a lord of a doughty keep;
   And when I thought that birds and grass   10
   Might bring some joy to the precious lass,
   As well as the delicate new season,
   And that she'd listen to my speech,
   Suddenly her manner changed.

3. Her eyes began weeping by that spring,   15
   And sighs from the heart came issuing:
   "Jesus!" she said, "King of this world,
   For *your* sake my great sadness grows.
   It's *your* fault that I'm all confused,
   For the finest man on all the earth   20
   Goes serving you—and this you like.

4. "With you he goes, my gentle friend, .
   The handsomest, noblest, richest of men!
   And here he leaves me in great distress,
   With constant crying and constant care.   25
   Ach! curses on that King Louís!
   He issued the summons and sermons too
   That let this pain come rushing in!"

---

52. Pastourelle in terms of dramatic action, but a Complaint on the Crusade in terms of the woman's lyric. The King in line 26 is Louis VII of France, who organized the Second Crusade in 1147. The last two lines admit several interpretations.
    *Original text appears in Section IX, from Paden, *Medieval Pastourelle*, I, No. 10.

5. When I had heard her make her lament
   I walked to the brookside radiant: 30
   "Beautiful," said I, "too many tears
   Spoil your features and complexion.
   It isn't good to be dejected,
   For he who makes the woodland bloom
   Can give you plenty of joy."   35

6. "Milord," said she, "I firmly believe
   That God will grant mercy to me
   In that other age for evermore
   As he will to sinners by the score;
   But *here* he's snatched away the thing   40
   That brought me joy; I just can't pray
   Because that man's too far away. . . ."

JAUFRE RUDEL

[53*] *Lanqan li jorn son lonc en mai*

1. In May when the days are long
   I like the sound of birds far away,
   And when I depart from their songs
   I remember my love who's far away.
   Head hanging I go, grief-torn.   5
   No song, no flowering hawthorn
   Do I admire more than winter ice.

2. And lord I'll rightly call the one
   Who'll help me see my love so far!
   But now instead of good I've won   10
   Two evils: he and I so far!

53. Jaufre Rudel (*fl.* 1140–1150). A noble from Blaye, on the Garonne River, believed to
have taken part in the Second Crusade from a mention by Marcabrun. Hero of a romantic
legend based on this poem, which states that he fell in love with the Princess of Tripoli from
hearsay, crossed the sea to find her, and fell dead in her arms; out of sorrow she reputedly
became a nun. Celebrated by Rostand's play, *The Far-Away Princess*. Only six poems usually
attributed to him. For recording, Harmonia Mundi HM 398B and 566; Archiv 14068 APM;
Elektra EKL 31; Philips A 00773, etc.

   *Original text appears in Section IX, taken from *The Poetry of Cercamon and Jaufre Rudel*, ed.
G. Wolf and R. Rosenstein (Garland, 1983), No. 6; music, Plates 1, 2, ed. Hendrik van der
Werf.

Ah, I'd take to the pilgrim's way
And stand with a staff, arrayed
In a cloak, reflected by her eyes!

3. For the love of God, what bliss   15
   To seek out her hostel far away,
   Where, if she wants, I'll insist
   On lodging by her, now far away.
   Then talking will be truly dear
   When this far-off lover, near,   20
   Hears speech that brings me solace's prize.

4. Half joyed, half pained would I depart
   From sight of my love so far away;
   But now! when can I even start?
   Our lands are so very far away!   25
   O I'd just get lost in the maze
   Of those many lanes and highways. . . .
   But—in God the matter lies!

5. Never will I know happiness
   In love, without my love who's far.   30
   She's the most graceful, very best,
   In any place, either near or far.
   For her, so fine beyond comparison,
   Even in the realm of the Saracens
   I'd gladly suffer the captive's cries!   35

6. God who made all that comes and goes
   And created this far-off love:
   Over me strength and courage dispose
   So that I really see my far-off love
   Abiding in such a dwelling place   40
   That her room, that her garden space
   Will always assume palatial size!

7. You're right if you say I lust or
   Burn for my far-off love.
   All other joys lose their luster   45
   Compared to that from my far-off love.
   But what I want is now denied
   Just as my godfather prophesied:
   I'd love but not feel love's reprise.

8. So what I want is now denied.   50
   Curse that godfather who prophesied
   I'd love but not feel love's reprise!

[54] *No sap chantar qui so non di*

1. He can't sing who can't make tunes;
   He can't write verse who can't work words,
   And he doesn't fathom the ways of rhyme
   If he can't encompass the sense itself.
   But my song starts like this: 5
   The more you hear it, the more it'll mean.
   Ah, ah!

2. Nobody should wonder about me
   If I love a thing that will never see me,
   For my heart never found any other joy   10
   Except in that one I've never seen,
   And for no joy does it laugh so much,
   And I don't know what good will come—
   Ah, ah!

3. Blows of joy strike me, they kill—   15
   And the prick of love starts stripping off
   My flesh, so my body's soon all bones;
   Never was I so gravely stricken,
   And for no other blow have I languished so,
   For it's no comfort, nor fitting either—   20
   Ah, ah!

4. Never did I sink sweetly to sleep
   But that my spirit wasn't soon there;
   Never did my heart feel such wrath here
   But it soon found itself again back there;   25
   And when I wake up in the morning,
   All my good knowledge deserts me,
   Ah, ah!

5. I know I never found joy in her
   And never will she be rejoicing for me,   30
   Nor ever consider me her friend;
   Nor will she make me a pact to herself;
   She never told me truth, nor lies,
   And I don't know if she'll ever do it:
   Ah, ah!   35

6. Good is the verse—I never once failed—
   And everything here stands in its place,
   And he who wants to learn from me
   Should guard against jostling, breaking it,

54. Riddle Poem. Music: Wolf-Rosenstein, Plates 9, 10, ed. H. van der Werf, recorded on Elektra EKL 31; lyrics, No. 3.

For this way they'll get it in Quercy,   40
Sir Bertran and the Toulousain Count:
Ah, Ah!

7. Good is the verse—and there they'll do
   Something of which a man can sing.
   Ah, Ah!   45

BERNART DE VENTADORN

[55*] *Can vei la lauzeta mover*

1. When I see the lark moving
   His wings with joy toward the light,
   Then forget and let himself fall
   From the sweetness that enters his heart,
   O! what great envy I feel   5
   Toward whomever I see who's glad!
   I wonder why my heart
   Doesn't melt right away from desire.

2. Alas! how much I thought I knew
   About love, and how little I know!   10
   For I can't keep myself from loving
   Her who'll give me nothing in return.
   She's stolen my heart and all of me
   And all herself and all the world;
   And after she robbed me, left me nothing   15
   Except desire and a longing heart.

3. Yes, I lost all power over myself,
   I wasn't mine from that moment on
   When she let me look into her eyes,

55. French: Bernard de Ventadour (*fl.* 1140–1180). Supposedly the son of a furnace-tender of Ebles (II or III) of Ventadorn (modern Ventadour, a ruined castle). After alleged misadventures with Ebles' wife, he was befriended by Henry II of England and Queen Eleanor in London; possibly joined Eleanor during her return to Poitiers. Later resided in Toulouse and Narbonne; believed to have died in the Monastery of Dalon. About 45 works survive. Tristan in stanza 8 is either the secret name for the poet's lady (masculinized in keeping with the term Milord) or the name of a jongleur. Rhyme: *ABABCDCD*. For music: Telefunken Das Alte Werk 6.41126(1); Harmonia Mundi HM 566; Elektra EKL 31; Philips A 00773R; Nimbus N 5002.

*Original text appears in Section IX, taken from the classic edition of Carl Appel (Niemeyer, 1915), No. 43.

Into a mirror I like so well.   20
Mirror, since I first saw myself in you,
Deep sighs have murdered me,
And I lost myself the way
Handsome Narcissus lost himself in the pool.

4. About women I feel great despair.   25
   Never again will I trust them.
   And although I used to protect them,
   From now on, I'm defecting,
   Since I see not a one will help me
   Against her who destroys and upsets me.   30
   I despair of them all, distrust them all,
   For I know very well that they're all like that!

5. And so My Lady's acting like a "woman"
   (And I blame her for it!),
   For she doesn't want what a man ought to want   35
   And whatever a man forbids, she does.
   I've fallen into very foul grace.
   I've carried on like the fool on the bridge,
   And I don't know why it's happened:
   Did I climb too high on the hill?   40

6. All grace is lost—it's true—
   (And I never even tasted it!)
   Since she who ought to have it most
   Has none; where will I find it?
   O! how bad it seems (if you see her)   45
   That she who owns this longing slave
   Who'll never have anything good without her
   Lets me die, won't lend me her aid.

7. Since prayers, thanks, and the rights I own
   Can't help me gain Milordess,   50
   And she doesn't care a bit
   That I love her, I'll never tell her of it.
   No, I'll leave her. I'll give her up.
   She's murdered me. As a corpse I speak.
   I'm going away since she won't retain me   55
   Downcast, to exile, I don't know where.

8. Tristan, you'll get nothing more from me.
   I'm going away, downcast, I don't know where.
   I'm through with songs, I'm giving them up.
   I'm hiding myself from love and joy.   60

[56] *Tant ai mo cor ple de joya*

1. I have a heart so filled with joy
       Everything changes its nature:
   Flowers white, crimson, and gold
       Seems the frost,
   For with the wind and the rain   5
       My fortune keeps on growing;
   Ah yes, my worth keeps mounting,
       My song's improving too.
   I have a heart so full of love
       And joy and sweetness,   10
   That the ice appears to me a flower,
       And the snow lies green.

2. I can go out without my clothes,
       Naked in my shirt,
   For fine, true love will keep me safe   15
       From wintry blasts.
   But a man's a fool to lose measure
       And not to toe the line,
   And so I've taken special care
       Ever since I fixed on   20
   The most pretty love who ever lived,
       From whom I expect great honor.
   For in place of the wealth of her
       I'd not take Pisa.

3. She can cut me off from her friendship,   25
       But I rest secure in my faith
   That at least I've carried away
       The beautiful image of her.
   And I have for my own devices
       Such a store of happiness   30
   That until the day when I see her,
       I'll feel no anxiousness.
   My heart lies close to Love and
       My spirit runs there too,
   Though my body's anchored here, alas!   35
       Far from her, in France.

4. Still I have steady hope from her
       (Which does me little good),
   For she holds me as if in a balance
       Like a ship upon the waves,   40
   And I don't know where to hide myself
       From woes besetting my senses.

56. Secular parody of Christian "contempt for the world." Rhyme: *abababbabcccb*. Ed.
Appel, No. 44.

All night long I toss and I turn
    Heaving upon my mattress:
I suffer greater torment in love   45
    Than that archlover Tristan,
Who underwent so many pains
    To gain Isolde the Blonde.

5. O God! Why am I not a swallow
    Winging through the air,   50
Coming through the depths of night
    There inside her chamber?
My good, joy-bearing lady,
    Your lover here's expiring.
I'm afraid my heart may melt   55
    If things go on like this.
Lady, because of your love
    I join my hands and adore:
Beautiful body with healthy hues,
    You make me suffer great woe.   60

6. There isn't any affair of the world
    That can occupy me more
Than the mere mentioning of her;
    Then my heart leaps high
And light suffuses my face, and   65
    Whatever you hear me say of it,
It will always appear to you
    That I really want to laugh.
I love that woman with such good love
    That many a time I cry,   70
And to me my sighs contain
    A far better savor.

7. Messenger, go on the run:
    Tell to my pretty one
The pain, O yes the grief   75
    I bear—and torment.

[57] *Lo tems vai e ven e vire*

1. The seasons come and turn and go
Through days and months and years,
And I, alas! have nothing to say,
For my desire is always one.
It's always one; it never changes: 5
I want the woman I've always wanted,
The one who never gave me joy.

57. Ebles in line 23 is probably Ebles III of Ventadorn (1148–70). Rhyme: *ABABCCD*.
Ed. Appel, No. 30.

2. Because she never ceases mocking,
   I'm rewarded grief and loss,
   For she made me sit at such a game   10
   That I've been the loser, two to one;
   Yet this kind of love soon is lost
   When only one side maintains it,
   Unless somehow a pact is reached.

3. I should stand my own accuser   15
   Indicting myself with every right,
   For never was man of woman born
   Who served so long, yet all in vain.
   And if she doesn't punish me for it,
   My folly will keep on doubling still,   20
   For a fool never fears till he's taken.

4. Never again shall I be a singer
   Nor part of that school of Lord Ebles,
   For all my songs aren't worth a jot,
   Nor my voltas, nor my melodies.   25
   And not a single thing I do
   Or say would seem to work me well:
   No, I see no improvement there.

5. Even though I make show of joy,
   My heart is filled with wrath.   30
   Who ever displayed such penitence
   Before he even committed a crime?
   The more I beg her, the harder she is,
   But if she doesn't soon relent,
   We'll come to a parting of the ways.   35

6. And yet it's good that she should bend me
   And make me subject to her will,
   For even if she dallies wrongly,
   Soon, I'm sure, she'll pity me.
   For so declares the Holy Scripture: 40
   A cause that has a happy outcome
   Makes the day worth a hundred more.

7. Never would I part from my life
   As long as I am safe and sound,
   For after the bran has blown away,   45
   The straw keeps fluttering a long, long time.
   And even if she isn't eager yet,
   Never would I take her name in vain
   If, from now on, she mends her ways.

8. Ah, my good, my coveted lover,   50
   Body well-shaped, delicate, smooth,

Lively features all rosy-hued,
Which God created with his very hands,
All this time I've desired you,
And nothing else has pleased me.   55
No other love do I want one bit.

9. Sweet and well-instructed creature,
   May he who formed you grant to me
   The happiness I long for.

[58] *Chantars no pot gaire valer*

1. A song cannot in any way have value
   If the singing doesn't spring from heart,
   And the singing cannot well from breast
   Unless its source is fine, true love.
   And so my verse looms high,   5
   For I have joy from love, devoting there
   My mouth and eyes, my heart and mind.

2. Dear God, I pray: never grant the might
   To ward away this rage for love.
   And if I knew I'd never have a thing,   10
   And every day would bring worse ill,
   Still I'd have my good heart at least;
   For I have much more enjoyment:
   Yes, good heart, and the strength to strive.

3. Foolish folk in their ignorance curse   15
   The work of love; yet no loss!
   For love is not about to crumble,
   Unless it's that "vulgar" kind;
   For that's not love; it's acting
   With the name, it's sheer pretense;   20
   There nothing's loved except what's grabbed.

4. And if I wanted to tell the truth,
   I know from whom comes all this deceit:
   From ladies who love for mere possessions,
   Who are nothing but common whores.   25
   I should be a liar—yes, false,
   But instead I speak the truth shamefaced,
   And I'm worried that I can't tell lies.

5. In mutual pleasure and in common will
   Resides the love of two fine lovers.   30
   And nothing good will ever come
   If the desire is not an equal thing.

58. Rhyme: *ABACCDD*. Ed. Appel, No. 15.

And he's a natural-born idiot
Who reproaches love for what it wants
And asks for a thing that's not quite right.   35

6. I know I've rightly placed my hope
   Whenever she shows me a cheerful face,
   The one I desire, want most to see,
   That noble, sweet, true, faithful one
   By whom even a king would be saved: 40
   The lovely, gracious, perfectly shaped
   Who raised me from nothing into wealth.

7. I've nothing dearer, fear no one more,
   And there's no task that's burdensome to me
   If it should please my lady master.   45
   That day will seem like Christmastime
   When she gives me one sure look
   With those beautiful, those spiritual eyes—
   So slow, that day will last a century.

8. The verse is polished; it's natural too,   50
   And good for the man who gets it all,
   And better for him who expects his fun.

9. Bernart de Ventadorn has made the plan;
   He spoke and made it; he expects his fun.

[59] *Lo gens tems de pascor*

1. The sweet season of rebirth
   With its freshening green
   Draws for us flower and leaflet
   With many a different hue;
   And therefore every lover   5
   Is gay and full of song—
   But me, I cry and clamor
   Without a taste of joy.

2. To all I lament, good men,
   About Milordess and Love,   10
   For I placed my faith in them—
   Those ever treacherous two—
   And they've turned my life to grief;
   And the good and all the honor
   I have rendered to the fairest   15
   Counts for nothing, gives no aid.

59. The "*pascor*" of the opening line means either spring or Easter. Heavy monorhyme. Ed. Appel, No. 28.

3. Pain and grief and damage
   I've had, and I have a lot;
   And yet I've borne it all.
   And I don't even think they're harsh,   20
   For you've never seen any other lover
   Offer better without deceit:
   No, I don't go around changing
   The way those women do.

4. Since we both were children,   25
   I have loved her, courted her well,
   And my joy goes ever doubling
   Through each day of every year.
   And if she doesn't offer me
   A welcome-look and her love,   30
   Then when she's aging, let her beg
   Me to offer my desire then!

5. Woe's me! What good is living
   If I can't see day by day
   My fine, true, natural joy   35
   In her bed, stretched under a window,
   Body pure white from head to toe
   Like the snow at Christmastide,
   So that we two lying together
   Can measure each other's sides!   40

6. Never was a loyal lover seen
   Who enjoyed a worse reward;
   For I love her with sincere love,
   And she says: "What do I care?"
   In fact, she says that's why   45
   She shows me her deadly rage,
   And if she hates me for this cause,
   Then *she's* guilty of a mortal sin.

7. Surely there'll some day be a time,
   My lady beautiful and good,   50
   When you can pass me secretly
   The sweet reward of a little kiss:
   Give it only on the grounds
   That I am taken with desire.
   One good is worth two others   55
   If the others are gained by force.

8. When I behold your features,
   Those gorgeous eyes full of love,
   I can't help wondering to myself
   How you can answer me so vilely.   60

And I consider it high treason
When a person seems honest and pure
And turns out puffed with pride
In places where he is strong.

9. Pretty Face, if my above-all   65
   Didn't stem from you alone,
   I'd long ago have left my songs
   Through the ill of the evil ones.

[60] *Can la frej'aura venta*

1. When biting breezes blow
   Out of your demesne,
   It seems to me I feel
   A wind from Paradise
   Because of my love for the noble one   5
   Toward whom I bow my head,
   To whom I pledge my will
   And direct my feelings;
   From all other ladies I part:
   So much she pleases me.   10

2. Even if she only gave me
   Her beautiful eyes and noble face,
   And never granted further pleas,
   Still she'd have conquered me.
   Why should I lie about it?   15
   (For in no way am I sure.)
   Hard it would be to show repentance
   After that time she told me
   That a good man gathers his strength
   While a bad one crouches scared.   20

3. The ladies, it seems to me,
   Are making a big mistake
   Because in no way at all
   Do they love their sincere lovers.
   I know that I shouldn't accuse them,   25
   Should say what they want to hear,
   But it pains me when a cheater gets
   Some loving out of sleight of hand,
   Or even more or just the same
   As a fine, true, noble lover.   30

4. Lady, what are you trying to do
   To me who love you so?

60. Rhyme: *abababba.* Ed. Appel, No. 37.

For you see how I'm suffering
And how I'm dying of desire.
Ah! noble woman, debonaire,   35
Give me a pleasant look,
One to lighten up this heart,
For I'm racked with many woes
And I shouldn't have to pay the price
Just because I can't break free.   40

5. If it wasn't for evil people
   And savage smooth-tongued spies,
   My love would be guaranteed to me,
   But instead I'm tugged back.
   She is human to me in her comfort   45
   When time and place are right,
   And I know that underhandedly
   I'll get a lot, lot more,
   For the blessed man sleeps in peace,
   And the unlucky one in pain.   50

6. I'm a man who never scorns
   The good that God creates for him:
   For in that selfsame week
   When I parted from her side,
   She told me in clear, plain terms   55
   That my singing pleases her much.
   I wish every Christian soul
   Could have the same kind of joy
   That I had then and have:
   It's the *only* thing to brag of.   60

7. And if she guarantees me this,
   Another time I'll believe her;
   If not, never will I believe
   Another Christian lady.

RAIMBAUT OF ORANGE

[61] *Escotatz, mas no sai que's es*

1. Listen, lords! but I don't know what it is
   That I'm trying to say;
   It's not a love poem, not a satire,
   Nor an estribot; in fact, I can't find a name;
   And I don't know exactly how I'll carry it off   5
   If I don't know quite what it is,
   > Because nobody ever saw such a poem written by a man or a
   > woman in this century or any other gone by.

2. I know you think I'm a fool,
   But I just can't stop myself
   From telling you what I want.   10
   Nobody should blame me for it.
   But I don't care two little bits
   Except for what I can see
   > And I'll tell you why (if I don't carry this thing through to the
   > end, you'll be sure I'm mad): because I'd rather have six deniers
   > in my fist than a thousand sous in Heaven.

3. I beg my lady friend not to worry   15
   That she'll do something to bother me.
   If she doesn't want to offer help right away,
   Then let her offer it after some waiting.
   Nobody else could deceive me
   As easily as she who's won me.   20
   > I'm saying all this about a woman who makes me languish with a
   > few pretty words and long expectations—and I don't know why.
   > Do you think she'll be good to me, my lords?

4. Four months have passed by now—
   Yes, and it seems a thousand years—
   Since she guaranteed, she promised
   She'd give me what's most precious to me.   25

---

61. Or Raimbaut d'Aurenga (*ca.* 1144-1173). Lord of Orange and Courthézon, who squandered most of his patrimony in gambling, warring, and partying. Left about 40 poems, mostly in the complex *trobar clus* style. This self-styled "I-Don't-Know-What-It-Is" ridicules the notion of genres, as well as religion. It contains prose endings for every stanza. An "estribot" in line 4 is a mixed song, with some satire. The Latin in line 28 says: "In the name of the Father and the Son and the Holy Ghost!" See Walter T. Pattison, *Life and Works of the Troubadour Raimbaut d'Orange* (U. Minnesota, 1952), No. 24.

Lady, since you clutch my heart,
Sweeten up this bitter love.
> O God help me, in *nomine Patris et Filii et Spiritus Sancti!* Lady,
> what will become of all this?

5. Because of you, I'm gay, yet full of grief;
   Happy, sad, you make me sing;   30
   And I've just left three women the likes of whom
   The world has never seen—except for you.
   And I'm such a good-mannered but mad singer
   That people even call me a jongleur.
   > Lady, do with me what Lady Emma did with the shoulder bone
   > when she stuck it into her box whenever she wanted.   35

6. And so I've finished my Don't-Know-What-It-Is,
   For so I'd like to baptize it!
   Since I never heard the likes before,
   Let everyone call it by this name.
   And let them recite it by heart after learning it   40
   Whenever they want to have pleasure.
   > And if anyone asks who wrote it, answer: "A man who can do
   > anything he wants, when he happens to feel like it."

[62] *Ar vei bru, escur, trebol cel*

1. Now I see brown, dark, troubled heavens
   Where the wind in the sky hisses and lashes,
   And snow is falling with ice and frost,
   And the sun that was hot and strong and harsh
   Has a warmth now diminished and feeble,   5
   And leaf and flower fall down from branches
   So that neither in hedgerow nor grove of oak
   Do I hear a song—only cries in houses;
   And so I'm singing a little bit grim.

2. But wind or rain or even the ice   10
   Would not detain me more than the spring
   If I ever dared to open the book
   Of my deeds of love with their darkish words;
   Fear holds me back like a coat of mail,
   Though wrath makes me call Milady and complain.   15
   For never again of Love that hooks me
   Should I be singing in any fashion
   Until a pact comes between us two.

62. An extraordinary sample of *trobar clus* verging toward a kind of Satanism. The secret
name of the lady, Demoniada (60), is *not* typical of troubadour names; poem almost seems like
a premonition of the poet's death. Ed. Pattison, No. 10.

3. But I can sing well of that bitterness
   That I know is causing me such ill: 20
   Of those false ones, sharper than vipers,
   Envious, talkative, damnable scamps,
   For each one bites and constantly tries
   To make a fine lover's Joy go lame;
   And wherever you find some pork or beefsteak,   25
   They'll take their fill with unwatered wine;
   And then they issue shrieks, roars, and brays.

4. I know a traitorous, faithless bowman
   Who seems to have less sense than an ox—
   Yes, he's one of those villainous hayseeds   30
   Who takes pain as he carefully draws his bow
   To insack the heart of his master;
   And if his lord got poisoned in a field
   I don't think he'd run for an antidote;
   O no! he'd strive with all of his might   35
   To hang him up with some good strong bonds.

5. For even Cain, who murdered Abel,
   Didn't understand treachery one jot
   Like him—but I know that I sound drunk,
   'Cause I'm telling him why I feel so old,   40
   And it weights my shoulders and bludgeons me;
   And so much the hunger and pain are grieving
   Whenever I think of that Raca-bitch—
   Why, I couldn't begin to run down her lies
   The minute I think of that wicked Satan!   45

6. And yet my singing should smack of honey
   In this poem I've fashioned around New Year,
   When the galingale and the ginger-root
   Have their season with guzzling wassailers;
   And my Stirrup-Ring, who lives on past Jaca,   50
   Wouldn't act like this for two great damns
   (The way I act in this low, muddy rhyme)—
   Not even if Acre and Tyre were his (hers?),
   Or up this way, Poitou and Rouen.

First tornada
And now as I suffer Yule-branch blows,   55
If she (he?) isn't lying with darkened words,
It's *I* who am going to end up lame!

Second tornada
My verse is now completely leashed up
And I'd like to see it carried secure
To my Demon-Girl, may it make her grim!   60

[63] *Amics, en gran cossirier*

1. Friend, I stand in great distress
   Because of you, and in great pain;
   And I think you don't care one bit
   About the ills that I'm enduring;
   And so, why set yourself as my lover   5
   Since to me you bequeath all the woe?
   Why can't we share it equally?

2. Lady, Love goes about his job
   By chaining two friends together
   So the ills they have and the lightness too   10
   Are felt by each—in his fashion.
   Yes, I think—and I'm no gabber—
   That all this deep-down, heart-struck woe
   I have in full on my side too.

3. Friend, if you had just one-fourth   15
   Of this aching that afflicts me now,
   I'm sure you'd see my burden of pain;
   But little you care about my grief,
   Since you know I can't break free;
   But to you it's all the same   20
   Whether good or bad possesses me.

4. Lady, because these glozing spies,
   Who have robbed me of my sense and breath,
   Are our most vicious enemies,
   I'm stopping: not because desire dwindles.   25
   No, I can't be near, for their vicious brays
   Have hedged us in for a deadly game.
   And we can't sport through frolicsome days.

5. Friend, I offer you no thanks
   Because my damnation is not the bit   30
   That checks those visits I yearn for so.
   And if you set yourself as watchman
   Against my slander without my request,
   Then I'll have to think you're more "true-blue"
   Than those loyal Knights of the Hospital.   35

6. Lady, my fear is most extreme
   (I'll lose your gold, and you mere sand)
   If through the talk of these scandalmongers
   Our love will turn itself to naught.

63. Debate Poem (*tenso*) between Raimbaut and a nameless Lady, often identified as the
Countess of Dia, but the manuscripts list only Raimbaut as the author. Ed. Pattison, No. 25.

And so I've got to stay on guard 40
More than you—by St. Martial I swear!—
For you're the thing that matters most.

7. Friend, I know you're changeable
In the way you handle your love,
And I think that as a chevalier 45
You're one of that shifting kind;
And I'm justified in blaming you,
For I'm sure other things are on your mind,
Since I'm no longer the thought that's there.

8. Lady, I'll never carry again 50
My falcon, never hunt with a hawk,
If, now that you've given me joy entire,
I started chasing another girl.
No, I'm not that kind of shyster:
It's envy makes those two-faced talk. 55
They make up tales and paint me vile.

9. Friend, should I accept your word
So that I can hold you forever true?

10. Lady, from now on you'll have me true,
For I'll never think of another. 60

COUNTESS OF DIA

[64] *Estat ai en greu cossirier*

1. I've suffered great distress
From a knight whom I once owned.
Now, for all time, be it known:
I loved him—yes, to excess.
His jilting I've regretted, 5
Yet his love I never really returned.
Now for my sin I can only burn:
Dressed, or in my bed.

64. La Comtessa de Dia (1150–1200?). Mysterious poetess often identified as Beatritz, wife of Count William I of Valentinois (1158–1189), but without convincing proof. Only four or five poems attributed to her. Text: Hill-Bergin *Anthology*, No. 65. See William D. Paden, ed., *Voice of the Trobairitz* (U. Pennsylvania, 1989).

2. O if I had that knight to caress
    Naked all night in my arms,   10
    He'd be ravished by the charm
    Of using, for cushion, my breast.
        His love I more deeply prize
    Than Floris did Blancheflor's.
    Take that love, my core,   15
        My sense, my life, my eyes!

3. Lovely lover, gracious, kind,
    When will I overcome your fight?
    O if I could lie with you one night!
    Feel those loving lips on mine!   20
        Listen, one thing sets me afire:
    Here in my husband's place I want you,
    If you'll just keep your promise true:
        Give me everything I desire.

[65*] *A chantar m'er de so qu'ieu no volria*

1. I have to sing about something I'd rather not:
    I'm very upset about the man who's my friend,
    Since I love him more than anything else in the world.
    But my kindness and my courtesy to him are as nothing,
    Like my beauty and my virtue and my good sense;   5
    For I've been deceived and mistreated,
    The way I'd be if I were totally loathsome.

2. But still I feel consolation, my friend,
    Because I never failed you in any way—
    No! I love you more than Seguin did Valensa.   10
    And I'm very glad that I surpass you in love,
    Dear friend, because you're an outstanding man;
    But to me you're arrogant in word and deed,
    Even though you're open toward everyone else.

3. I stand in awe at how your heart grows cold,   15
    Dear friend, toward me—good reason why I grieve.
    It just isn't right for someone else to seize you
    For anything that she may say or do;
    Ah, just think back of those first happy days
    Of our affair! May God never will it   20
    That I should be the cause of any parting.

65. Sung in an Andalusian manner on Telefunken Das Alte Werk 6.41126(2), where the tornada, in an Arabic manner, is spoken; cf. London International V 91116 and Harmonia Mundi HMC 90396. See *The Writings of Medieval Women*, trans. Marcelle Thiébaux (Garland, 1987), 183–191. Seguin and Valensa were legendary lovers in a lost romance.
    *Original text in Section IX.

4. The great prowess that in your body resides
    And your rich virtue now hurt me,
    Since there's not a lady near or far
    Who, wanting loving, wouldn't be drawn to you.   25
    But you, my friend, are truly discriminating
    And you can tell who's the finest of them all;
    Just think of those covenants we exchanged!

5. My own noble worth and lineage should assist me,
    As well as my good looks and refined nature,   30
    And so I'm sending this poem as my messenger
    Over there where you hold your estate;
    I'd like to know, my fine fair friend,
    Why you're so savage to me and so cruel:
    Is it your proud nature or just ill will?   35

6. But, messenger, I want you to say one thing more:
    Many a man has suffered greatly for foolish pride!

AZALAIS OF PORCAIRAGUES

[66] *Ar em al freg temps vengut*

1. Now we've arrived at the frigid season
    With ice and snow and slush,
    When the birds remain all mute,
    As not one breaks out in song;
    And the branches through the woods are brittle   5
    Since not a flower or leaf will bud,
    And no nightingale cries out,
    Which I love and which always wakes me.

2. My inner self is so disrupted
    That I act foreign to everyone else;   10
    And I know that it's much easier
    To lose than to win at a game;

66. Azalais de Pourcairagues, near La Grand-Combe, or Portiragues, near Béziers (later 1100s). Only one poem survives. Little is known about her except for her love of Orange, whose Roman Arch (with other little-known details) is celebrated (see Plate 3), along with her "fright" of a lover (Raimbaut of Orange?). The tornada may praise that famous patroness of poets, Viscountess Ermengarde of Narbonne. For music with text: Harmonia Mundi HM 397A.

If I lose by speaking truthful words,
That "fright of Orange" has caused this,
Making me stand here all amazed   15
Losing some part of my consolation.

3. A lady places her love at great risk
   If she enters competition with a wealthy man
   Who is higher in rank than a vavassor;
   And if she does this, she's a blatant fool,   20
   At least that's what they say in Velay:
   That you should never fool around with wealth,
   And a lady who plays that game
   They judge to be quite villainous.

4. I have a friend of great value   25
   Who has mastery over a great deal,
   And he doesn't show a trickster heart
   Toward me, since he offers me his love.
   I assure you that my love belongs to him,
   And I hope that God will cast a hex   30
   On anyone who says that I lie,
   Since I consider myself quite secure.

5. My sweet friend, with unwavering will
   I pledge that I'm yours for evermore—
   You with the noble, handsome face—   35
   Only please don't ask me for too much;
   Soon we'll be coming to a test
   When I should surrender to your mercy;
   You have already pledged to me your faith,
   So please don't ask me now to err.   40

6. I commend my Bel Esgar (Pretty Face) to God
   And also the entire city of Orange
   And the Glorieta and the Caslar
   And the Lord of all Provence
   And all who wish me well there,   45
   And the Arch which shows a great triumph.
   I've lost the man who owns my life,
   And forever I'll be afflicted.

7. Jongleur, you who have a happy heart,
   Carry my song over there   50
   Toward Narbonne with this ending
   For her who is guided by joy and youth.

GUIRAUT DE BORNELH

[67] *Reis glorios, verais lums e clartatz*

THE COMPANION OUTSIDE:

1. Glorious King, true light and clarity,
   Almighty God, Milord, if it please thee,
   To my companion be a faithful friend;
   I haven't seen him since the night came on—
   And soon will come the dawn.   5

2. My dear companion, whether you wake or sleep,
   Rouse yourself up; it's time to vigil-keep;
   For in the orient—I know it well—
   I see the star that makes the day come on—
   And soon will come the dawn.   10

3. My dear companion, singing I call your name:
   Sleep no more, for I've heard the bird exclaim
   That goes in quest of day throughout the wood;
   And I fear the jealous one will make you pawn,
   For soon will come the dawn.   15

4. My dear companion, open the window wide—
   Look at the stars waning in the sky!
   See if I bring a true picture to your eyes;
   If you don't rush, all hope will soon be gone,
   For soon will come the dawn.   20

5. My dear companion, since you parted from me,
   I haven't slept, haven't left my knees;
   No, I have prayed to God, St. Mary's Son,
   To let your loyal companionship go on—
   For soon will come the dawn.   25

6. My dear companion, here on the terrace stones,
   You begged me not to sleep, to lie alone
   And keep my watch all night into the morn.
   My song, my love are things you'd soon see gone—
   But soon will come the dawn.   30

67. Or Giraut de Borneill (*ca.* 1155–*ca.* 1205). Considered in his own day "The Master Troubadour," but condemned by Dante and most moderns for his artificiality. This religious Dawn Song shows his skill. Of humble origin, perhaps from the hamlet of Bourneix in Dordogne, he traveled widely into Aragon and Navarre, leaving about 80 pieces. The last stanza is sometimes considered a crude interpolation and thus omitted. For music: ECM 1368; Atomic Theory 1102; Harmonia Mundi HM 441; Hispavox HH (S) 6; Columbia CBS 76038, etc.

Plate 4. The Castle of Altafort (now Hautefort) in Périgord, fought over by Bertran de Born and his brothers (see No. 68). The modern castle is larger than its medieval beginning. (Courtesy of Kenneth Alcock)

THE COMPANION INSIDE:
7. Ah, dear companion, I now know such delight;
   I want to see no morn, I want the night.
   The loveliest lady on whom Sun ever shone
   Lies in my arms. I say—to Hell be gone
      Those jealous ones and dawn!   35

BERTRAN DE BORN

---

[68] *Un sirventes on motz no faill*

1. I've made a sirventes where not a word
   Will fail, and it didn't cost me an onion,
   And I've learned the art of living so
   That with brothers, first and second cousins,
      I'll share an egg or a copper piece,   5
   And if later they try to grab my share,
      I'll toss them out of the tribe.

2(5). All my thoughts I keep in my safe,
      Although they've caused me trouble galore
      Between Sir Aimar and Sir Richard;   10
      A long time they've watched me distrustfully,
         But they're making such a ruckus
      That their babes, unless the King parts them,
         Will get it in the guts.

3(4). William of Gourdon, a muted clapper   15
      You've attached there inside your bell,
      And I like you—God help me, yes!

68. Bertran de Born (*ca.* 1140–*ca.* 1214). Master of the witty, satiric sirventes. Unfairly condemned by Dante as a sower of discord in *Inferno* XXVIII.113–142, and re-created by Pound's monologues in *Personae*. Lord of the castle of Hautefort (Altafort) in Périgord, shared with his brother Constantine, who had acquired it through marriage. His outcries against Richard the Lion-Hearted, Philip Augustus of France, various Spanish lords, and the local barons reflect the historical turbulence shown in this poem. About 47 poems survive, many of them preceded by prose explications (*razos*), which I omit. Here the primary contestants are Aimar (Ademar) V of Limoges, Richard, Elias VI of Périgord (nicknamed Talleyrand); affairs best dated in 1182. In the last line, the peacock warned the daw not to surpass the limits of measure. Rhyme: *AABBCBC*. Text: *Poems of the Troubadour Bertran de Born*, ed. William D. Paden, Jr., Tilde Sankovitch, and Patricia H. Stäblein (U. California, 1986), No. 3; the stanzaic order follows that of most other editors, showing the Paden order in parentheses.

But as a lunatic and a fool
   They count you, those two viscounts
Who made the pact; yet they yearn   20
To lock you in their buddyhood.

4(2). Every day I'm struggling, I'm brawling;
   I joust, I beat back, I contend;
   And they light my land and they burn it,
   And they turn my orchard to a pile of twigs,   25
      Blending my barley with my straw,
   And there's not one coward or diehard
      Who's not assailing my door.

5(7). Every day I resole, I regird,
   I recast those barons, I heat them up   30
For I want to send them hot to war.
Yet I'm a fool even to consider it
      Because their workmanship's worse
Than the chains that bound St. Leonard;
      A man's a damned fool to bother!   35

6(3). Talleyrand can't leap, he can't trot,
And he can't even move from Arenalh;
He can't pitch a lance or a dart:
No, he's living like a Lombard
      So stuffed up with inertia   40
That when other folks splinter away,
      He just stretches out and yawns.

7(6). At Périgueux, up to the wallwork
As far as a man can throw with mace,
I'll come armed on my horse Bayard,   45
And if I find some paunchy Poitevins,
   They'll find out how this sword cuts,
For I'll cover their heads with mud
   And mix their mail with brains.

8. Barons, God save you, God watch out,   50
   And help you, see you all wax hale;
And may he tell you to tell Lord Richard
   What the peacock said to the daw.

[69] *Be·m plai lo gais temps de pascor*

1. How I like the gay time of spring
   That makes leaves and flowers grow,

---

69. Pleasure Song, with war as theme. Doubtfully attributed. Ed. Paden et al., No. 30, who add some stanzas on love after st. 5; music, 495–497. See the author's *Seven Troubadours* (Penn State, 1970), pp. 154 ff. for an attempt to see more than warmongering here.

And how I like the piercing ring
Of birds, as their songs go
Echoing among the woods. 5
I like it when I see the yield
Of tents and pavilions in fields,
And O! it makes me feel good
To see arrayed on battlefields
Horses and horsemen with shields. 10

2. And I like it when the scouts
   Make people with property flee,
   And I like it when I see the rout
   Of a swarm of opposing armies;
   And O! how my spirits adore 15
   The sight of strong castles attacked
   With barricades broken and hacked
   And troops waiting on the shore
   That's completely encircled by ditches
   With strong-staked rows interstitched. 20

3. And likewise I like a lord
   Who's the first man out in the fray,
   On horse, armed, fearlessly forward,
   Inspiring his men to obey
   With his valiant deeds; 25
   And when the battle's fierce
   Everyone's prompt to pierce
   And freely follow his lead,
   For a soldier is soon forsaken
   Unless he's given many blows, and taken. 30

4. Maces, swords, helmets—colorfully—
   Shields, slicing and smashing,
   We'll see at the start of the melee
   With all those vassals clashing,
   And horses running free 35
   From their masters, hit, downtread.
   Once the charge has been led,
   Every man of nobility
   Will hack at arms and heads.
   Better than taken prisoner: be dead. 40

5. I tell you: no pleasure's so large
   (Not eating or drinking or sleep)
   As when I hear the cry: "Charge!"
   Or out of the darkened deep
   A horse's whinnying refrain 45
   Or the cry: "Help! Bring aid!"
   As big and little in turn cascade
   Into ditches across the plain,

And I see, by the corpses whose sides
Are splintered, flags unfurling wide.   50

6. Barons, put up as pawns
   Those castles, cities, and villas well-stored
   Before bringing each other war!

[70] *Miez sirventes vueilh far dels reis amdos*

1. About two kings I'll write half-a-sirventes,
   For shortly we'll see which one has more knights:
   Brave Alfonso of the Castilian throne
   Will come to look for hirelings, if I hear right.
   Richard will let his gold and silver fight   5
   By the bushel and peck; to him's no great fuss
   To lavish and spend; who cares about trust?
   Why, war's more to him than a quail to a kite!

2. If both these kings prove strong and hale,
   Soon we'll see strewn among our fields   10
   Helmets, swords, shields, and mail,
   And bodies, spear-split from belt to brain,
   And stallions running unmounted, unreined,
   And many a lance through thigh and chest,
   With tears and joy, sorrow and happiness.   15
   The loss'll be great; greater still the gain.

3. Trumpets and drums, banners and flags,
   Standards and stallions of every hue
   Soon we'll see as our great age drags
   The holdings from every usurious Jew.   20
   Down no highway will go no laden mule
   Trusting the day, no burgher unaskance,
   Nor any merchant heading out from France.
   No, he'll be rich who grabs as he chooses.

4. If Alfonso comes, I'll put my faith in God: 25
   Either I'll live or lie hacked on the sod.

5. And if I live, great will be my bliss;
   And if I die, thank God for what I'll miss!

---

70. Self-styled "Half-A-Sirventes." Richard the Lion-Hearted's opponent was Alfonso
VIII of Castile. Dating June 1190 by Paden et al., No. 38.

[71] *Belh m'es quan vey camjar lo senhoratge*

1. Ah, how I like to see great power pass
   As young men gather in the estates of old
   And everyone, with babies by the mass,
   Bequeaths hope for a leader brave and bold.
   Then I think that the age will soon renew   5
   Better than any flower or bird's refrain,
   For knowing that certain lords and ladies are through,
   We allow the young to take up hope again.

2. You can tell a lady's old by her balding hair;
   She's old, I say, when she hasn't any knight,   10
   Or if she takes her lovers by the pair,
   Or if she takes a lover full of spite;
   Old she is if she loves in her estate,
   Or if she uses magic as a crutch.
   I call her old when jongleurs irritate   15
   And certainly she's old if she talks too much!

3. A lady's young when she values noble rank
   And likes good deeds whenever good's been done;
   I call her young if her heart is fine and frank
   And she casts no evil eye on valor won.   20
   She's young if she keeps her body well looked after,
   Young if she knows exactly how to behave;
   I call her young if gossip brings her laughter,
   And if she can keep herself with her lover safe.

4. A man is young if he'll risk his hard-won hoard,   25
   He's young if he's ever suffered need or want.
   I call him young if he spreads an expensive board
   Or if his gifts approach the extravagant.
   He's young when he burns all his chests and treasure
   And wars and jousts and hunts and rambles.   30
   He's young if he knows every woman's pleasure,
   And young he is if he yearns to gamble.

5. A man is old when he's scared to take a dare
   And stores away his bacon, wine, and wheat.
   I call him old if he offers eggs and Gruyère   35
   On days when he and his friends are allowed meat.
   He's old when he shivers under both cape and cloak,
   Old, if he rides on a horse he hasn't tamed;
   Old, if a day of peace doesn't seem a joke,
   Or if he runs away from a gory game.   40

---

71. Self-styled "Young-Old Song," conceived partially in the genre of the Pleasure Song. Ed. Paden et al., No. 24. Some would like to make the jongleur in line 41 Arnaut Daniel.

6. Arnaut jongleur, take my song "Young-Old"
   To Richard, let him watch it, see it's sung:
   Let him not care a damn for gold that's old,
   But only prize his treasures when they're young!

[72] *Dompna, puois de mi no·us cal*

1. Lady, since your heat is not for me
   And you've drifted from my side
   Without the slightest reason,
   I don't know where to search,
   For never again   5
   Shall such rich joy be garnered
   By me; and if I can't find another
   Of the same kind who meets my liking,
   Worth the same price as you I've lost,
   Never again will I have a lover.   10

2. And since I'll never find your like,
   One who's both beautiful and good,
   Whose body's richly full of joy,
   With lovely manners
   And ever gay,   15
   Whose worth is wealthy and ever true,
   I'll go around subtracting
   One pretty feature from every girl
   To make my Lady Self-Conceived,
   Who'll last me till I have you back.   20

3. That healthy, fresh complexion
   I'll take, pretty Cembelis, from you,
   And also that sweetly loving look;
   And yet there's superabundance
   Of things I leave,   25
   For pretty things you're never lacking.
   Milordess Aelis, from you I beg
   Your graceful mode of conversation,
   For you could give Milady help;
   Never will she be fool or mute.   30

4. And I wish the Viscountess of Chalais
   Would give me in full possession
   Her throat and both of her hands.
   And then I'll direct my career
   Without false turn,   35

72. Often referred to as "The Song of the Self-Conceived Lady." Magnet (Aziman) could either be a woman or the troubadour Folquet of Marseille, as interpreted by Paden et al., No. 7. Ezra Pound made much of this poem in "Near Périgord."

Flinging myself straight to Rochechouard
To ask Milady Agnes' hair,
For even Isolde, beloved of Tristan,
Who is celebrated for all her parts,
Never owned locks of higher praise. 40

5. And Audiart, though she wish me ill,
   I hope she'll give me a feature, too,
   For she's put together in a noble way:
   No, she hasn't any fault,
   For her loving 45
   Never faltered, never turned bad.
   And from my Better-Than-Good I beg
   Her young, upright body of highest price,
   So fine that one can see in a glance
   How wonderful to hold her nude! 50

6. And also from my Lady Faidida
   I'd like that gorgeous set of teeth,
   Her welcome and that gentle response
   She bestows so generously
   In her abode. 55
   My Beautiful Mirror, I bid she grant
   Her gaiety and her beauty fair:
   She always knows how to maintain
   Good standing; she's most informed:
   Never does she twist or change. 60

7. Pretty Lord, from you I ask naught:
   No, I'm as desirous of the one
   Who's self-conceived as I am of you:
   I feel a very avid
   Love being born 65
   Which has seized my entire heart;
   But I'd rather just keep asking you
   Than clench another with a kiss.
   Why does Milordess refuse me thus,
   Since she knows I love her so? 70

8. Papiols, take this song of mine
   And run to tell my Magnet
   That love here's no longer known,
   But has fallen from high to humble.

[73] *Si tuit li dol e·lh plor e·lh marrimen*

1. If all the grief and sorrow, the strife,
   The suffering, the pains, the many ills
   That men heard tell of in this woeful life
   Assembled, they would count as nil
   Compared to the death of the young English King,   5
   Who leaves behind youth and worth in tears
   In this dark world beset with shadowy fears,
   Lacking all joy, abounding in doleful spite.

2. Grievous and sad, sensing the bitter wrong,
   Stand his noble soldiers, left behind;   10
   His troubadours, his jongleurs sing no song,
   For death's bereft the warrior from mankind:
   Still they salute their young English King,
   Who makes the generous seem steeped in greed.
   He never did, nor will he now, take heed   15
   To repay this wicked world its tearful spite.

3. O boundless death, abounding yet in pain,
   Brag, brag you've got the finest cavalier
   Who ever stalked upon this broad terrain,
   Who, needing nothing, never knew his peer,   20
   For peer there never was to that English King.
   God, it's more just, if ever you would grant:
   Let *him* live, instead of all those tyrants
   Who never pay with worth—just doleful spite.

4. Since Love now flees this jaded age, downweighed   25
   By grief, I consider all its joys a lie,
   For nothing lasts that doesn't pass away,
   The way tomorrow feels today slip by.
   Let everyone admire the young English King!
   Who in all the world of valiant men was best.   30
   It's gone—that body full of lovingness,
   And all that are left are grief, discord, spite.

5. You who desired to counter all this pain
   By entering this world with its many snares,
   And suffered death that we might live again—   35
   We cry out in your just and humble name:
   Show mercy upon our young English King!

---

73. Lament for the Young King: Prince Henry of the Short Mantle (1155–1183), son of
Henry II of England and Eleanor; he died of fever at the age of 28 in France. One of three
manuscripts attributes this moving Planctus to Bertran; the others to Peire Vidal and Richart
de Berbezilh. Text: Carl Appel, *Lieder* (Niemeyer, 1932), No. 43.

Pardon, if pardon pleases, toward this end:
That he may stand among his honored friends
There where grief never goes—nor spite. 40

PEIRE VIDAL

[74] *Ab l'alen tir vas me l'aire*

1. With every breath I draw to me the air
   That wafts upon me over from Provence,
   And all that comes to me is wondrous fair,
   And each report of excellent provenance
   Sets me listening with an inner glow; 5
   Yes, from a single word I want much more.
   It's beautiful when all is going well there.

2. There is no haven more surpassing fair
   Than from the banks of Rhone to alpy Vence;
   There is no joy abounding anywhere 10
   Like that between the sea and blue Durance.
   And there among the people good and kind
   I've left my heart ajoying still behind
   With her who sets the wrathful folk adance.

3. No man could call that day an evil one 15
   When he of her has a happy souvenir,
   For she is source and cause of earthly fun,
   And whoever whispers flattery in your ear
   Will just be telling truth, not packs of lies,
   For she's the best—I'll brook no bold reprise— 20
   The fairest in the world, without a peer.

4. And anything I do or ever say
   I owe to her, for she's the one who imparts
   The knowledge and the skill to guide my way,
   And therefore I am gay, and so songs start. 25

74. Peire Vidal (*fl.* 1170–1204). Popular troubadour with a simple style, who attracted many legends: supposedly dressed himself in wolfskins to woo Loba (She-Wolf) de Pennautier, and was almost torn apart by her dogs; reputedly married the daughter of the Byzantine Emperor on Cyprus and assumed imperial pretensions, including the royal title. Probably the son of a furrier in Toulouse, he visited many dignitaries in Spain and Italy; served Count Raymond V of Toulouse. 50 poems survive. Text: Hill-Bergin *Anthology*, No. 87. For a tape: *Peire Vidal, A Troubadour in Hungary*, Hungaroton HCD 12102.

And anything I do that finds good end
Is inspired by the sweet body of my friend,
Including all reflections of good heart.

RICHART DE BERBEZILH

[75] *Atressi com l'olifanz*

1.   Just like the elephant
        Who, when he falls, can't rise
        Till others have upthrust him
        With their cranelike cries,
        I'll take up his custom: 5
I know my troubles are pachydermally heavy
And if that Court at Puy with its tycoon
And all its loyal-loving lords and ladies
Don't lend a hand, I'll wallow in my swoon.
Lords and ladies, get pity for my pain   10
From her who makes laments and logic vain!

2.   If you fine noble lovers
        Can't help my joy come back,
        Then poetry—I'll spurn it.
        It just can't fill my lack.   15
        Or else I'll become a hermit
Alone with no companion (for whom I'm burning).
My life's too full of misery and despair.
Joy's turned to grief, happiness to mourning.
My God, I'm not in any way like the bear!   20
When I'm abused or clubbed with a heavy bat,
I don't thrive, don't prosper—don't get fat.

3.   O I know Love's strong enough
        To help the tried but true man
        (Even if my love's more than "nice").   25
        Still, I never carried on like Simon
        Pretending to be Christ!
Wanting to soar to the very heavens above,
But shoved the other way for his sinful pride.

75. Or Rigaut de Barbezieux (*fl.* 1170–1207). From Saintonge; attached to Marie of Champagne, daughter of Eleanor. Only 10 poems remain, this one with fantastic conceits drawn from bestiaries. Two short *tornadas* (final refrains) omitted. Text: Hill-Bergin *Anthology*, No. 62.

My pride is such a simple thing—just love. 30
Ergo, let pity give what love's denied.
For there's a place where reason conquers pity.
The place where reason fails is not so pretty.

4.   I'll shout to all the world
      About myself, prolix, profuse. 35
      If I could only imitate
      The phoenix (O what's the use?),
      Who burns himself to procreate,
Then I'd burn all this misery and be purged.
I'd even burn those poems, bald untruths. 40
Then, in a chorus of sighs and tears I'd surge
Up where all virtue, loveliness, all youth
Reside—where pity's never in absentia,
Where all good forces hold annual convention.

5.   Song, be my middleman 45
      Over there where I dare not go
      Nor even look, except cross-eyed.
      My penning-in's so thorough
      That no one's on my side.
Better-Than-Woman, I ran from you two years 50
Wildly, like a deer running at chase.
Now I've come back, brimming over with tears,
Ready to die from the shouts of your huntress face.
Deerlike I come to you, lady, for your grace.
Do you care? Is love's memory so soon erased? 55

ARNAUT DANIEL

[76] *L'aura amara*

1. The bitter breeze
Makes the leafy copses
Whiten
That the soft one thickens with leaves,

76. Arnaut Daniel (*fl.* 1170–1210). Primary exponent of *trobar clus*, the hidden or abstruse style. A native of Ribérac near Périgueux, he was a poor jongleur until he won acclaim from Richard the Lion-Hearted and various lords of Aragon and Italy. Hailed by Dante in *Purgatorio* XXVI.115ff. as "the better craftsman of our maternal tongue," thus preferring him to Guiraut de Bornelh. Translated by Ezra Pound. The rhyme in this poem proceeds from stanza to stanza rather than within the strophes, as I have been forced to render it. Sense difficult in many places. See the author's *Poetry of Arnaut Daniel* (Garland, 1981), Nos. 9, 1, and 10.

And the happy   5
Beaks
Of birds on branches
It holds stammering and mute,
Both paired
And unpaired.   10
And so I strive
To do and say
Pleasant things
To many, because of her
Who has turned me from high to low,   15
So that I fear to die
If she doesn't heal my torments.

2. It was so clear,
   My first bright glimpse,
   When I selected   20
   Her for whom the heart believes the eyes.
   I don't value
   Base
   Messages worth two angevins;
   By another very rarely   25
   Is my prayer
   Drawn forth;
   And so it's a delight
   For me to hear
   Good will,   30
   Good words with nothing harsh
   For her for whom I exult so
   That at her service
   I stand from the feet up to my hair.

3. Love, look!   35
   I'm truly conquered;
   So I fear
   To make heard (if you reject me)
   Those kinds of
   Sins   40
   That it's better to cut yourself off from;
   Since I'm a fine lover,
   Sincere
   And unveering,
   But my firm, unflinching heart   45
   Makes me cover up
   Many true things:
   For despite the snow
   I'll need a kiss to refresh
   My ardent heart,   50
   Since no other balm suffices.

4. If she protects me—
   To whom I've handed myself over—
   In ease
   (For she's the citadel of value),   55
   From the quiet
   Prayers
   That I have inside in rows,
   I'll openly set out for her
   My thoughts   60
   All clear:
   For I would be dead,
   But hope makes me
   Bear on,
   And so I pray her to be brief for me,   65
   Since that hope keeps me glad and gay;
   For enjoyment from others
   Is joy not worth an apple to me.

5. Pretty face
   With every desired quality,   70
   For you
   I'll have to suffer many affronts;
   For you're
   The limit
   To all my follies,   75
   From which I have many bad
   Partners
   And scoffings.
   Wealth doesn't wrench me away
   Or make me part   80
   From you,
   For I never loved anything
   So much with so little vanity;
   Indeed, I desire you
   More than the men of Doma God.   85

6. Now get prepared,
   My song and melody,
   To run
   To the King who will receive you.
   For Worth,   90
   Dry here,
   Over there wells doubled,
   And gift-giving
   And feasting
   Are well-maintained.   95
   Carry yourself there with joy!
   Admire his ring
   If he raises it,

    For I never stayed a day
    Out of Aragon without wanting   100
    To go there with a leap,
    But here Rome has called to me.

7. The accord is made,
    And I contemplate in my heart
    Every evening   105
    The one whom I am courting
    Without a rival—I, Arnaut—
    For in other thoughts
    My aim's not strong for the summit.

[77*] *En cest sonet coind'e leri*

1. In this little song, pretty and joyful,
    I create my words, and I plane and hew them,
    And they will be exact and certain
    When I've passed the file over them,
    Since Love for me [at once] smooths down and gilds   5
    My singing, which emanates from her
    Who maintains and governs Value.

2. A thousand masses I hear and I proffer,
    And I burn a light with wax and oil,
    So that God may give me a good outcome   10
    From her where no shielding protects me;
    And when I gaze on her blondish hair
    And the graceful and young body she has,
    I love her more than one who'd give me Luserna.

3. I love and desire her so with all my heart   15
    That I think that with too much yearning I'll
        lose her
    (If a man loses anything through good loving).
    Her heart totally floods down over mine
    And does not ever disperse to the winds;
    She's made such a great new loan indeed   20
    That she owns the craftsman and the shop.

4. Every day I improve and grow more perfect
    Because I serve and revere the noblest one
    In the world—this I tell you openly;
    I am hers from my feet up to my top,   25
    And although the chilly breeze may blow,

    77. For a tape featuring Gérard Zuchetto, Gallo CD 529. Luserna in line 14 and the people in line 35 are unidentified.
    *Original text in Section IX, taken from Wilhelm, No. 10.

Love, which inside the heart rains over me,
Keeps me warm where it's wintry most.

5. Never because of the pain that I suffer
   Do I pull myself away from loving her   30
   Well (instead I speak out openly);
   Yet even if I write myself words in rhyme,
   I fare worse in loving than a man who labors;
   For never did he love a single bit more,
   That man of Moncli his Lady Audierna.   35

6. I do not want the Empire of Rome
   Nor anyone to make me the Apostle,
   For to her I would have no turning again
   For whom the heart burns and rends me;
   And if she doesn't heal this suffering   40
   With a kiss before the New Year,
   She kills me, and she goes to Hell.

7. I am Arnaut, who hoards the wind
   And chases the rabbit with the ox
   And swims against the swelling tide.   45

[78] *Lo ferm voler qu'el cor m'intra*

1. The fervent will that into my heart enters
   No beak can scratch, nor can tear the nails
   Of lying spies who through gossip lose their souls;
   Because I dare not bat with stick or rod
   (Except on the sly), there where I have no uncle   5
   I'll find joy: in the orchard or the chamber.

2. O when I recall that chamber
   Where I know to work me ill no man will enter,
   But everyone will be more than brother or uncle,
   All of my limbs start trembling, even my nails,   10
   Like some little kid about to face the rod:
   Such fear I have she'll be too much for my soul.

3. Would she were of body and not of soul!
   And would agree to hide me inside her chamber!
   She wounds my heart more than a switch with a rod   15
   Because this slave, where she is, dare never enter;
   Forever I'll be with her in flesh and in nail,
   And never trust the chastising of friend or uncle.

78. Sestina, a form that relies on the repetition of six end-words of stanzas rather than upon internal rhyme. The Virgin is alluded to in line 25. Stanza 7 brings all end-words together in a compressed form. Music ed. Hendrik van der Werf in Wilhelm, Plates 1, 2. Tapes: Nimbus N 5002 and Gallo CD 529.

4. Even the very sister of my uncle
   I never loved more or as much as her, on my soul!   20
   I'd like to be as near as the finger to the nail,
   If it pleased her, there deep inside her chamber.
   This love can treat me (which in my heart now enters)
   More at its will than a strong man with weak rod.

5. After the fruition of the Dried-Out Rod,   25
   After Sir Adam, there never moved nephew or uncle
   With the fine true love that into my heart enters:
   I don't think it's been contained in a body or soul.
   Wherever she is—in the plaza or inside her chamber—
   My heart is clinging, as if it had fingernails.   30

6. Yes, thus it hangs with its nails,
   My heart gripping her, like a bark around a rod;
   Of joy she is my tower, palace, and chamber;
   So much I never loved brother, father, or uncle;
   And in Paradise joy will double for my soul   35
   If ever a man through good love there should enter.

7. Arnaut sends over his Sestina Uncle-Nail
   For the pleasure of her from the rod down to the soul,
   His Desired One, whose worth in the chamber enters.

THE MONK OF MONTAUDON

[79] *Molt mi platz deportz e gaieza*

1. Ah, how I like fun and fooling around,
   Good eats and gifts and men who have some guts;
   Girls who are straight, but dig the high-class ways
   And know how to give a comeback that's just right;
   And I like the rich who are not always up-tight   5
   But are genuine bastards toward their foes.

79. Lo Monge de Montaudon (*fl.* 1180?–1215?). Rollicking poet whose actual identity is
masked. His vida claims that he came from Vic in the Auvergne and that he became the Prior of
Montaudon (although the name varies widely in the manuscripts). Sometimes identified as the
Prior of Vic, known as Peire of Vic. His poems include a debate with God and arguments
among the saints. Genre: Pleasure Song. Text: Hill-Bergin *Anthology*, No. 100. For recordings of his Displeasure Song: Harmonia Mundi HM 566, Hispavox HH (S) 6.

2. And I like a guy who talks to me nice
   And gives me presents without any catch;
   Rich kooks who aren't always going around bitching;
   And I swear I like a good, intelligent hassle,   10
   And a snooze when it thunders and lightnings,
   And a big fat salmon in the midafternoon.

3. And I like to stretch out in summertime
   Along the banks of a river or a brook
   When the fields are green and the flowers ripe   15
   And the birds are piping their little peeps
   And my girl friend sneaks up on the sly
   And gives it to me one time quick!!

4. And I like a guy with wide-open arms
   But without that faggot two-facedness;   20
   And I like the cool of my little pal,
   Her smooches—and everything I can get.
   And if my enemies all go to Hell,
   I like it—yeah! when I give the shove.

5. And O how I like my buddies   25
   When they're sitting there with my foes
   And I hear someone call for my work,
   And they clap and they shout and they yell!

RAIMBAUT OF VAQUEIRAS

[80] *Gaita ben, gaiteta del chastel*

1. Watchman from the castle wall, guard well,
   When I've what I most deeply prize
       Here in my arms—until the dawn.
   Let the day come! But never, never tell.
       New games arise   5
   To snatch away the dawn, the dawn, O yes, the dawn.

80. Raimbaut de Vaqueiras (*ca.* 1155–*ca.* 1210). Born to a poor knight in a castle near Orange. Spent much time in Spain and then in Italy, serving Boniface II of Monferrat, whom he followed on the Fourth Crusade in 1202. Believed to have died in Salonika. More than 40 poems extant in a variety of styles; here, a Dawn Song. Text: Hill-Bergin *Anthology*, No. 114.

2. Watchman friend, wake and shout "Oyé!"
   O I'm rich and what I want I own.
       My only enemy's—the dawn.
   And the ruthless havoc of the risen day   10
       Makes me moan
   More than the dawn, the dawn, O yes, the dawn.

3. But guard yourself, watchman on the tower,
   From that jealous man—your evil lord—
       Who envies more than does the dawn.   15
   And softly, softly, speak of Love's great power.
       Fear comes toward
   Us only from the dawn, the dawn, O yes, the dawn.

4. Lady, good-bye! I'm sorry I can't stay!
   It hurts me, but I simply have to leave.   20
       O it pains me so—that dawn—
   As I watch its slowly rising ray.
       Deceiver!
   That's all he is, the dawn, the dawn, O yes, the dawn.

[81*] Kalenda maya

1.   Not the kalends of May
            Nor the leaf of a beech
   Nor the song of a bird   nor a gladiolus
            Can bring me enjoyment,
            My fine, gay lady,   5
   Until I receive   a message express
   From your lovely person   that will promise me
   The new pleasures   that love attracts me to
            And it delights me
            And leads me   10
   To you,   my true lady;
            And may the jealous one
            Be struck with a blow
   And fall—   before I go.

2. My lovely friend, (15) / may God never allow / that "jealous one" / to laugh at
   my loss; / no, he'll pay dearly / for his jealousy / if he causes two lovers / ever
   to part; (20) / for I'd never be / happy again, / since joy without you / I'd
   consider woe; / I'd take to / such a road / that no one again / would ever see
   me; (25) / I'd die / that day, / my fine lady, / when I lost you.

   81. Estampida or stomp-dance, extraordinary for its powerful end and internal rhymes.
Rousingly rendered on Telefunken Das Alte Werk 6.41126(2); cf. Archiv 14018 APM;
Elektra EKL 31; Philips A 00773 R; Concord CRD 4006; Nimbus N 5002. *Erec and Enide* is
a romance about a married couple by Chrétien de Troyes. English Lord is Boniface II of
Monferrat.
   *Original text in Section IX, taken from Carl Appel, *Provenzalische Chrestomathie*, 6th ed.
(Reisland, 1930; rpt. 1971), No. 52.

3. How can a lady / be lost or regained (30) / when she's never been possessed? / For a boyfriend and girlfriend / don't exist like thoughts; / but when a courter / becomes a true friend, / the honor that accrues to him / is very great; (35) / but our fair appearance / has aroused bad talk, / though I never held you / naked / in my arms / or in any other way; / I have wanted you (40) / and I have trusted you, / without any other ploys.

4. Scarcely would I exult / in parting from you, / my Beautiful Chevalier, / with any anger; (45) / neither my heart nor my desire / is veering off / or pulling me away / because I want no other; I know it would make / our slanderer happy, / lady, since nothing else / can cure him; (50) / if he saw / and felt / my pain, / he would thank you for it, / as he stares at you / and schemes (55) / presumptuously— / making my heart sigh.

5. My gracious lady, / everyone shouts and praises / your high worth, / which is resplendent; / and to anyone who'd forget you, (60) / life would have little value. / Why do I adore you, / my chosen one? / I selected you / as the loveliest / and the very best, / replete with virtue; / I have courted you (65) / and served you / more nobly / than Erec did Enide. / And so, English Lord, / I've worked on / and now finished / my estampida.

[82] *Altas undas que venez suz la mar*

1.   High waves who ride upon the sea,
Rolled by the will of the wind in every way,
Bring some news of my belovéd to me;
He's never come back after that farewell day.
    And the God Amór, O!   5
One hour gives me joy and then gives sorrow.

2.   O gentle breeze blowing over there
Where my good friend lives and sleeps and lies,
Carry me one breath from his body fair!
Send me a draught to make this desire die.   10
    And the God Amór, O!
One hour gives me joy and then gives sorrow.

3.   Wrong loving makes him vassal in foreign lands,
And so I weep as I think of his games, his smile.
I never thought I'd be parted from my man,   15
For I always gave whatever could beguile.
    And the God Amór, O!
One hour gives me joy and then gives sorrow.

82. Love song from a woman to a man, a model for the Galician-Portuguese *cantigas de amigo*. Text: Hill-Bergin *Anthology*, No. 113.

FOLQUET OF MARSEILLE

[83] *Vers Dieus, el vostre nom et de Sancta Maria*

1. In the name of Saint Mary, in yours, True Lord,
    Let me awake as the morning star moves toward
    Me from Jerusalem, lending me these words:
        Rise up, up and away,
        All who the Lord obey,   5
        For the morning's under way
        As the night expires.
        May the Lord be praised
        And adored in every way
        As together we pray   10
        For peace, our lives entire.
    Day comes, Night flies
    The clear, tranquil sky
    As the dawn's not shy
    But comes in full attire.   15

2. Lord God, born of Mary the pure,
    To restore us to life with death's cure,
    To harrow Hell, that the Devil thinks secure,
        O Cross-wise raised,
        Thorn-crowned, abased   20
        By the bile's taste—
    Lord, honored men desire
        Their sins erased,
        Knowing your mercy chaste
        Pardons sin's waste.   25
    Amen, Lord, may it transpire!
    Day comes, Night flies . . .

3. O you ignorant of prayer, be diligent!
    Listen to what I say; grasp my intent:
    Lord, to you, beginning of all events   30
        I offer thankful praise
        For that love and grace
        You've offered me always,

83. Or Folc de Marseilla (1150–1231). Son of a rich merchant of Genoa, he lived in southern France, squandering his patrimony in riotous living. Renounced secular life and in 1205 was installed as Bishop of Toulouse. Played a harsh role in persecuting heretics during the Albigensian Crusade. Defended Simon de Montfort at the Lateran Council of 1215. Died in seclusion in 1231, hated by most South French. However, stories of his miracles were common, and Dante awarded him with a place in his heaven of love: *Paradiso* IX. Genre: religious Dawn Song. Text: Hill-Bergin *Anthology*, No. 97.

    And pray, Lord, pity inspire
    You to guard my days   35
    From wrong-taken ways:
    O keep the Devil at bay
    With his subtle fire!
    Day comes, Night flies . . .

4. God, grant me wisdom and sense to apprehend   40
   Your holy laws, to heed, to comprehend;
   Grant mercy to nourish me and to defend
      From worldly ways,
      From sin-fall safe!
      Lord, I believe, I praise   45
      You as you rightfully desire.
      In a sacrifice's place
      Accept my faith.
      So offering, I beg grace:
      O make me, torn, entire!   50
      Day comes, Night flies . . .

5. To glorious God who gave his body for sale
   To buy us life, I pray: over us veil
   That Holy Spirit, over all evil prevail:
      Let me be raised   55
      To the ranks of the saved
      And there, where you hold sway,
      Live beneath the pavilion's spire!
      Day comes, Night flies . . .

PEIRE CARDENAL

[84] *Tartarassa ni voutor*

1. Not a buzzard, not a vulture
   Can smell the stink of rotting flesh
   Like those clerics and those preachers
   On the sniff for earthly wealth.
   Right away they're rich men's servants,   5

84. Or Peire Cardinal (*ca.* 1185–*ca.* 1275). Greatest poet of the Albigensian Period, with some seventy songs surviving, mostly *sirventes*, as here. Born in Puy Nôtre-Dame, he attached himself to the courts of Raymond VI and VII of Toulouse. Also worked for James I of Aragon and Alfonso X of Castile. "Died at about one hundred years of age," claims his vida-writer, who is more reliable than most. Text: Hill-Bergin *Anthology*, No. 141.

And when they sense disease's swipe,
Then they cozen out bequeathings:
The relatives have nothing left.

2. The Franks and the clergy get the praise
   For evil, since they're masters there;   10
   And the usurers and the traitors
   Own the age about half and half;
   For with their lying and their cheats
   They have so upset the world
   There's not a religious order left   15
   That hasn't mastered the lesson too.

3. Know what happens to all that loot
   Belonging to those who get it ill?
   Up there springs a mighty robber:
   Nothing will he leave behind.   20
   Name is Death; O how he beats them!
   In just four ells of linen cloth
   Off he rolls them to his mansion
   Where they find other evils galore.

4. Man, why perpetrate such folly,   25
   Why transgress those commandments
   Of God, who is your rightful Lord
   And formed your body out of nothing?
   He who battles against his Master
   Would sell a good sow in the marketplace;   30
   Yes, his earnings will be those
   Won by that other villain, Judas.

5. Our true God, who is full of sweetness,
   Master, be our guarantor!
   Keep us from the hellish tortures,   35
   Hold us sinners from torment safe;
   Unravel those out of the evils
   In which they're caught, in which bound:
   Yield them then your truthful pardon
   In return for their true confessions.   40

[85] *Una ciutatz fo, no sai cals*

1. There once was a city (I know not which)
   Where rain had fallen in such a way
   That all the inhabitants of the town
   Who were touched went suddenly mad.

---

85. Fable Poem. A few final lines omitted. Text: Hill-Bergin *Anthology*, No. 145.

2. They all went crazy, except for one: 5
   That one escaped (there was no more)
   For he was safe inside a house
   Asleep when all this was going on.

3. When he woke up after his sleep
   And saw that the rain had gone away,   10
   Outside he went among the folk.
   They all were acting completely mad.

4. One wore a cloak, another was nude;
   Another was spitting up at the sky;
   One threw stones, and another sticks;   15
   Another stood tearing at his gown.

5. One was striking, another hit back;
   Another was acting like a king
   And held himself regally in the hips;
   Another leaped through the market stalls.   20

6. One was threatening, another cursing;
   One was swearing, another laughed;
   One spoke, and didn't know what he said;
   Another made constant startled looks.

7. And the man who still had his wits   25
   Was wondrously struck by these fits
   And saw that they all were crazy,
   And he looked up, and he looked there,

8. To see if one wise man existed,
   And yet he could not spy a single one.   30
   And so he stood gaping at them all.
   And they showed greater wonder at him,

9. Amazed by his tranquillity.
   They thought he must have lost his mind
   Because he wasn't aping them,   35
   For to them it all appeared

10. That they were wise and full of wit
    And that he was utterly deranged.
    One strikes his cheek, the other his neck:
    He couldn't keep himself from tumbling.   40

11. One man presses, another shoves:
    He thinks he's going to flee the mass,
    But one man tears, another pulls;
    He takes the blows, rises—falls.

12. Then, lifting up with giant strides,   45
    He rushes home on double time,
    Muddy and battered and halfway dead,
    And glad to be out of their clutches.

13. This little fable concerns this world:
    It's like the people you meet today.   50
    This age of ours is that very town
    That's full to the limit with lunatics.

14. For the greatest reason man can have
    Is to love and fear his God,
    And to hold to his commandments;
    But now that sense is wholly lost.   55

[86] *Un sirventes novel vueill comensar*

1. I'd like to start a sirventes that's new,
   One I'll recite upon the Judgment Day
   To him who made me, formed me from the void.
   And if he plans to hold me in account,
   And if he wants to cast me to devilhood,   5
   Then I'll reply: "Master, mercy! no!
   For in a wicked age I groaned my years.
   And guard me now, I beg, from all those torturers."

2. Then I shall make his court all stand in awe
   As they attend the pleading of my case: 10
   For I'll say he's the guilty party then
   If he plans to cast his own to hellish pain.
   For he who loses the things he ought to gain
   Rightfully wins a lack for his vileness;
   For he should be sweet, as well as generous,   15
   In holding on to souls who have transgressed.

3. Those devilish types he ought to dispossess
   And then he'd have a running stock of souls,
   And the clearing out would gladden all the world,
   And he himself could give himself his pardon: 20
   Yes, willingly could he destroy them all,
   Since everyone knows he owns the absolution.
   "Beautiful Master Lord, go and dispossess
   Those enemies who are vicious and are vile.

4. "Never should you deny the open door,   25
   For Peter, who is porter there, receives
   Shameful remarks: instead, every soul who treads
   Past those portals should walk in with a grin.

86. Complaint to God. Text: Hill-Bergin *Anthology*, No. 144. Recording: Hispavox HH
(S) 6.

For never was there a court one calls complete
Where one man laughed and yet another cried. 30
And though you are monarch powerful and bold,
Unless you open, I'll issue a complaint.

5. "I have no wish to voice you my despair;
Instead, I place in you all of my faith
In hope that you defend me from my sin; 35
It's *your* burden to save me, corpse and soul.
Now let me offer you a pretty choice:
Either send me back where first I saw the day
Or pardon me for the wrongs that I have wrought.
Never would I have sinned had I not been born. 40

6. "If I suffer evil here and more in Hell,
By faith! that would surely be a sinful wrong,
And I'd have a rightful reason to reproach you,
For I've a thousand sufferings for every good."

7. —"Mercy I beg of you, Holy Lady Maria: 45
Offer good witness for me unto your Son,
That he may lift this father and his children
And place them there in grace beside St. John."

SORDELLO

[87] *Planher vuelh en Blacatz en aquest leugier so*

1. I want to mourn for Lord Blacatz with this lighthearted sound,
With a heart that's sad and sore beset, for there are reasons for it:
In him I lost a good, true friend and a worthy lord,
And all the manly virtues are gone with him.

87. Provençal: Lo Sordels (*ca.* 1215–*ca.* 1270). Most famous Italian who wrote in Provençal. Born at Goito near Mantua; became notorious for abducting the beautiful Cunizza, sister of the powerful Ezzelino da Romano, away from her husband, Rizzardo di San Bonifazio. Abandoning her later, he went to Spain and finally Provence, where he was patronized by Blacatz, lord of Aups, who died between 1235 and 1240. In his Lament for Blacatz, Sordello summons the following to eat his lord's heart, in respective order: Emperor Frederick II, Louis IX of France, Henry III of England, Ferdinand III of Castile, James I of Aragon, Thibaut of Navarre (see No. 141), Count Raymond VII of Toulouse, and Count Raymond Béranger of Provence. Returned to Italy with Charles of Anjou in 1266. Fought at the battle of Benevento and in Sicily; was rewarded with some land in the Abruzzi region, where he died. Dante made him guardian of his Vale of Princes (*Purgatorio* VI, VII), and he appealed to Browning and Pound because of his intense energy and fierce scorn for corruption. Texts from the author's *Poetry of Sordello* (Garland, 1987), Nos. 26 and 3.

Ah, the loss is deadly! for I think I'll never see   5
A return of any goodness, unless it comes just so—
Let everyone split up his heart—yes, let those barons eat!
For they're all heartless men who could stand a cordial treat!

2. Ah, number one comes the Emperor of Rome, a man
   Who needs some hearty food if he wants to overtake   10
   Those Milanese by force, for they think he's a loss—
   He's got no inheritance, even with his friendly Germans.
   And after him let the King of France step up to the banquet,
   For he wants to win back Castile that he lost through foolishness:
   But let him think of his mother; she won't touch a piece—   15
   No, she's too dignified to do anything that distasteful!

3. I like that English King, for he's a man of little heart,
   And if he'll just sample some, he'll be valiant and good,
   And he'll win back the land snatched by the King of France,
   Who knows he's a good-for-nothing and leaves him in disgrace. 20
   And that Castilian King! I think he should eat for two!
   For he holds two domains, and is not good enough for one!
   But if he wants a nibble, he should eat secretly,
   For if his Mamma catches him, she'll flail him with her rod.

4. And the King of Aragon should have a taste, I do believe,   25
   For it will help to purge him of the shame
   That he gets over here from Marseille and from Millau,
   For he gets not a jot of honor for anything done or said.
   And next I want the Navarrese King to step up to the feast,
   For he was a worthy count before he was crowned, I hear.   30
   It's terrible when God helps a man to mount in wealth
   And then weakness of heart makes him tumble in price.

5. The Count of Toulouse needs a good big bite of heart
   If he thinks of what he had and what he has now;
   For if this new infusion doesn't help him recoup his losses, 35
   It's lost for good with that old heart in his breast.
   And the Count of Provence should eat if he'll recall
   How a man who's disinherited isn't worth a damn
   And although he fights and defends himself with guts,
   He still should dine on this heart for the burdens he bears. 40

6. The barons will curse me for the evil I've said here,
   But they know I think they're as low as they think me.

7. Beautiful Restorer, in you alone I may find my grace,
   And I scorn every man who won't hold me as his friend.

[88] *Atretan deu ben chantar finamen*

1. I should sing just as beautifully about winter
   As I do about summertime, and with good reason—
   Because in the cold I want to create a happy song,
   Since, if my heart can be seized by song in the spring
   Because the rose resembles her whom I sing about,   5
   So too the snow resembles her fair complexion;
   And so I ought to exalt her love in both seasons,
   So forcefully do the rose and the snow make me
       remember her.

2. Above all others I love my lady, who is fine and noble,
   Who makes me need a heart that's rich year-round   10
   In loving well, since moderation preaches
   That one should have a heart according to the deeds he
       does;
   And because I undertook such a love that wherever I go
   Other lovers have ladies far inferior to mine,
   I have a heart that will surpass the best in loving well   15
   And the valiant in acting, if I can, in a better way.

3. When I think deeply in my rich meditations
   About who she is to whom I pledge and yield myself,
   I love her so much, since she surpasses all pleasures,
   That in ways of love, I consider other women lower;   20
   And since I don't know any so worthy in all this world
   From whom I could get my pleasure—lying and
       kissing—
   Therefore I don't want to savor any other fruits
   By which the sweet would change for me to bitter.

4. I detest mirrors: to me they're most annoying   25
   Because of her who makes me languish in her keep,
   For when she gazes on her face and figure,
   Thinking how great all is, she values my torment little;
   And so the eyes go stirring up inside the heart
   That pride by which she lays my loving low;   30
   She thinks me vile, and considers herself quite precious
   Because she lives without an equal in worth and
       beauty.

5. He who does everything good that he can do
   By serving his lady, as the rule of love prescribes,
   Can surely make a request for his recompense,   35
   And she should yield it, if she knows the laws;
   And so I beg "milord," crying out for her mercy,
   Since I don't demand a reward by any laws,
   Because she's worth so much that no servitude
   Could ever equal her rich compensation.   40

6. Just as the sun, when it shines, eclipses
   All other brightness, so the Countess of dear form,
   She of Rodez, goes eclipsing other women
   Of merit, without ever quite effacing my lady.

7. The Countess shouldn't detest me in any way   45
   If I love and prize her for whom I'm a vassal without
       any peer.

GUIRAUT RIQUIER

[89] *A Sant Pos de Tomeiras*

The Sixth Pastourelle by Sir Guiraut Riquier in the Year 1282

1. To St.-Pons-de-Thomières
   I came the other day
   Totally rain-soaked,
   To the domain of two landladies
   Whom I'd never met;   5
   In fact I was rather surprised
   Because the older one was laughing
   And telling the younger one
   Some sly joke;
   But both of them offered me   10
   All the comforts they had
   Until I was pleasantly lodged;
   And then I regained my memory
   Of the time that had passed
   And I regained my recognition   15
   Of the old one—which pleased me.

2. I said to her: "You're the person
   Who was once a shepherdess
   And teased me so."
   She said to me, not maliciously: 20

---

89. Guiraut Riquier (*ca.* 1233–1292). Born in Narbonne, but spent 10 years in the court of
Alfonso IX of Castile. Left over 100 poems, often with dates, as with this sixth and last in a
series of Pastourelles. Often rather perfunctory, he said of himself: "I have come too late." The
town in line 1 is in the Department of Hérault; the Count in line 98 is Bernard IV of Astarac.
Note the shift to "Lady" in line 93. Text: *Medieval Pastourelle*, ed. W. D. Paden, II, No. 139.
For a tape: *Last of the Troubadours*, Nimbus 45008.

"Sir, I'll never willingly
Be your opponent again."
"Good woman, I see that you
Still maintain a manner
That ought to be reproved." 25
"Sir, in those days I was always
Light-hearted because I had
A ready market for my wares."
"Good woman, was that remark made
By someone passionate for easing?" 30
"No sir; because now I'm close
To a man whom I don't love."

3. "Good woman, a man who loves
A young thing like you has to be
Extremely high-spirited." 35
"Lord God! He wants me
As his wife, but I'm not
At all eager for that."
"Good woman, now's the time
To put your low condition behind 40
If someone comes along who's rich."
"Sir, we could get along very well,
But I know that my friend's
The father of seven kids."
"Good woman, you'll be beautifully 45
Taken care of when they grow up."
"Sir, yes, but now I'm bothered
Because not one of them is ten."

4. "Ah, what a silly woman!
You escape from one evil 50
And go around searching for a worse."
"Sir, no; I'm really quite sensible
And my heart doesn't lead me
On to causing my own trouble."
"Good woman, your're looking for 55
Some twisted path that could lead
To death, I think, inside of a year."
"Sir, this girl standing here before you
Is the thing that comforts me
And is the portal of my joy." 60
"Good woman, I do believe
That she's your daughter."
"Sir, you stumbled on us
Near L'Ile last year."

5. "Good woman, then she should 65
Give me some recompense
For the many pains you've dealt me."

"Sir, you have to wait
Until her husband might agree,
And then you can do your business."   70
"Good woman, your teasing around
Hasn't played itself out,
But instead goes on as bad as ever."
"Sir Guiraut Riquier, I'm all worn out
Because you insist on following   75
The tracks of these silly songs."
"Good woman, old age has made
These songs seem bitter to you."
"Sir, old age is not your problem
Since you don't act like other old men!"   80

6. "Good woman, you're not going to make
   Me afraid of your wicked talk;
   Your words sound to me like a joke."
   "Sir, I find it hard to believe
   That you'd ever try to conjure up   85
   An evil intent on my part."
   "Since I'm on your turf,
   You should show some patience
   Toward anything you find in me."
   "Sir, it doesn't make me happy   90
   To go around arguing
   Or to make you uncomfortable."
   "Lady, you couldn't if you wanted
   Because I can't stop loving you."
   "Sir, as long as you keep doing that,   95
   I'll keep on honoring you."

7. "Our argument is very amusing
   To the good Count of Astarac,
   Milady, and all should praise him."
   "Sir, his excellent value   100
   Makes all the people speak
   His name with loving friendship."
   "Lady, if you saw him here,
   Would you know how to receive him?"
   "Sir, you will hear indeed   105
   What I have in my heart to do."

[IV] ITALIAN LYRICS

Italian literature is remarkable for its sudden flowering in the thirteenth century, without any visible antecedents. Yet the appearance is fully understandable in terms of literary connections with Provençal. The troubadours were born wanderers, and many of them ventured into northern Italy, especially after the Albigensian Crusade impoverished the nobles at home and dictated an exodus. Sordello, who is grouped with the Provençals, was an Italian, as were many others who wrote in Old South French.

When literature written in Italian did at last appear, it naturally bore a strong trace of its southern French heritage. The first group of writers in the native tongue was the so-called Sicilian School, which flourished from the time of the coronation of Emperor Frederick II (1220) to his demise (1250). Frederick was reputedly himself a poet, but the few bland works that come down with the notation "King Frederick" are now usually ascribed to his son, Frederick of Antioch. Still, the Hohenstaufen Emperor did support poetry, and it flourished from Naples to Palermo. Each of the five poets in Poems 91 to 95 is believed to have worked for him: Pier was his right-hand man and Re Enzo, or King Heinz (to use the German equivalent), was Frederick's bastard son. Thus the antipapal, freethinking, heretical emperor casts his shadow over the early development of Italian song.

The differences between Provençal and Italian lyrics are as obvious as the likenesses. For one thing, the *canso* form (in Italian, *canzone*) yields very fast in popularity to the more abbreviated, more epigrammatic *sonnetto* (sonnet), which is totally lacking in Provençal literature. No one knows why or how this form became so widespread—was it a reflection of popular songs?—but a look at Petrarch's output will attest to the eventual dominance of the genre.

If one had to theorize, one might say that the genius of the Provençal lyric lay in its continual exploration of the poet's mind, with emphasis upon the madness of love and playful disorder. The Provençals placed great stress upon wit, gaiety, and the casual things of life: Duke William's "I'll write a poem, then take a nap." The Italians, on the other hand, are often extremely serious. Giacomo's poem (No. 91), perhaps the world's oldest extant sonnet, states a proposition somewhat whimsically: he would like to see his lady in heaven. When he is called to account for this proclamation, he does not retract. In fact, he insists upon putting her there, just as Dante places his Beatrice in the final circle of the blessed in the company of Mary, Jesus, and the saints. Similarly Guinizelli in No. 103 is challenged by God for his pretensions, and although many feel that he withdraws completely, one can read the last stanza of his poem in a semidefiant way: "*You* take the blame for making my lady so beautiful."

The fact that the term for "my lady" in Italian can be *madonna*, the epithet of the Virgin, no doubt promotes this equation of the holy with the

profane. Imagistically, the Italians seize upon the rose and other accouter-
ments of Mary, even in the earthy *Contrasto* (Debate Poem) of Cielo d'Al-
camo, No. 92. Italian lyrics are filled with expressions that might have been
drawn from a laud to the Perfect Lady. It is not at all surprising that a
Tuscan poetess appears with that very name, although some consider her a
fiction (No. 98). In sum, Italian poetry is far more metaphysical than
courtly in its tone and diction. Perhaps the fact that the literature begins
with the loving St. Francis of Assisi, who saw an easy correspondence
between the human and the divine, establishes the ethos from the start. To
an Italian like Iacopone da Todi, the Virgin is a warm, dramatic, living
mother, not a remote abstraction. Religion in Italy is either conveyed very
movingly, as in the Umbrian School, which includes St. Francis and Iacopone, and which was the product of the Papal States, or it is contested
frankly, as in Rinaldo d'Aquino's Complaint Against the Crusade (No. 94)
or in the work of the important Tuscan School, which dominated the period
after 1260.

This last great movement was fathered by Guido Guinizelli, whose
famous *Al cor gentil* (No. 103) was the poetic manifesto of Dante's circle
and succeeding generations. A term often used to describe this poetry is
dolce stil nuovo or "sweet new style," which is taken from the mouth of
Bonagiunta da Lucca in Dante's *Purgatorio*. It is difficult to stipulate the
exact doctrines of this school, but Dante tells Bonagiunta that his mode of
composing was as follows:

> . . . I am one who,
> When Love breathes on me, take note, and in the mode
> He dictates to me inside, I go making meanings. (XXIV. 52–54)

Bonagiunta replies:

> O brother, now I see the knot
> That held Guittone and the Notary and me
> From gaining the sweet new style that I hear.
> I see well how your pens ran straight
> Behind the great dictator, and certainly
> That was not the case with ours.
> If anyone else looks further carefully
> That is the only difference between our styles.

The passage seems to indicate that freshness of conception and adherence to
a guiding structure (following the dictator) are the features that made
Guinizelli, Cavalcanti, and Dante great. These were lacking in the self-
conscious, rhetorical work of Bonagiunta and Guittone d'Arezzo, as their
selections may indicate (99, 100).

Certainly there is freshness in Guinizelli. His Poems 101 and 102 approach the woman with a beautiful blend of natural imagery—the morning
star of Venus, the green banks of pastoral poetry—along with an insistence
upon an ideal system that the woman suggests, a system that is clearly
Christian-Neoplatonic. The famous correspondence of the lady-angel is
made in *Al cor gentil* in such a way that we can see the whole structure of the

Divine Comedy emanating from the work. In fact, in the *Vita Nuova* Dante freely acknowledges his debt to the first Guido in his imitative canzone "Love and the noble heart are a single thing" (No. 113). In his other poems from that early work (Nos. 112, 114) one can see Beatrice entering the realm of God, where Guinizelli's lady might well have feared to tread. My selection of Dante's work emphasizes the point to which he takes his woman beyond Guinizelli, for Dante is properly the epic poet. No collection of lyrics can express his achievement, which was to make his love for Beatrice mesh with his love for the divine.

Cavalcanti, however, is a mystery. This "second Guido" was Dante's best friend, as we are told in the *Vita Nuovo* III. It was he who persuaded Dante to compose in Italian, not Latin. When Dante put Cavalcanti's father in his Circle of Heretics in *Inferno* X, he was perhaps giving us a clue about this rather enigmatic poet. For the difficult *Song of Love* (No. 108) does not present love in the optimistic, idealized treatment established by Guinizelli. Love is an accident, a movement in substance (not a miracle or divinely motivated occurrence). It is analyzed psychologically and even physiologically rather than theologically: "Love is not virtue. . . ." Furthermore, Cavalcanti's love does not lead to heaven: "his pleasures/ Last but a little, for he stays not long." Still, Guido insists, love is responsible for whatever good is done on earth, and even without access to a metaphysical system, it is the antecedent of virtue.

In his less difficult poetry, the objective, realistic side of Cavalcanti can be seen. His Pastourelle (No. 104) is a frank representation of the sexual act as a precursor to a magic vision. In this brilliant evocation of the sensual, one feels the door to the refined new paganism of the Renaissance opening. Lest we align Cavalcanti with the rationalists as opposed to the idealists, we must mention selections 105 to 107, which show his kinship with the writers of the *dolce stil nuovo*. Poem No. 105 shows the gradual stages whereby the natural is transformed into the supernatural; it is like Diotima's speech in Plato's *Symposium* set to music.

Poem 108, however, reestablishes the tragic tone that runs throughout much of Cavalcanti's work, where love is as often disaster as triumph, death or suffering more than redeeming vision. In the poignant Farewell Ballata (No. 109), perhaps written before his untimely death in Sarzana on the Ligurian coast in 1300, the woman seems more like the abstract goddess Wisdom, a handmaid of art, than an actual woman of Tuscany. In his *Decameron* VI.9, Boccaccio describes Guido as having been "one of the best logicians and natural philosophers in the whole world." The emphasis on humanistic values is explicit in his work.

Aside from writing the masterpiece of the Guinizelli tradition, Dante wrote some poems which fascinate because of their strangeness. His Invitation to Guido and Lapo (No. 110) to embark on a magic ship shows a skillful blend of the romantic with the mystical: Merlin rubbing shoulders with Plato. His Sestina of the Rock Lady (No. 111) is utterly baffling unless one interprets her as the Dark Lady antithesis to Beatrice. It is an early poem and shows perhaps a wavering on the poet's part; he is still in the dark wood with which the *Comedy* opens. Lastly, the *Tenzone* or Debate Poem with Forese Donati (No. 115) shows the virulent, choleric side of the poet that is often concealed under the role of the timid Everyman in the epic poem. He slashes Forese so mercilessly here and in other poems that he apologized later by placing his victim among the redeemed in *Purgatorio* XXIII.

The brawling, boisterous side of Italian literature—what we expect when we move from a southern French castle to a Tuscan city bursting with energy—is continued by the man of Siena, Cecco Angiolieri. He puts Dante down in the witty sonnet No. 119, and establishes his general hatred of life in 116, saving most of his invective for women, and especially for his particular woman, the crude, lowly born Becchina (No. 117). As the Black Mass accompanies the sacred one, so Cecco and Becchina accompany Dante and Beatrice to complete the medieval world view.

Other poets of the period include Folgore of San Gimignano, who wrote a beautiful sequence of sonnets on the twelve months of the year, showing a fine handling of realistic detail. Lapo Gianni and Cino da Pistoia are two other members of the *dolce stil nuovo* who were capable of writing verses that stand out from the rather vague, abstract poetry of many of their peers.

Francesco Petrarca is, of course, the culminating genius of the Italian lyric tradition of the Middle Ages. In him the sonnet found the hands of the master shaper, for he made it the vehicle that was most appealing to the poets of the Renaissance. To assess Petrarch's intellectual achievement is not easy, however. He was acquainted with the work of most of the foregoing writers, as well as with the troubadours, yet he managed to strike an original style. His poems written to Laura depart from those of the *dolce stil nuovo* because of the way in which he portrays her realistically and insists on singing about the unhappiness of love, as well as the joy. After Laura's death (see No. 130), the *Canzoniere* or *Songbook*, the collection of his sonnets and other poems, tells about his moving away from earthly preoccupations to the divine.

Throughout the *Songbook*, which he called his *Rime Sparse* (Scattered Rhymes), Petrarch creates the persona of the lover as a wandering, melancholy figure. Putting humor aside entirely and reducing metaphysical overtones to rhetorical conceits (usually with paradox), he found the medium that proved fascinating to later generations. To many moderns, such as Ezra Pound, Petrarch seems contrived, self-serious, and even morbid; yet he did catch the figure of the brooding poet, alternately at home with and displaced in nature, who marks the change from medieval romance to later romanticism.

Unless otherwise indicated, texts are from Gianfranco Contini's two-volumed *Poeti del Duecento* (Ricciardi, 1960).

ST. FRANCIS OF ASSISI

[90] *Canticle of the Creatures: Altissimu, onnipotente bon Signore*

1. Most mighty and most powerful, Good Seigneur,
   Thine be the praise, the glory, and the honor and every blessèd word.

   Thou alone, Most Mighty, canst all claim,
   And no man is worthy to speak thy name.

2. Praise to thee, Milord, with all thy creatures,   5
   Especially Messér my brother Sun,
   Who day makes and who lights us all alone.
   And he is beautiful and shiny with great splendor;
   Thy meaning, Mighty, to mankind he doth render.

3. Praise be thine, Milord, for sister Moon and all the stars;   10
   In Heaven didst thou cut them precious and pretty and shining far.

4. Praise be thine, Milord, for brother Wind
   And for Air and Cloud, Fair Weather and for Rain,
   By which thou givest creatures what doth sustain.

5. Praise be thine, Milord, for sister Water,   15
   Who is precious and chaste, thy useful, humble daughter.

6. Praise be thine, Milord, for my brother Fire,
   By whom thou lightest the night;
   And he is handsome and happy, full of vigor and might.

7. Praise be thine, Milord, for sister Our Mother Earth,   20
   Who doth rule us and yield us from her girth
   And to fruits with colored flowers and grasses doth give birth.

8. Praise be thine, Milord, for those who pardon with thy love
   And bear infirmities and tribulations;

9. Blessed are they who will suffer in peace,   25
   For by thee, Most Mighty, they shall be crowned.

90. San Francesco (1182?–1226). Founder of the Franciscan Order. After a spoiled youth, he was converted to Christianity in his twenties, espousing the cause of the poor. Granted his order by Innocent III. Received the stigmata on his limbs in 1224. Reportedly composed the *Canticle* before his death at San Damiano. Life recounted by Thomas of Celano and St. Bonaventure. Text in Contini, *Poeti del Duecento*, I, 33–34.

10. Praise be thine, Milord, for our sister Bodily Death,
    Whom no living man can ever outrun.
    Woe to those who in mortal sin take their last breath,
    But blessed those living in thy most holy will,   30
    For a second death shall never work them ill.

11. Men, praise and bless My Lord, and in servility
    Work for him, and thank him with humility.

GIACOMO DA LENTINI, THE NOTARY

[91*] *Io m'aggio posto in core a Dio servire*

I've put it in my heart to serve my Lord
So that I may rise into his Paradise
To that holy place where, so I've heard,
Are games and laughter, everything that's nice.
Without Milady I would not wish to go there,   5
For without her I could find no delectation—
She with the shining face, the golden hair—
Sad would I be at my lady's separation.

But I'm not saying this to take a dare
And commit a voluntary mortal sin,   10
As if I had to have her bearing fair,
Her visage lovely from the brow to chin—
Still, it would prove great solace for my care
To see my lady stand in full glory there!

---

91. Or Iacopo da Lentino, nicknamed Il Notaio (*fl.* 1230–1245). Considered the father of the sonnet, of which this may be the oldest extant sample. Worked for Frederick II as *notarius* and *scriba* in 1233 and 1240.

    *Original text appears in Section IX, taken from *Poetry of the Sicilian School*, ed. and trans. Frede Jensen (Garland, 1986), No. 10.

CIELO D'ALCAMO

---

[92] *Rosa fresca aulentissima*

1. HE: Fresh, sweet rose, my summer sprout,
    Adored by virgins—and missuses too—
    I'm in hellish fire. Pluck me out!
    Lady, I know no peace night or day
    Because my thoughts all turn your way.   5

2. SHE: Buzzing around this rose is insanity.
    Go plow the ocean. Harrow air with seed.
    Hoard the age's wealth with great vanity!
    I'll never be yours in this earthly life.
    I'd rather be God's shaven wife.   10

3. HE: If you were a nun, I'd ask Death's pardon,
    For I would lose my solace and my joy.
    O when I see you, rose of the garden,
    You give me pleasure constantly.
    Why not place our love in unity?   15

4. SHE: I don't care a hoot for your unity;
    If Daddy and my kin should see you here,
    They'll chase and catch you easily.
    Well, you found access to my door.
    Pray your exit's lucky as before.   20

5. HE: Bah! if they find me, what's the bother?
    My defense is two thousand *augustali*.
    Properties in Bari wouldn't help your Father.
    Thank God the Emperor's in health!
    Sweetheart, do you know the power of wealth?   25

6. SHE: Lord, how you pester me night and day!
    Why, I've got byzantine coins of the finest gold.
    Give me all the Sultan's tucked away
    And double the loot of the Mussulmans—
    Still, I'll never let you touch my hands.   30

7. HE: Many women have heads carved out of stone
    But men can still master and persuade them.

---

92. Or Ciullo dal Como (*fl.* 1230–1250). Unknown Sicilian poet. His *Contrasto* (Debate Poem: the usual word in Italian is *Tenzone*) is dated from its mention of *augustali* in line 22), which were issued in 1231. Text: Jensen, *Sicilian School*, pp. 136–147, with a more conservative translation.

The chase is hot. The catch comes home.
Who wants to be a lonely quarry?
Don't resist, dear. You'll be sorry.   35

8. SHE: Me be sorry? Why I'd rather be slain
Than disgrace all womankind. Last night
Why'd you prowl around here half-insane?
Go home, troubadour. Sit.
I don't like your talk one little bit.   40

9. HE: O me! it's not the first time I felt the lash.
I feel it every day when I make my rounds.
No other girl ever made me act as rash
As you do, my envied rose sublime.
I still think that Fate will make you mine.   45

10. SHE: If *that's* my fate, I'll leap off a cliff
Rather than waste my beauty in your hands.
I'll cut my hair, if that's destiny's drift,
And really become a nun
Before I'd let you have your little fun.   50

11. HE: If you're a nun, girl of the shiny face,
I'll go to your convent and become a monk;
I'll get you. Who cares about disgrace?
And stay with you each waking hour.
I've simply got to have you in my power.   55

12. SHE: O God, poor me! What fate could be worse?
Almighty Jesus, you must be mad at me,
Pitting me against a pagan like him—perverse!
Go see the world. It's big enough.
You'll find some girl with much better stuff.   60

13. HE: I've hunted through Tuscany, Calabria, Lombardy,
Apulia, Constantinople, Pisa, Syria,
Germany, Babylonia, and all of Barbary,
But never found a girl so courtly;
That's why I chose you to be my lady.   65

14. SHE: Well, you worked hard. Why not promise this?
Go ask my hand from my mother and my father.
Then to the church—if they say yes—
And marry me before all of our folks.
That's the only way I'll bear your yoke.   70

15. HE: My life, your proposition doesn't help you well;
No, I know the gist behind your talk.

You wanted feathers, but your angel wings fell
As I have given you an earthly shove.
Well, if you can—keep your countrified love!   75

16. SHE: Don't try to frighten me with your catapult.
I'm gloriously safe in this strong fortress.
You know, sometimes you talk like a young colt.
If you don't get up and go home to bed,
I'd be very happy to see you dead!   80

17. HE: Aha, my life, you want me killed for you!
Well, I can be hacked or torn to bits
But I won't leave till I've got that fruit
Sequestered in your garden of delight.
That's what I desire day and night.   85

18. SHE: My fruit's not been had by knights or counts
Though it's been sought by many marquises and judges,
Who didn't get it, no matter how they flounced.
Listen carefully to what I say:
Your money's just a needle in the hay.   90

19. HE: I've got the lettuce, but not for you those stocks!
Don't scoff, my pretty, till you've toted up the sum.
Fair winds can change and drive you on the rocks.
Remember these words of mine, though brief:
Your stubbornness causes me much grief.   95

20. SHE: If grief suddenly made you totter off your feet
And people rushed in here on every side,
Yelling: "Help this poor man!" I'd retreat.
I wouldn't lend a hand with any hope,
Not if you were Sultan—or even Pope!   100

21. HE: Life, if God willed my death here in your house,
I'd be consoled by my daily hauntings.
People would shout: "See that treacherous louse
Keeping a dead man in her room!"
With words alone, you can seal my doom.   105

22. SHE: If you don't take away your evil curses,
My brothers are going to find you in our manse.
What do I care if your life gets worse!
You came to preach all by yourself
Without any friends or relatives to help.   110

23. HE: True, I don't have any relatives to aid me.
I'm all alone among your gentle clan.

It's now a year since I first saw you, lady,
Stepping out in your fancy party dress.
Beautiful, that was the start of my distress.   115

24. SHE: Ah yes, you fell in love, you traitorous Jude,
With all my purple, scarlet velvets and silks.
Even if you swore on the Gospel you'd be true,
You'll never in this life own little *me*.
I'd rather pitch myself into the sea.   120

25. HE: If you jumped into the sea, my lady grand,
I'd search for you all along the beach;
I'd find your corpse somewhere on the sand
And then I'd end where I'd like now to begin:
Locked with you even in death—in sin.   125

26. SHE: Forgive him, Father, Son—St. Matthew too—
I swear I never heard those evil words.
He's no heretic—no son of a Jew.
Lord, whenever a woman's dead and done,
She can't offer a man any pleasure or fun.   130

27. HE: I know but I can't take another stand.
If you won't help me, I'll give up my song.
Lady, please help! You know that you can!
I love you even unloved, forsook:
You've caught me. I'm a fish upon your hook.   135

28. SHE: I know you love me, and my own love's palatine;
Get up and go. Come back tomorrow morning.
If you do what I say, I'll love you well and fine.
I promise this without any lies.
I pledge this: you have me as your prize.   140

29. HE: Dear, I still can't go. Please, I beg:
Take this knife. Slit me down the throat!
Do it quicker than you can fry an egg.
Beautiful, grant me what I implore:
My heart and soul are waging constant war.   145

30. SHE: I'm sure your soul's as hot as a man half-cooked.
Well, I know only one cure for this disease.
Why not swear you're mine on the Holy Book?
Look, you could even cut off my head:
I'm not going to go just *anywhere* I'm led!   150

31. HE: Sweet, I have the Gospel in my chest.
(I took it when the church priest wasn't looking.)
I swear that with me you'll never be depressed.

Now show your love here with charity.
Lady, my soul shines with genteel clarity. 155

32. SHE: Sir, since you've sworn, I've no defender.
Suddenly my body's setting me on fire.
I wronged you, but—mercy! I surrender.
Now quick! upstairs let's turn and bend
And give this long, long talk a happy end. 160

PIER DELLA VIGNA

[93] *Amore, in cui disio ed ho speranza*

1. Love, by which I have desire and hope,
   Has given me, beautiful, a reward from you,
   And now I'm waiting till my happiness comes,
   Firmly expecting a good time in good season.
   Like a man at sea who's hoping to ride the swells 5
   And the time is right, and out he flings his sails,
   And the hope he has is true with no betraying—
   Just so am I, my lady, as I move toward you.

2. Ah, if I could reach you, loving lady,
   Like some thief asneak, and not be seen! 10
   If Love would grant me just this little gift,
   I'd think that I had grasped some good-omened joy.
   Ah, I would speak with you graciously, my lady,
   And tell you how I've loved you this long while
   More sweetly than Pyramus did his Thisbe, 15
   And I'll love you for as long as I have life.

3. Your love it is that holds me in desiring
   And gives me hope for some great joy,
   For I don't care if I grieve or if I suffer,
   For I'll remember the hour I came to you; 20
   And if I delay too long, I think I'll perish,
   O perfumed breath! and you will lose me too.
   And so, my beauty, if you wish me well,
   See that I don't die in my hope for you.

93. Or Piero da le Vigne (*ca.* 1182–1249). Close counselor to Frederick II and secretary of the imperial chamber. Studied at Bologna; assumed imperial duties after 1220. Disgraced and imprisoned in 1249; committed suicide. Movingly described by Dante in *Inferno* XIII. Ed. Jensen, pp. 72–75. For Pyramus and Thisbe, see Ovid, *Metamorphoses* IV.55 ff.

4. In hope of you I live, my lady fair,   25
    And still my heart goes on in quest of you,
    And it seems to me the hour is getting longer
    That true love spends in sending me to you;
    And I'm searching for a time that will be right
    To loose my sails in your direction, rose,   30
    And anchor in a port where I'll repose
    With heart intent upon your mastery.

5. Go, little song, and carry these laments
    To her who holds my heart within her power;
    Go, count for her the pains that I have felt   35
    And tell her how I'm dying with desire,
    And let her send a message back to tell
    How I can console this love I bear for her;
    And if I ever did a thing debased,
    Let her give me penance as she wills.   40

RINALDO D'AQUINO

[94] *Già mai non mi conforto*

1. Never again that comfort,
    Never that joyous heart.
    The ships down in the harbor
    Are straining to depart.
    Away runs the noblest one   5
    To the land across the sea.
    But me—poor weeping thing—
    What shall become of me?

2. Away, away he runs,
    Not one word does he write,   10
    Leaving me here spurned;
    All day, all the night
    Many are the sighs
    That assail me constantly.
    Not in heaven, not on earth   15
    Does life exist for me.

94. Rinaldo d'Aquino (*fl.* 1235–1279?). Aristocrat from the Campagna, possibly a
brother of St. Thomas Aquinas. Perhaps the imperial falconer of Frederick II. Wrote this
Complaint Against the Crusade (of 1227–1228). Ed. Jensen, pp. 56–59.

3. O Holy, Holy Savior
   Who from Mary came our way!
   Watch, protect that lover,
   Since you're taking him away.   20
   O reverenced and feared
   Power from above!
   In your hands I place
   My tender love.

4. O cross that saves mankind,   25
   You plummet me to error,
   Twisting my grievous mind
   Beyond all hope of prayer.
   Why, O pilgrim cross,
   Why this destructive turn?   30
   Bowed beneath my loss,
   I kindle; O I burn.

5. The Emperor who rules the world
   In his peaceful sway
   Ravages poor little me   35
   By taking my hope away.
   O reverenced and feared
   Power from above!
   In your hands I place
   My tender love.   40

6. When he took up the cross,
   I didn't know the end was this:
   Whatever love he gave me
   I repaid him kiss for kiss.
   Now I'm thrust aside—   45
   Yes, condemned to prison—
   Now I'm forced to hide
   In lifelong derision.

7. The ships are in their moorings.
   Soon they'll depart.   50
   With them and their people
   Sails my heart!
   O Father, O Creator,
   Guide them to holy haven.
   By your sacred cross   55
   They're all enslaven.

8. And O Darling, I beg you:
   Take pity on my hysteria.
   Write me a little sonnet.
   Send it to me from Syria!   60

Night and day I'll know
Only this bitter strife.
In lands beyond the ocean
Lies my whole life.

RE ENZO

[95] *Tempo vene chi sale a chi discende*

Time comes for one descending to ascend,
A time for standing mute, a time for speech,
A time to listen for one to apprehend,
A time for not fearing fearful things.
There is a time for obeying one who reprehends,   5
A time for foreseeing future events,
A time to punish one who offends,
A time to make pretense that one can't see.

And thus I hold him a wise and knowing man
Who guides himself always with his reason   10
And knows how to conduct himself with the time,
And with the people stands always in good season,
And never offers any grounds for doubt
That might let his deeds be suspect of any treason.

95. Or King Heinz, Heinrich (*ca.* 1220–1272). Bastard son of Frederick II from an unknown mother. Married Adelasia in 1238, thereby claiming rights to the Kingdom of Sardinia. Captured by the Bolognese at the battle of Fossalta (May 26, 1249) and imprisoned in the Central Square of Bologna, where his castle quarters still stand; never freed. This poem, attributed also to Guittone d'Arezzo, based on Ecclesiastes 3:1–8. Ed. Jensen, p. 120.

IACOPONE DA TODI

[96] *Donna de paradiso*

MESSENGER:
Lady of Paradise,
Your Son's in custody,
The blessèd Jesus Christ.
Run, Milady, and see:
They beat him mercilessly!   5
He'll die, it seems to me,
The whip so cruelly bites!

VIRGIN:
Tell me, how can it be?
He never acted wrongly.
Did they bind him strongly—   10
O my one hope, Christ!

MESSENGER:
For a thirty-denier dole,
Milady, Judas sold,
Betrayed for the love of gold—
That was his heavy heist!   15

VIRGIN:
Help, my Magdalene!
Suddenly I've pain!
O God, he goes on rein—
As someone once prophesied.

MESSENGER:
Help, Madonna, quick!   20
Look! the people spit!
They shove, won't let him sit!
Now he's at Pilate's side.

VIRGIN:
O Pilate, don't allow
My Son to suffer now.   25
I can show you how
All his accusers lied.

96. Jacopone of Todi (1236–1306). Born in the Umbrian city of wealthy parents. Renounced the world for Franciscan orders after the sudden, tragic death of his wife at an elegant ball. This Dialogue Poem is part of his *Lauds* to Christ and Mary. Text in Contini, *Poeti del Duecento*, II, 119–124.

CROWD:
Crucify, yes crucify
This "King" who tries to falsify
The laws that we all live by,   30
And Rome he has defied!

VIRGIN:
Please, O please attend me!
See how this grief will end me . . .
A change of heart would lend me
A little peace of mind.   35

CROWD:
Let's drag the thieves outside,
Companions for homicide.
A crown of thorns there'll be
For the self-claimed monarchy!

VIRGIN:
O my Son, my Son, my Son!   40
Lovely lily, amorous one!
Son, who can make languish
This heart now filled with anguish?
Son, with eye ever dancing,
Son, why aren't you answering?   45
Son, why have you pressed
Away from this suckling breast?

MESSENGER:
Milady, look! they bring
The Cross of suffering
On which the Light of Things   50
Will be hanged high.

VIRGIN:
What are you doing, Cross?
Snatching him to my loss?
What charges do you toss?
No sin he ever tried.   55

MESSENGER:
Help, grieving mother of worship—
Your Son is being stripped.
The nails are next—the whips—
For they will crucify.

VIRGIN:
O if they tear off his clothes,   60
That body will disclose
Those cruel and brutal blows—
The blood I'll have to spy.

MESSENGER:
Lady, they're lifting his hand—
Now on the Cross it stands. 65
The pounding they command—
Straight to the board he's plied.
The other hand they're snatching—
Out on the Cross it's stretching.
His face his pain is etching, 70
And that's now multiplied.
Lady, his feet now go,
Nailed on the wood down low.
They wrench and maul him so,
His joints are gaping wide. 75

VIRGIN:
Ah, I begin my lament.
Son, my one true enjoyment,
Who ordered your life spent?
My one delicate pride.
Better if they had pressed 80
This heart out of this breast
Than I should see you trussed
And agonized—

CHRIST:
Mother, and are you there?
You're causing me even more care 85
With all of this despair
That grips you in its vise.

VIRGIN:
Son, do you cast me blame?
Husband and father in name,
Son, who will make you lame? 90
Who has bared your hide?

CHRIST:
Mother, why now complain?
I want you to remain
And serve the friends I've gained
Through the world wide. 95

VIRGIN:
Son, this is not to ask!
Son, I refuse the task!
Son, with you I'll pass,
Until my breath's expired.
A single grave will mark— 100
Son of a mother made dark—
The place where we both embark,
Choked by this homicide.

CHRIST:
Mother with heart perplexed,
I want you to stand erect   105
With John, who is my elect,
As your new son he'll abide.
John, take my mother there;
Hold her with great care;
Her heart has felt a tear—   110
So hold her tender and tight.

VIRGIN:
Son, your soul's departed.
Son of one brokenhearted,
Son of a woman martyred,
Son who was mortified.   115
Son who is rosy and fair,
Son beyond all compare,
Son, where for me? where?
Son, have you left my side?
Son who is blond and white,   120
Son with a face of delight,
Why did the world show spite,
Son, why were you despised?
Son who was pleasant and sweet,
Son of a woman with grief,   125
Son whom the masses treat
In a wicked wise.
Now, my new son, John—
Your belovéd brother is gone;
The knife for him was drawn,   130
As was long prophesied,
Which killed both Son and Mother;
Cruel death did them smother
Lying wrapped round each other
In each other's arms gripped tight.   135

[97] *Senno me par e cortesia*

1. To me it seems sense and nobility
   To worship Messiah with imbecility.

2. It seems to me great intelligence
   To worship God by losing your sense;
   In Paris you will never see   5
   Such a great philosophy.

97. Text in Contini, II, 73–74; this attack on knowledge is as stunning as his prayer for
sickness: Contini, II, 135–138.

3. Who for Christ becomes all mad
   Seems afflicted, troubled, sad;
   But a master he will be
   Of nature and theology.   10

4. Who for Christ acts all hazy
   Seems to the people utterly crazy;
   He who hasn't known insanity
   Thinks divine madness is all inanity.

5. He who wants to enter this school   15
   Will have to learn a new set of rules;
   Unless you experience madness directly
   You can't practice it correctly.

6. He who wants to join this dance
   Will witness love in great abundance;   20
   A hundred days' pardon is the fee
   For all who curse him wickedly.

7. But he who puts ambition above
   Will not be worthy of Christ's love;
   For Jesus dangled willingly   25
   With thieves accused of villainy.

8. He who seeks with true humility
   Will arrive with great agility;
   Go no more to Bologna University
   To master doctrines of perversity.   30

THE PERFECT LADY OF FLORENCE

[98] *Lasciar voria lo mondo e Dio servire*

I want to go away from vanity
And leave the world and serve my God
Because I see on every side of me
Madness and unchecked evil and great fraud:
Sense and courtesy are ever expiring   5
And fine value and goodness of every kind;
And so I want no husband, want no sire;
Leaving the world is all that's on my mind.

   98. La Compiuta Donzella di Firenze (latter 1200s). Otherwise unknown poetess often considered a construct of the male poets of the day. This Sonnet in Contini, I, 435.

When I recall how man with ill's adorned,
I suddenly am disdainful of all the race   10
And toward my God all of my body's turned.
My father makes me stand with pensive face.
He turns me away from service to my Christ.
What man will come to claim my dowry's price?

GUITTONE D'AREZZO

---

[99] *Tuttor ch'eo dirò "gioi," gioiva cosa*

Every time I say "joy," my joyous thing,
You'll understand what I mean,
For you're the joy of all joyous beauty
And the joy of fine and enjoyable pleasures,
And a joy in which joyous events reside,   5
A joy of adornments and lovely body,
With a joyous and loving look
That is truly a joy to see.

You are joyous in your will and in your thought,
A joy in your speech and making enjoyment,   10
And a joy in all your joyous movements;
And so, my joyous joy, I find myself
So desirous of you that I'll never know any joy
If my heart doesn't rest amid your joy.

99. Brother Guittone from Arezzo (*ca.* 1230–1294); member of the order of Frati Gaudenti (Jolly or Joyous Brothers) after 1265. Given to using awkward Provençal and Sicilian rhetoric (as here), he was severely criticized by Dante in *De vulgari* II.4.8 and through the voice of Bonagiunta da Lucca in *Purgatorio* XXIV.56. Text: Contini, I, 244.

BONAGIUNTA DA LUCCA

---

[100] *Voi, che avete mutata la mainera*

>   To Guido Guinizelli

You, who have changed the style
Of writing pleasing love songs
From the form and essence of before
In order to surpass all other poets,
Have acted like a beacon   5
Casting your light into dark quarters,
But not here where a sublime sphere illuminates,
Which surpasses everything else with its splendor.

You so surpass all other writers in your subtlety
That there isn't anyone who can explain you,   10
Since your style is so obscure!
It seems to me very strange that from Bologna,
Which has long been noted for its rational sense,
You squeeze love songs out of turgid prose.

GUIDO GUINIZELLI

---

[101] *Vedut'ho la lucente stella diana*

I have seen the blazing morning star
Appear before day hands us dawn,
Shaped like a woman standing afar,
More splendid than any other one—
Snow-white face with scarlet glow,   5
Gay, sparkling eyes, full of love for earth;

100. Bonagiunta Orbicciani of Lucca (*fl.* 1242–1257). With Guittone, helped to bring earlier modes of poetry to northern Italy. In this *sirventes*, he criticizes the father of the "sweet new style," but Dante makes him atone for this in *Purgatorio* XXIV.20 ff. Text in Robert Edwards, *Poetry of Guido Guinizelli* (Garland, 1987), No. 19a.

101. Or Guido Guinicelli (*ca.* 1230–1276). Acknowledged father of the *dolce stil nuovo*. Judge in Bologna, descended from wealthy Ghibellines; driven into exile after the Guelph victory in 1274. Died near Padua. Immortalized by Dante in *Purgatorio* XXVI, where he introduces Arnaut Daniel. Texts in Robert Edwards, *Poetry of Guido Guinizelli* (Garland, 1987), No. 7; next poem, No. 10.

Plate 5. The Piazza Maggiore or main square in Bologna, with the Church of San Petronio on the left, the Municipio (Town Hall) in the background, and part of the Castle of Re Enzo (No. 95) on the right, where he was imprisoned. The famous University of Bologna, where Guido Guinizelli (Nos. 101–103) taught and Dante (Nos. 110–115) studied, was in the left foreground. Many early poems were written on legal documents in the Municipio in the Middle Ages. (Courtesy of the Archivio di Stato di Bologna)

No worldly Christian girl I know
Can match her beauty and her worth.

By the love of her I'm so assailed
With a battle of sighs that rages fierce,   10
Before her I'd stand by fear impaled:
O if she knew how desires pierce
And, wordlessly, would get me some gain
From the pity she should pass upon my pain!

[102] *Io vogl' del ver la mia donna laudare*

I truly wish to give my lady praise
And liken her to lily and to rose:
Brighter than morning star she comes and glows
And makes me think of all that heavenly blaze.
Green banks I compare with her, I compare the skies,   5
Flowers of every color, yellow and green,
Azure and gold, the richest jewels to be seen;
Through her even Love feels his value rise.

She passes in the streets, noble, adorned;
She humbles the pride of any with her greeting,   10
And skeptics to believers quickly are turned;
No wicked man with her would risk a meeting;
And still I say: her powers are even keener.
No man thinks evil once that he has seen her.

[103*] *Al cor gentil rempaira sempre amore*

1. Love always repairs to the noble heart
      Like a bird winging back into its grove:
   Nor was love made before the noble heart,
      Nor did nature, before the heart, make love.
   For they were there as long as was the Sun,   5
      Whose splendor's ever bright;
   Never did love before that shining come.
   Love nestles deep inside nobility
      Exactly the way
   One sees the heart within the fiery blaze.   10

2. Fire of love in noble heart is caught
      Like power gleaming inside a precious stone.
   The value does not come down from the stars
      Until the Sun has blenched the stone all pure.
   Only after the might of the Sun   15
      Has drawn out all that's vile
   Does the star bestow its noble power.

*Original text appears in Section IX, taken from Edwards, No. 4.

Just so a heart transformed by nature pure,
    Noble and elect,
A woman starlike with her love injects.   20

3. Love for this reason stays in noble heart
    Like a waving flame atop a burning brand,
Shining, its own delight, subtle and bright;
    It is so proud, it knows no other way.
Yet a nature which is still debased   25
    Greets love as water greets the fire,
With the cold hissing against the heat.
Love in noble heart will find a haven
    Like the shine
Of a diamond glinting in ore within the mine.   30

4. Sun beats against the mud the livelong day;
    Mud it remains; Sun does not lose its ray;
The haughty one says: "I am noble by my tribe."
    He is the mud; Sun is the noble power.
Man must never believe   35
    That nobility exists outside the heart
In the grandness of his ancestry,
For without virtue, heart has no noble worth;
    It's a ray through a wave;
The heavens retain the sparkle and splendor they gave.   40

5. Shines among the powers of heaven
    God the creator, more than Sun in our eye;
Each angel knows the Maker beyond its sphere,
    And turning its circle, obeys God's noble power.
And thus it follows at once: 45
    The blesséd tasks of the Master transpire.
In the same way, in all truth, the beautiful lady
Should behave, for in her eyes reflects the desire
    Of a noble man
Who will turn his every thought to her command.   50

6. Lady, God will ask me: "Why did you presume?"
    When my soul stands before his mighty throne.
"You passed the heavens, came all the way to me,
    And cheapened me in the light of profane love.
To me is due all the praise   55
    And to the Queen of the Royal Realm
Who makes all fraudulence cease."
I'll tell him then: "She had an angel look—
    A heavenly face.
What harm occurred if my love in her was placed?"   60

GUIDO CAVALCANTI

[104] *In un boschetto trova' pasturella*

1. Once within a little grove a shepherdess I spied;
   More than any star of sky beauteous did she prove.

2. Ringlets she had, blonde and curly locks,
   Eyes filled with love, a face of rosy hue,
   And with her staff she led her gentle flocks,   5
   Barefoot, with their feet bathed by the dew.
   She sang, indeed, as if she were enamored;
   She had the glamour of every pleasing art.

3. I greeted her, and asked her then at once
   If she had any company that day;   10
   She answered sweetly: "For the nonce,
   Alone throughout this grove I make my way."
   And added: "Listen, but when the gentle bird is heard,
   A friend should have my heart."

4. And when she told me of this state of mind,   15
   Suddenly I heard birdsongs in the wood.
   I said to myself: "This surely would be the time
   To take from this shepherdess what joy I could."
   Grace I requested—just to kiss her face—
   And then embrace if she should feel like me.   20

5. She took my hand, seized with love's old power,
   And said she'd give me her heart too;
   She led me then into a fresh green bower,
   And there I saw flowers of every hue.
   And I was filled so full of sweetened joy   25
   Love's godlike boy there too I seemed to see.

[105] *Fresca rosa novella*

1. Fresh newborn rose,
   My beauteous Spring,
   Through field, by river,

104. Guido Cavalcanti (*ca.* 1255–1300). Florentine member of the rich merchant classes: Guelph and White in politics; banished to Sarzana in Liguria, where he contracted malaria; died in August, 1300. His mistress, Giovanna (Vanna), is mentioned in the *Vita Nuova*, where Dante tells us that her secret name was Primavera or Spring (see No. 105, line 2). The heroine of this Pastourelle is a simple peasant girl. Text in Lowry Nelson, Jr., *Poetry of Guido Cavalcanti* (Garland, 1986), No. 46; next poem, No. 1.

> Gaily singing,
> Your noble worth I set, In nature.   5

2. Your truly noble worth
   Renews itself with joy
   In agéd man or boy
   With every setting forth;
   Birds chant to it their vows,   10
   Each in his own Latin,
   From vespers into matins,
   On their greenish boughs.
   The whole world's now with song,
   Since it's your season,   15
   And, with proper reason,
   Hymns your majesty,
   For you're the most heavenly Of creatures.

3. Heavenly features
   In you, my lady, rest;   20
   O God, how wondrous blessed
   Now seems my desire.
   Lady, your glad expression,
   Whenever it comes and passes,
   Nature and custom surpasses   25
   In wonderful expression.
   Together women admire
   Your truly godlike form,
   For you are so adorned,
   Your beauty's not transcribed,   30
   For can't it be described: Beyond nature?

4. Beyond our human nature
   God made your excellence
   To show by its very essence
   That you were born to rule.   35
   Now, so your noble face
   May stay forever near,
   To me keep ever dear
   Your most abundant grace,
   And if I seem a fool   40
   To set you as my queen,
   Know that I don't blaspheme,
   For Love makes me courageous
   Which still no force assuages
         Nor measure.   45

[106*] *Chi è questa che vèn, ch'ogn'om la mira*

Who is it comes whom every man admires,
Who sets the air with clarity atremble?
Bringing Love too, so no man dare dissemble,
By speech, but each can only now suspire?
O how to catch her from the eye's swift gyre? 5
Love tells me: "No, you'd only bumble,
Because of women she's so far most humble
That any other you must then call 'ire.'"

No one could count her many charms, though modest,
For toward her bends every noble power; 10
Thus Beauty sets her forth to be her goddess.
Still my mind is not so high and grand,
Nor have I felt the grace at any hour
To encompass her and say, "I understand."

[107] *Avete 'n vo' li fior' e la verdura*

You have in you the flowers and the verdure
And all that's light or beautiful to sight,
So far outshining Sun, that nurture
No man knows who knows not your delight.
In this world live no other creatures 5
So full of beauty or of countless pleasures;
Whoever fears Love needs but view your features,
To rest assured of all his many treasures.

The ladies who now lend you company
Much please me because of their respect for you, 10
And so I beg them, for their courtesy:
Whatever they can, that much honor show
And hold with love your loving mastery;
Because of all the rest, you are the best.

[108] *Donna me prega, per ch'io voglio dire*

1. A lady asks me; therefore, I'd explain
   An accident that often fiercely smarts
   And is so high it claims Love for its name.
   Now who'd deny, let him hear its fame,

*Original text appears in Section IX, taken from Nelson, No. 4.
107. Text in Nelson, No. 2.
108. *The Song of Love* (*Canzone d'Amore*). Difficult text, edited by Mario Casella, *Studi di Filologia Italiana*, 7 (1944), with emendations by J. E. Shaw, *Guido Cavalcanti's Theory of Love* (University of Toronto, 1949). An "accident" in stanza 1, line 2, is a Scholastic term meaning "a movement in a substance." In stanza 10, the "one who to truth is sworn" is his unnamed philosophical source: Aristotle, Albertus Magnus, Averroes?

Though I can't hope to teach a lowly heart;   5
I'd reach some men with knowledge in their brains,

2. Who bring to reason some intelligence.
   Because without a bit of natural science
   I have no will or wit to try to prove
   Where Love is born, or who created Love,   10
   What is his virtue or his potency,
   How he might move or what his essence be,
   His delights which by "to love" are known
   Or if Love's ever to men's sight been shown.

3. In that part where memory has its locus   15
   He takes his state and there he is created,
   Diaphanous by light, out of that dark
   That comes from Mars and then takes lasting focus;
   And once he's made, he has a name sensate,
   Taking desire from heart, from mind his mark.   20

4. He comes from an image seen and comprehended
   That's apprehended in the Possible Intellect;
   There he waits in subject, without wandering,
   And in that part his vigor has no force,
   For Love's never from pure quality descended;   25
   And yet he shines, himself his own effect,
   Without delight, unless it's that of pondering,
   Because he cannot breed from his own source.

5. Love is not virtue, but he takes his course
   From what we call perfection—   30
   Not rational but emotional, I say:
   Outside of health he steers his judgment's force,
   Lets ecstasy gain reason's predilection,
   Choosing poorly friends to vice's way,
   Pursuing his power often to death's end.   35

6. Yet if by chance his power is turned aside
   To guide instead along the other way,
   He was not made by nature to go astray:
   However far from the perfect good he bend,
   By that much is the lover life denied: 40
   Stability can fail the mastery it's gotten;
   Love can't prevail when reason's all forgotten.

7. Love comes to be whenever desire's so strong
   It can't keep bearing nature's measures;
   Then leisure can't long please, and so Love veers,   45
   Changing complexions, turning smiles to tears,
   Twisting the face with fear; his pleasures
   Last but a little, for he stays not long.

8. And yet you'll find him most in men of worth
   Where his new qualities create new sighs   50
   And make men gaze at uncreated spaces,
   Arousing ire to burn in fiery faces
   (No man can imagine it until he tries).
   Love does not move, though arrows whistle forth;
   He does not twist to find his jests at all;   55
   Nor does he search for great wisdom, or small.

9. Like looks and tempers attract their kindred parts,
   And make Love's pleasures then appear the surer.
   No man can ever cower from his spear.
   Never was nymphlike Beauty like his darts,   60
   For coyer passions expire in such furor.
   Still, a reward awaits the spirit speared—

10. Though not a trace appears on the lover's face.
    For Love's no object, neither black nor white;
    Look at a lover; you find no form for seeing   65
    Unless some emotion from Love's form takes its being.
    Outside of color, likewise cut off from space
    This form out of darkness sheds faint light;
    Beyond all fraud, says one who to truth is sworn,
    So that only by this Love is true compassion born.   70

11. Go now, my song, where you aspire,
    Securely, for I've so upraised
    You, you'll be praised
    Most highly for your sense
    By all who own intelligence: 75
    To stand with others you have no desire.

[109] *Perch'i' no spero di tornar giammai*

1. Because I never hope to go once more,
       Ballata, into Tuscany—
   You go soft and gently
       Straight to my lady's door,
       And she, from her high courtesy,   5
       Will do you honor.

2. Go, and carry with you tales of sighings,
       Filled with long pain and grievous fear;
   Beware only of hostile spyings
       From those who hold nobility not dear.   10

109. Commonly called the "*Farewell Ballata*," probably written in exile at Sarzana shortly
before death. Adapted by T. S. Eliot in "Ash Wednesday." Ed. Nelson, No. 35.

For certainly from my estate so low,
   To see you ill-dispatched
   Or by cruel hands snatched,
Which cause me now so many anguished breaths,
   Would cause me after death   15
   Grief and fresher woe.

3. You feel, Ballata, now how death
   Forces me to put my life behind;
You feel my heart pounding with every breath,
   Sensing the end of every reasoning mind.   20
   Now my body's so totally torn apart
      That pain's not even fervent;
      If you would be my servant,
   I ask: take my spirit with you
      (And this I beg you too:)   25
      Soon, when it leaves my heart.

4. Alas, Ballata, to your kindly company
   This soul that trembles I too recommend:
Take it along, out of your piety,
   To that sweet lady where I send.   30
   Alas, Ballata, say with sighings more
      When you've at last drawn near,
      "I am your servant here,
   And I have come to stay
      From one who's gone away,   35
      But was Love's servant long before."

5. You, my voice, now weakened and dismayed,
   Which issues crying from this saddened heart,
With soul, and with this song that I have made,
   From ruined mind now reason wide apart.   40
   You'll find that lady pleasing to the sense
      For her sweet intellect;
      And out of charmed respect
   You'll always stand before her;
      Spirit, you too adore her   45
      Forever for her excellence.

DANTE ALIGHIERI

[110] *Guido, i' vorrei che tu e Lapo ed io*

Guido, I wish that you and Lapo and I,
Spirited on the wings of a magic spell,
Could drift in a ship where every rising swell
Would sweep us at our will across the skies;
Then tempest never, or any weather dire   5
Could ever make our blissful living cease;
No, but abiding in a steady, blessèd peace
Together we'd share the increase of desire.

And Lady Vanna and Lady Lagia then
And she who looms above the thirty best   10
Would join us at the good enchanter's behest;
And there we'd talk of Love without an end
To make those ladies happy in the sky—
With Lapo enchanted too, and you and I.

[111] *Al poco giorno e al gran cerchio d'ombra*

1. To slender daylight and a vast circle of shade
   I've come, alas! and to whitening of the hills,
   Where all the coloration is lost from the grass;
   And yet my desire has thus not lost its green,
   For it is founded on a hard, hard rock   5
   Which speaks and hears as if it were a woman.

2. Similarly this most extraordinary woman
   Stands frozen like the snow beneath the shade;
   She's never moved, unless it's like a rock,
   By the sweet season that heats up all the hills   10
   And makes them turn from whitening into green,
   Because it covers them with flowers and grass.

3. Whenever she wears a garland hat of grass
   She draws attention from every other woman,
   Because the blend of curly gold and green   15
   Is beautiful; Love stands within their shade,

110. Dante Alighieri (1265–1321), author of the monumental *Divine Comedy*. Wrote many lyrics in his youth, some collected in his youthful biography, the *Vita Nuova* (New Life); No. 15 in *Dante's Lyric Poetry*, ed. K. Foster and P. Boyde, an Invitation to Lapo Gianni (with Lagia) and Guido Cavalcanti (with Giovanna) to ride in a magic ship with Merlin (11) and Beatrice (10).

111. Sestina to a mysterious "Rock Lady," No. 78 in the Foster-Boyde edition.

And locks me in between these little hills
More tightly than the limestone locks the rock.

4. Her beauty exerts more power than magnetic rock,
   And her blows cannot be cured by any grass;   20
   For I have fled through fields and over hills
   To try to escape the clutches of such a woman;
   And yet her light won't grant me any shade,
   Under mound or wall or any frond of green.

5. I've seen her already dressed up in her green   25
   So stunningly that she would have moved a rock
   With the love I offer even to her shade;
   And so I've wanted her in a pretty field of grass
   To fall in love like me, like any woman,
   Surrounded by a circle of the highest hills.   30

6. But the rivers will run upward to the hills
   Before this wood that's dewy and is green
   Takes fire, as would any pretty woman;
   I'd take my life and sleep out on a rock
   And go around pasturing on the grass   35
   Just to see where her garments cast their shade.

7. Whenever the hills cast down a blackened shade
   In a fair green this youthful woman makes them
   Disappear, like a rock that's hidden under grass.

[112*] *Donne ch'avete intelletto d'amore*

1. Ladies who have intelligence of love
   With you about my lady I'd discourse,
   Not that by talk I'd reckon up her worth,
   But speech can often ease the burdened mind.
   I say: whenever her worth looms high above,   5
   Love makes me feel his presence sweetly, so
   That if I didn't gradually lose his glow,
   I'd teach the entire world to feel her love.
   And yet I should not be talking overmuch,
   For later fear will make me vilely quake;   10
   No, I shall treat her most genteel estate,
   Compared to what she is, with light-handed touch
   In talk to you, my loving ladies and lasses—
   It's not a thing for sharing with the masses.

112. Canzone from the *Vita Nuova* XIX.
*Original text appears in Section IX, taken from Foster and Boyde, No. 33.

2. An angel proclaims to the divine intellect,   15
   Saying, "My Master, upon the earth I heed
   A miracle in act that now proceeds
   Out of a soul which this far casts its splendor."
   Heaven, which has suffered no other defect
   Except the lack of her, to its Lord exclaims   20
   And every saint cries out in mercy's name.
   Pity is my only staunch defender,
   Saying in God, who my lady comprehends,
   "Delights of mine, suffer now in peace,
   For although your hope is one that can only please,   25
   Still there's a man who's waiting for her end
   And he will say in Hell: 'O spirits hexed,
   These eyes have seen the great hope of the blessed.'"

3. My lady is desired in highest Heaven.
   Ladies, become acquainted with her power: 30
   I say: she is the gentle lady's endower,
   So go with her whenever she passes by.
   Love casts a frost upon hearts which are craven,
   And every thought then icily petrifies;
   But he who can stand and fix on her his eyes   35
   Will become a noble thing—or else, will die.
   Whenever she finds a man who shows his worth
   For seeing her, he experiences her grace;
   She humbles him, all injuries to erase,
   And changes into happiness all that hurts.   40
   For even more grace God has given a donation:
   Certain salvation after her conversation.

4. Love says about her: "How can she possibly be
   A mortal thing, since she's beautiful and pure?"
   He looks at her and inwardly is sure   45
   God wants to set her forth as something new.
   Almost the color of pearl she has, to the degree
   A woman should, certainly within measure;
   She has all good that lies in nature's treasure;
   Her very existence proves that Beauty is true.   50
   Out of her eyes, whenever she moves them round,
   Issue spirits of Love encased in blaze
   Which strike the eyes of all who on her gaze
   And penetrate till the heart of each is found:
   Love you will see upon her visage painting;   55
   No one dare look there long or he'll be fainting.

5. Song, I know that talking you'll make your way
   To many ladies, once I've set you free.
   Now I admonish: I've reared you up to be
   A little daughter of Love, sweet and simple,   60

And wherever you go, you must always say:
"Show me the road; for I am being sent
To one whose praise explains my embellishment."
And if you don't want to act like an imbecile,
Stay away from people who are base,   65
Contriving, if you can, to show true grit
Only to ladies and to gentlemen of wit
Who will guide you quickly over the straightaways.
When you find Love in her company,
Never forget to offer him greetings from me!   70

[113] *Amore e 'l cor gentil sono una cosa*

Love and the noble heart are a single thing
(So said wise Guinizelli in his rhyme):
One without the other can have no fling,
As reason and soul are joined forever in time.
Nature creates them when with love it abounds.   5
Love is the sire, his mansion is the heart;
Deep inside he lies with sleep wrapped round;
Sometimes it's long or soon before he starts.

Beauty appears as a lady seeming wise,
Wakening desire from his heavy sleep,   10
Striking the heart through windows of the eyes.
Desire has lasted so long within the deep
It rouses the spirit of Love as best it can.
Thus too a lady is acted on by a man.

[114] *Oltre la spera che più larga gira*

Beyond the sphere that circles us most wide
Passes a sigh that issues from my heart.
A new intelligence that Love imparts
With tears will be its upward guide.
When it arrives where it most desires,   5
A lady receiving honor it will see,
Shining with a splendor so dazzlingly
The pilgrim spirit will marvel at her fire.

Such he sees. But when he crosses the breach,
I can't comprehend; he talks with subtlety   10
To my mourning heart, which demands his speech.

113. Sonnet from the *Vita Nuova*, XX. Strongly indebted to Guinizelli; ed. Foster and
Boyde, No. 34.
114. Final Sonnet of the *Vita Nuova*, XLII, affirming the ascension of Beatrice into
Paradise; ed. Foster and Boyde, No. 57.

I know only: he describes that noble lady
Because he often utters, "Beatrice . . ."
That, my dear women, is one thing I can reach.

[115] *Ben ti faranno il nodo Salamone*

Solomon's knot will soon be wrapping you in,
Bicci Junior, with those precious necks of quail.
Those expensive cuts of mutton will make you wail
Your sins duly recorded on the dead sheepskin.
Your house'll be even closer to St. Simon's Jail,   5
Unless, of course, you make a quick getaway.
But now (I fear) it's just too late to repay
Those debts—unless that appetite should fail;

They tell me, though, you've got a clever hand.
Well, if it's true, maybe you'll be like new   10
Because you can make a hoist of some thousand grand.
Perhaps this art will ease your gluttony's grief:
You'll pay your debts, and stay in Florence too.
What's better, Bicci? To be glutton or be thief?

CECCO ANGIOLIERI

[116] *S'i' fosse foco, arderei 'l mondo*

If I were fire, I would burn the world.
If I were wind, I'd buffet it wide.
If I were sea, I'd drown it in swirls.
If God, I'd boot it on the Devil's side.
If I were Pope, what a gay thing I'd be!   5
I'd toss all those Christians into jail.
If Emperor, know what would pleasure me?
To slice off every head from every tail.

115. Debate Poem (*Tenzone*) with Forese Donati. "Solomon's knot" is a symbol of usury. The last line is freely rendered; in Foster and Boyde, No. 73: "But thievery didn't help Stagno's sons(?)." For Forese's poems, Foster and Boyde, Nos. 72a, 73a, 74a.

116. Cecco Angiolieri (*fl.* 1281–1312). Cynical poet of Siena. Member of an important family. Military deeds documented from 1281; known dead in 1313. Wrote only sonnets. Figures as a duped character in *Decameron* IX.4. Texts in Maurizio Vitale, *Rimatori comico-realistici del Due e Trecento* (UTET, 1968), pp. 398, 351, 391, 420.

If I were Death, I'd go to visit Papa;
If I were Life, I'd bid him fond adieux.   10
And frankly I'd do the same for dear ole Mamma.
If I were Cecco, as I am and cannot choose,
I'd snatch the chicks who are young and happy too,
And all the old ugly broads I would leave to you.

[117] *Becchin' amor!—Che vuo', falso tradito?*

"Becchina, my love!" "What do you want, you lout?"
"Pardon me!" "You don't deserve it a bit."
"Please! O God!" "You're looking all washed-out."
"I'll serve forever—" "What do I get for it?"
"My good faith." "Ha! That you've got in droves."   5
"Always for you." "Peace! I know what's fraud."
"How'd I go wrong?" "A bird told me in the grove."
"Tell me, my love!" "Go! in the wrath of God!"
"Want me to die?" "It'd take a thousand years."
"Ah, you talk bad." "*You* want to teach me good?"   10
"No. I'll just die." "God, you're a screw-up, dear!"
"God pardon you!" "O hell! go—like you should!"
"Ah, if I could . . ." "Shall I lead you by your seat?"
"You've got my heart." "And with torment that I'll keep."

[118] *La stremità mi richer per figliuolo*

Misery calls out to me: "Hi, Sonny!"
I answer back: "How goes it, Mother, there?"
I was bred by a stud named Grief—not funny!—
And Melancholy delivered me from the mare.
My swaddling clothes were woven from a thread   5
That's called Disaster by the common folk.
From the bottoms of my soles up to my head
There's not a thing in me that's not a joke.

When I grew up, to make a restoration,
They gave me a wife; she's the one who yells   10
As far as the starry heavens feel vibrations:
Her yap's a thousand tympanums with bells.
A man whose wife is dead enjoys purgation:
He who takes another goes straight to Hell.

[119] *Dante Alleghier, s'i' so bon begolardo*

Dante, if I'm a big loud-talking cuss,
It's 'cause you've got your sword against my guts;
If I have lunch with someone, you have dinner;
I feed on fat, while lard-sucking makes you thinner;
If I shear out the cloth, you squeeze the carder;   5
If I run at the mouth, you gallop harder;

If I play gentleman, then you're downtrod;
If I'm the man of Rome, then you're a Lombard.

Okay! thank God at least we know we two
Are both to blame, me as much as you.   10
It's misery or bad sense that makes us run.
But if you want to carry on this fun—
Dante, I'll go until you're in the box;
For I'm the gay gadfly, and you're the ox.

FOLGORE OF SAN GIMIGNANO

[120] *I' doto voi, nel mese de gennaio*

In the month of January I will bear
Courtyards with the snap of kindled hay,
Warm rooms with beds of the loveliest array:
Silken sheets and coverlets of vair,
Asti spumante, sugared nuts, and sweets,   5
The finest clothes from Arras and Douai
To ward the chill and bitter blasts away
Of winter wind and rain, of snow and sleet.

We'll go out sometimes in the course of day
And toss some glistening, shiny snowy balls   10
At the little girls who'll follow on our way;
And when we're tired of all those skids and falls,
Back to the court we'll troop in disarray,
And with fine friends make restful festival.

[121] *D' april vi dono la gentil campagna*

For April I offer the gentle countryside
All flowering with blossoms bright and fresh,
Fountains of water that never can depress,
Maids and ladies over whom you can preside;
Stallions from Spain, chargers which boldly prance,   5
Company coutured in the latest Parisian style,
Instruments from Germany, lutes and viols
For tunes of old Provence and for the dance.

120. "The Splendor" of San Gimignano (*fl.* 1300–1332). Born Giacomo di Michele, but called Folgore because of his luxurious life-style. Cited for military successes in 1305, 1306. Sonnets to January and April; texts in Vitale, *Rimatori comico-realistici*, pp. 581–584.

And all around lie gardens by the score
Where everyone can lounge or wander on,   10
And each will bow with reverence and adore
The noble girl I place the crown upon
ˋWhich shines with finer jewels than does the hoard
Of Prester John or the King of Babylon.

LAPO GIANNI

---

[122] *Amor, eo chero mia donna in domino*

Love, I want my lady in my keeping,
The Arno River with finest balsam sweeping,
Silver encrustations on Florentine walls,
Rutted roads paved with finest crystal,
Battlemented citadels looming tall   5
And every Italian sworn to be my friend;
Roadways secure, world peace without an end,
Neighbors who have helping hands to lend,
Weather in every season moderate,
A thousand maids and ladies standing ornate,   10
With love their leading standard against wrong,
Ready both night and morn to join in song;
And gardens of great compass full of fruit,
With every wingéd thing that sings or hoots,
With quiet canals and places where I can shoot;   15
This way I would be as blessed as Absalom
Or like great Samson or even Solomon;
I'd choose mighty barons for menial things:
All my songs would be sung to viols and strings;
And then to make my heavenly entry sure,   20
I'd ask a life young, healthy, happy, secure,
To last as long as this world of ours endures.

122. Lapo Gianni (*fl.* 1298–1328?). Cited in No. 110, as well as in the *De vulgari*, as one
of Dante's closest friends. His lady was Lagia (Alagia or Adalasia). Probably held juridical and
political posts. Text in Contini, II, 603.

CINO DA PISTOIA

[123] *Io guardo per li prati ogni fior bianco*

Through all the fields I search for flowers white
In memory of what caused me such delight
That even sighing I go inquiring for more.
I still remember the white orbs with their sheen
Blending with a cut of brownish green   5
That Love himself once wore
At that time when with Mars and Venus gazing,
His keen-whittled arrow came blazing
Into the middle of my core;
And now when the wind has set the petals swaying,   10
I think of the whiteness of her lovely eyes
Which ignites this excitement that never dies.

PETRARCH (FRANCESCO PETRARCA)

[124] *Voi ch'ascoltate in rime sparse il suono*

You who hear in scattered rhymes the sound
Of sighs with which I nurtured once my heart
As youthfulness in error made its start—
A different man in part from this man now—
In many styles I weep and turn in mind   5
Among vain hopes and sadness also vain;
If there is one experienced in love's pain,
His pity with his pardon I would find.

Ah, to the masses I see I was but a name
They mouthed for quite a time, and yet   10
Within me now this thought arouses regret:

123. Cino Sigibuldi or Sinibuldi (*ca.* 1270–*ca.* 1337). Native of Pistoia who studied law with Francesco d'Accursio in Bologna and taught in Siena, Perugia, Naples. His legal writings survive along with numerous poems. Praised by Dante in *De vulgari*. Text in Contini, II, 686.

124. Francesco Petrarca (1304–1374). Italy's most famous medieval lyric poet. Biographies by Morris Bishop and Ernest Hatch Wilkins. No. 124 is the Introduction to the *Canzoniere* or *Songbook*, and the poems follow in chronological order. Texts in *Petrarca*, ed. F. Neri and others (Ricciardi, 1951), Nos. 1, 62, 126, 129, 164, 269, 311, 365.

The fruit of all my vanity is shame,
And penitence, for now the knowledge gleams
That all that delights the world are just brief dreams.

[125] *Padre del ciel, dopo i perduti giorni*

Father in heaven, after the squandered days,
After the nights misspent in vanity
With that desire always burning fiercely,
Looking at limbs shaped beautifully to craze—
With your light, may it please that I now turn   5
To a different life, to tasks of a nobler kind
And leave the nets spread out in vain behind,
Showing the Adversary that he's been spurned.

It's going, Master, into the eleventh year
Since I was bent beneath the yoke of cruelty   10
That heaps on the submissive a direr loss.
My restless thoughts to a better place please steer;
Take pity on my suffering, though unworthy;
Remind me how you hanged upon the Cross.

[126] *Chiare, fresche e dolci acque*

1. Waters clear and sweet and fresh
   In which those limbs would lie
   Of her alone who to me was a woman;
   The gentle trunk where she would press—
   Ah, memory's sigh!—   5
   Her flank against it as a column.
   Flowers and grasses as a dress
   Would lightly press
   Against her angel breast;
   The holy air forever at rest   10
   Where Love opened my heart to her loveliness—
   All of you, lend credence
   To these final words of grievance.

2. If it should be my fate
   (And Heaven should enter in)   15
   That Love should close these eyes now welling,
   May some great act of grace
   Bring you this body full of sin,
   While soul runs naked to its place of dwelling.
   Death will seem less distorted   20
   If this hope is transported
   Into that pass that is ever full of doubt;
   A soul that's all worn out
   Can find no port with any greater comfort
   Or grave with greater quiet   25
   To flee the trouble of bones and flesh's riot.

3. The time may yet return
   When that lovely one who's wild
   Comes tamely back to the haunts of former days;
   There on a blessèd morn   30
   Where she first beguiled
   My eyes, let her turn with a fond, desirous gaze
   Searchingly; and, mercy!
   Seeing me stretched adversely
   Among the stones, may Love inspire   35
   Sighs of soft desire
   So that she will get a little pity for me,
   And against Heaven prevail
   As she dries her eyes with her beautiful veil.

4. From pretty branches tumbled   40
   (Sweet to memory)
   A rain that filled her lap with gentle flowers;
   She sat there humbly
   Yet radiant in glory,
   Wearing a coverlet of that loving shower.   45
   Some flowers hemmed her dress,
   Some lay on a golden tress
   Like polished gold with pearl,
   Not seeming the hair of a girl;
   Some fell on earth and some the pool caressed;   50
   One drifted in a twisting disarray,
   Turning, as if to say: here Lord Love holds sway.

5. How many times I heard
   My fearful tongue repeat:
   "This one was born in Paradise for certain!"   55
   Her face, her every word,
   The sound of her laughter sweet,
   Had weighted me with a very heavy burden
   Of forgetfulness that brings
   Division from tangible things.   60
   Hearing myself muttering again:
   "How did I get here? When?";
   Believing myself in Heaven, not at that spring.
   The grass gave such release
   That nowhere else can I find an equal peace.   65

6. Song, if you had the embellishments you want,
   You'd bolt with great fastness
   Out of these woods, and run and join the masses.

[127] *Di pensier in pensier, di monte in monte*

1. From thought to thought, from mountain unto mountain
   Love guides me; and every road with signs
   I find contrary to a tranquil life.
   On solitary slope, by brook or fountain
   Where shadowed vale between two hills reclines,   5
   There the soul quiets itself from strife,
   And as Love then invites,
   It laughs or cries or fears or feels assured,
   And face, which follows soul wherever it guides,
   Shows upset, which subsides   10
   And in one state of being seldom endures,
   So that one who to such living is inured
   Would say: "He burns. His life is all unsure."

2. Through highest mountains, thickets wild with thorns,
   I find repose; every inhabited place   15
   Remains a mortal enemy to my sight.
   With every step a novel thought is born
   About my lady; the torment is replaced,
   Which I forever carry, by delight;
   Scarcely have I the might   20
   To change this life alternately bitter and sweet
   When I say: Love's keeping you in wait
   For a time propitiate;
   You hate yourself, yet another you will please.
   And in this pass I sigh and on I go: 25
   "When? And how? And is this really so?"

3. Wherever a hillock or high pine casts its shade
   I sometimes stop, and on a rocky mass
   I shape her lovely face within my mind.
   When I come to myself, my breast is bathed   30
   From passion, and I cry out: "O! alas!
   What have you come to? What have you left behind?"
   But as I hold inclined
   My thoughts upon the image I first made,
   With steady gazing my own self disappears   35
   And then as Love comes near
   The soul in its own delusion is swept away.
   Everywhere the beautiful one I adore
   I see; if this is error, I want nothing more.

4. Many a time (although now who will trust me?)   40
   I have seen her image upon the water appear,
   In the trunk of a beech, or where the grasses sway,
   Or in a white cloud, so that Leda would agree
   Her daughter Helen's beauty could not come near,
   Like a star that Sun eclipses with a ray.   45

The wilder the place
Or the more deserted the strand where I chance to be,
The more beautiful I cast her forth enshrouded.
Then when the truth's unclouded
The sweet deception, I sit continually   50
As cold as stone, dead rock on living rock,
Shaped like a man who thinks and weeps and talks.

5. Where the shadows of other mountains never reach,
   Ever upward toward the greatest, highest peak
   A strong desire pulls which I can't resist;   55
   Then as my eyes begin to measure the breach
   Of losses, I cry, but even as I weep
   I lighten this heart beset with its heavy mist;
   My thoughts will not desist
   From dwelling on the space that separates me,   60
   For she is always far, yet ever near.
   Softly within I hear:
   "What are you up to now, wretch? It could be
   That somewhere too your absence she is grieving."
   And with this thought, my soul begins its breathing.   65

6. Song, go beyond that mount
   Where the sky lies in happy serenity;
   You'll see me by some flowing fount
   Where the air wafts fragrantly
   From the fresh-scented laurel tree.   70
   There is my heart, and she who stole it from me;
   Here you will see just a mere effigy.

[128] *S'amor non è, che dunque è quel ch'io sento*

If love is not, what is this then I feel?
But if love is, O God, what then is he?
If good, where come these mortal jabs of steel?
If bad, why then this wondrous misery?
If I burn freely, why all this lamenting?   5
If it's forced on me, what can cries avail?
O living death, delight that quickly pales,
How can you master me without consenting?

And if I do consent, I wrongly feel the pain.
On contrary winds I sense the frail bark's terror   10
Blown out on open seas without a rudder,
Light in my knowledge, heavy in my error,
Myself not knowing what it is I'd gain:
The winter warms me; in midst of summer I shudder.

[129*] Or che 'l ciel e la terra e 'l vento tace

The earth and wind are quiet now, the sky,
Sleep bridles beast and bird without a sound,
Night leads his starry chariot on its round
And Ocean waveless in his bedding lies:
I see, I think, I burn, I also cry   5
As sight of my upsetter brings sweet woe;
War is my steady state, with wrathful throe;
Only the thought of her will pacify.

Thus from a limpid, living fountain's poured
This fare of bittersweet on which I feed;   10
The same hand heals that causes laceration.
Still that this martyrdom move ever forward,
A thousand times a day I'm born, I bleed;
So far am I removed from my salvation.

[130] Rotta è l'alta colonna, e 'l verde lauro

The Column's broken, the Laurel laid to rest
That granted shade upon my weary mind;
I've lost the thing I never hope to find
From Boreas to Auster, East to West.
Death, you've taken away my double treasure   5
That made me walk happily, head ever higher;
No oriental gem, no land or empire
Can bring her back—no, nor golden measure.

But if great destiny has given consent,
What can I do except keep feeling low,   10
Eyes forever wet, head forever bent?
O life of ours, so beautiful in show,
How speedily in one morning lies expired
Gain for many a year with pain acquired!

[131] Quel rosignuol che sì soave piagne

The nightingale who now so soft complains
Perhaps the deaths of children or a mate
Makes sky and field with sweetness reverberate
With the sound of her poignant, pity-filled refrain.
All the night long it seems she's at my side   5
And my sad fate she utters with each breath;

---

*Original text appears in Section IX, taken from *Petrarca*, ed. F. Neri and others (Ricciardi,
1951), No. 164.
    130. Sonnet on the deaths of Laura (the Laurel), April 6, 1348, and of his patron, Cardinal
Giovanni Colonna (the Column), July 3, 1348.

To myself alone my sorrow I confide,
For I thought goddesses were exempt from Death.

How easy to fool oneself who feels secure!
Those two pretty lights, sunlike as they penetrated— 10
Who thought they'd ever lie like earth, obscure?
And now I realize my savage fate
Wills that I live and learn with bitter tears:
Nothing down here endures and still endears.

[132] *I' vo piangendo i miei passati tempi*

I go weeping my time that now is past
Which I squandered in the love of a mortal thing,
Without rising to flight, though I had the wings
Perhaps to cut some example that would last.
You who survey my vile, worthless evil, 5
King of the heavens, deathless, invisible,
Help this soul unsettled and too fragile,
And all its lacks with your great mercy fill,

So that if I suffer warfare or a tempest
I'll die in peace and port; and if my stance 10
Was vain, at least my ending will be blessed.
In my little life that's left, I pray: advance
Your hand to me, as even in death I grope.
You know full well in others I have no hope.

GIOVANNI BOCCACCIO

[133] *Or sei salito, caro signor mio*

My most dear lord, now you have arisen
Into the realm where every soul awaits
Selection to be one of God's consecrates,
After departing from this earthly prison.
You're in the place desire pulled you toward, 5
Where you can cast your eyes on your Lauretta,
Who's sitting with my beautiful Fiammetta
Basking in the company of the Lord.

133. Boccaccio (1313–1375). Author of the *Decameron*; the first real master of Italian prose. Lament on the Death of Petrarch, in sonnet form. Fiammetta was Boccaccio's lady. Line 9 refers to Cino da Pistoia (see No. 123), and Petrarch's good friend Sennuccio del Bene.

With Cino and Sennuccio and with Dante
You're living now, assured of eternal rest,   10
Studying things for us too far above.
If I was dear in this world where value's scanty,
O draw me after! let me too be blessed
With the sight of her who kindled my first love.

[V] NORTH·FRENCH LYRICS

In northern France, lyric poetry took a very different turn from that in Italy. From the start the North French had a vital tradition of songs of the people: anonymous Spinning Songs, Workers' Songs, Spring Dances, and Songs of the Ill-Married. This popular bent, with its emphasis upon things of this world, is an important element in North French literature from the early folk songs to the writings of François Villon.

When formal love poetry was written, as by the *trouvère* (troubadour) Gace Brulé, the imprint of Provence was strong upon it, for the South French tradition had already developed fully. The basic situation of a suffering lover, an almighty and often uncooperative lady (and sometimes, but not always, a jealous husband) is the same in both. Unlike the Provençal poems, however, the North French lyrics tend to be devoid of metaphysical overtones. If service is mentioned, it is the service for a lady-lord and not for a lady-goddess; if joy is mentioned, it is usually secular fun and not religious ecstasy. In No. 139, for example, the situation is clearly social. We can see the girl in stanza 3 aligned with great demeanor, good company, beauty, and good sense; she is opposed to villainy. The reference is clearly courtly. Furthermore, we can detect a movement toward secular abstraction. One could easily capitalize the qualities cited above and create a social war, a *psychomachia* of the court, exactly as Jean de Meun and Guillaume de Lorris did in their *Roman de la rose*. In France the court takes precedence over the cathedral; the Gothic spirit of organization overcomes Romanesque suggestibility; and the madame of high society is more evident than the Madonna of another world.

Unfortunately the worldliness of North French poetry tended to work against its development. Rutebeuf stands out for his vigorous, Marcabrun-like morality, but many of the poets around him, who are not represented here, are jaded and effete. In the 1300s a revival took place under the leadership of Guillaume de Machaut and Eustache Deschamps. Although both men are greater musicians than poets, they kept the lyric alive by casting it in the highly musical form of the *rondeau*, as well as in the ever-popular ballade or chanson. Deschamps' indictment of Bohemia or his lovely praise of the city of Paris are sudden intrusions of realism into a highly artificial poetic world. When compared to her male counterparts, for example, Christine de Pizan sounds vigorous.

The dissolution of the tradition can best be seen in Charles d'Orléans, whose poetry is both graceful and fragile. Although his melancholy is tempered by the elegant form in which it is cast, it nevertheless verges upon morbidness. The artificial is so apparent in his work that nature itself seems almost man-made: the scenes in No. 157 are tailored by a designer of high fashion; the landscape in 158 is laid out by interior decorators. In short, the

Plate 6. The annual celebration on May 7 and 8 at Orléans in honor of Joan of Arc's freeing the city from the English in 1429. The city is associated with the poet Charles d'Orléans (Nos. 155–163), and Joan is mentioned in François Villon's No. 165. Villon was imprisoned for a time here. (Courtesy of the French Government Tourist Office)

haut monde is omnipresent. Even religion is reduced to social terms in the graceful and brilliant 163. Yet at this point, despite the skill and mastery, one feels that the medieval sensibility is exhausted. We are ready for a change.

This shift occurred in the writings of François Villon. His *Last Will* presents the brawling, tumultuous world of Paris outside the elegant salon and the dining hall. When we put Charles and François side by side, we see the stirrings of future revolution: Charles's poetry, on the one hand, is aristocratic, far removed from the people and their needs; François', on the other, is a howl of the lower classes who are verging on degradation. For all that he may sound like a Renaissance humanist, Villon is as medieval as Duke William of Aquitaine. He writes prayers for his mother, as well as love songs to his whore-mistress; even in the face of death, he does not despair, but prays movingly to his God.

North French literature never produced a crowning achievement like Dante's *Divine Comedy*, but in its adherence to the human condition, it helped to prepare the way for the modern world.

FOUR ANONYMOUS SONGS

[134] *Voulez vous que je vous chant*

1. Would you like it if I sing
   A song of love enchanting?
       One never made by a churl,
   No, but by a knight off parade
   In the spangled olive tree's shade   5
       In the arms of a little girl.

2. She wore a little kirtle of linen
   And a tunic made of white ermine,
       And a silken gown.
   Shoes were shod out of mayflower,   10
   Stockings came from an iris bower
       Tumbling tightly down.

3. She wore a beltlet made of leaf
   That grew all green when the rain was brief,
       With golden buttons riven;   15

134–137. From the 1100s and 1200s. The first, a Reverdie, song with fantastic imagery probably related to May Day or spring rites. Texts: Albert Pauphilet, *Poètes et romanciers du moyen âge* (Pléiade, 1958), pp. 863–864, 828–829, 825–826, 864.

Her little purse was made of love,
Flowers dangled down from above—
   For love it had been given.

4. She went on a mule that slowly trod,
Whose feet were all with silver shod,   20
   His seat with gold inlaid.
On his crupper in the flanks
Were three rose trees arranged in ranks
   To bring her shade.

5. Thus she travels throughout the land;   25
Chevaliers wait everywhere on her hand,
   Saluting with gentility!
"Pretty girl, where were you born?"
"I am from France, whom no man scorns,
   And from nobility.   30

6. "The nightingale gave me siring,
Who on the branch is always choiring
   In the dells deep.
A siren-mother gave birth to me
Whose cry rings over the salty sea   35
   On a cliff steep."

7. "Beautiful, you have a very great line!
Your parentage is truly fine,
   Your pedigree.
To God our Father above, I pray   40
That you may be given some day
   To marry me."

[135] *Trois sereurs seur rive mer*

1. Three sisters down by the side of the sea
   Are singing clearly;
The youngest one has brownish hair and
Cares for a brownish man:
"I am dark, so naturally   5
A darkish man should go with me."

2. Three sisters down by the side of the sea
   Are singing clearly:
The smallest one is sobbing
For her boyfriend Robin   10
   In despair:

135. Spinning Song (*Chanson de toile*).

"O in the woods
You got my goods—
O take me there,
    Take me there." 15

3. Three sisters down by the side of the sea
    Are singing clearly;
The eldest one declares:
"A man should always put
His tender maiden up above, 20
And always take good care
To guard her love."

[136] *Quant vient en mai, que l'on dit as lons jors*

1. When the time is May, and the days are lengthening,
The Franks of France ride from the court of the King;
Raynaud rides in the front ranks, up in the fore,
And passes beneath the mansion of Erembor;
He doesn't deign to glance to the rail above— 5
    Ah, Raynaud, my love!

2. Fair Erembor in the sunny window glowing
Holds on her knees her colored bits of sewing;
She sees coming from the court of the King the Franks
With Raynaud astride in the foremost of the ranks. 10
She breaks into speech, cannot restrain the mind:
    "Ah, Raynaud of mine!

3. "Raynaud my love, I've already seen the day
When if you passed our tower on your way
Without some word from me, you'd have been all sad." 15
"Yes, emperor's daughter, but you've been bad.
You took another man; you gave me the shove."
    Ah, Raynaud my love!

4. "Raynaud, good sir, now listen to my complaint:
I swear on a hundred virgins, by all the saints, 20
With thirty women who with me will take their stand—
Never, except for you, have I loved a man.
Here, take this oath-pledge; then a kiss from me.
    Ah, Raynaud ami!"

5. The Count Raynaud now mounts upon the stair. 25
Blond and tightly curling was his hair;

136. Spinning Song, called "Belle Erembourc."

His shoulders were broad, and yet his waist was slim;
No land had ever seen a lusty man like him.
When he sees Erembor, he sheds a tear—
    Ah, Raynaud my dear!   30

6. The Count Raynaud has mounted to the tower.
  He sits upon a couch with colored flowers.
  Beside him sits the beautiful Erembor.
  Their love goes on again as it had before:
    Ah, Raynaud amor!   35

[137] *Por quoi me bat mes maris*

1. Why is my husband always whacking
    Poor little me?
  I never give him lying quacking,
  Don't go around always squalling
  Except when my gentleman friend comes calling   5
    On the QT.
  Why is my husband always whacking
    Poor little me?

2. Why is my husband always whacking
    Poor little me?   10
  If he won't let me lead the life
  Of a good and trusted happy wife,
  Then I'll arrange for him the strife
    Of cuckoldry!
  Why is my husband always whacking   15
    Poor little me?

3. Ah yes, now the course is laid:
  With a vengeance I'll be paid:
  With my lover I'll parade
    Stark nakedly.   20
  Why is my husband always whacking
    Poor little me?

---

137. Song of the Ill-Married (*Chanson de mal-mariée*), which celebrates cuckoldry.

RICHARD THE LION-HEARTED

[138] *Ja nuls homs pris ne dira sa raison*

1. A man imprisoned can never speak his mind
   As cleverly as those who do not suffer,
   But through his song he can some comfort find.
   I have a host of friends, poor the gifts they offer.
   Shame on them if this ransoming should trail   5
      Into a second year in jail!

2. This they know well, my barons and my men,
   English, Norman, Gascon, and Poitevin,
   What I'd leave of my property in prison!
   O I'm not saying this to cast derision,   10
      But still I'm here in jail!

3. Here is a truth I know that can be told:
   Dead men and prisoners have neither parents nor friends,
   No one to offer up their silver and gold.
   It matters to me, but much more to my men.   15
   For after my death, they'll be bitterly assailed
      Because I'm so long in jail!

4. No wonder if I have a grieving heart
   When I see my land torn by its lord asunder:
   If he'll recall the pact in which we took part   20
   And remember the pledges we vowed we'd both live under,
   Truly within the year, without a fail,
      I'd be out of jail!

5. This they know, the Angevins and Tourains,
   Those bachelors there who are strong and own a lot,   25
   While I'm encumbered here in another's hands;
   They loved me lots, but now they don't love a jot;
   Over the plains I don't see a piece of mail
      Although I'm still in jail!

138. Richard Coeur-de-Lion (1157–1199). King of England from 1189 to 1199. Son of Henry II and Eleanor of Aquitaine. Played a dramatic but disastrous role in the crusades; imprisoned in Austria at Dürnstein (Plate 7), causing the payment of an enormous ransom. Composed his Complaint from Prison in North French. Swashbuckling and romantic, but ineffectual as a ruler. Killed in a meaningless raid on a second-rate castle in France. Envoi omitted from poem. Text in Pauphilet, pp. 841 f. Recordings: CEPEDIC CEP 104; Harmonia Mundi HM 441.

6. I've loved and I love still my companions true,   30
   The men of Cahiu and the men of Porcherain,
   But tell me, song, if they still love me too,
   For never to them was I double-faced or vain:
   They're villains if my lands they now assail—
       Since I am here in jail!   35

GACE BRULÉ

[139] *De bien amer grant joie atent*

1. Great joy from loving well I am awaiting,
   For this desire is very strong in me;
   And here's a truth that I find sure of stating:
   Love rules with such great majesty
   Double rewards it is always compensating   5
   To those who will treat it loyally,
   But a man who won't consent to serve
   Will find himself for nothing quite unnerved.

2. Never did I commit a sin
   Against Love voluntarily.   10
   At its command, I have always been
   And will be until life ends for me.
   He is one of the most desolate men,
   The one whom Love deserts completely.
   My lady has taught this lesson to me: 15
   Honor comes from loving loyally.

3. She is a person of great demeanor
   And she lends good company;
   She's wise among men who are meaner,
   The girl who seized control of me.   20
   Good sense and beauty in her are keener
   And she despises all villainy.
   The only thing that upsets my weal
   Is that she doesn't know how I feel.

139. Gace Brulé (*ca.* 1170–1212). Nobleman from Champagne, associated with Eleanor's daughter by Louis VII, Marie of Champagne. About 82 poems survive, edited by Samuel N. Rosenberg and Samuel Danon, with music edited by Hendrik van der Werf: *Lyrics and Melodies of Gace Brulé* (Garland, 1985), No. 12. The Count is probably Louis, who died in 1205.

4. Great Love will never mortify;   25
   The more it kills, the better you get;
   I would much prefer to live and die
   Than one day simply to forget.
   Lady, you could grant easily
   The great joy for which I fret;   30
   The thing that often makes me sigh
   Is that desire from pain will not die.

5. Lady, none of the others is your peer.
   Pretty and blonde, rightful receiver of lauds,
   You should never bend your ear   35
   To those false and depraved bawds
   Who with lies and guesses engineer
   To make lovers all distraught.
   And afterward they don't even know
   Exactly where they ought to go.   40

6. Lady, from you I've never concealed
   Any desire or any thought.
   My love for you is pure and real,
   More than for any other creature wrought.
   I want to be your servant leal,   45
   And for this end I feel so fraught
   That, without some mercy, I'm undone;
   Far away or near, I can't go on.

7. Count de Blois, unless like this you love,
   You can never soar in value above.   50

LE CHÂTELAIN DE COUCY

[140] *La douce vois du rossignol sauvage*

1. The sweet voice of the nightingale in dells
   That I hear night and day in trilling call
   Softens my heart again and sends me calm;
   Then I've desire in singing to outswell.
   Truly I should sing, since it makes fervent   5
   Her to whom my heart stands ever feal;

140. Le Châtelain de Coucy (d. 1203?). Probably Guy de Thurotte, who is said to have died in 1203 en route to the Fourth Crusade. Ed. Pauphilet, pp. 875–876.

I should have great joy, indeed great weal
If she would let me join her as her servant.

2. Never to her have I proved fickle, untrue
   (A thing that should put me in good standing);   10
   I love and serve and worship without bending,
   And yet my thoughts are things I must eschew,
   For her beauty puts me in such disarray
   That before her language always ceases;
   And I dare not regard her gentle features,   15
   So much I hate to tear my eyes away.

3. Firmly I've set my heart upon her serving;
   I think of no one else—God grant me joy!
   For never did Tristan, that potion-drinking boy,
   Love as loyally without a swerving.   20
   I put all there: body, heart, desire,
   Feeling and knowing—maybe like one who's crazed,
   And still I fear that as I course my days
   My service to her and loving might expire.

4. I will not admit I acted foolishly,   25
   Not even if for her I had to die;
   For the world finds none like her, pretty or wise,
   No one else who can equally pleasure me.
   I love my eyes: they made me see her;
   After I saw her, heart as hostage lay   30
   In her keeping for a very long stay,
   And even today, it refuses to leave her.

5. Song, go with this message over there
   Where I dare not go or bend my steps,
   For I fear the wicked people's depths   35
   Who guess before things even appear
   The goods of love. God give them ill,
   For to many they show ire and spite,
   And day by day I suffer this plight,
   For I'm forced to obey them against my will.   40

THIBAUT IV, COUNT OF CHAMPAGNE, KING OF NAVARRE

[141] *Por mau tens ne por gelee*

1. Not for icy wind or storm
   Neither for the morning chill,
   Nor for anything yet born
   Will I ever abandon my will
       To love the thing that's mine   5
       For I love her much indeed
       With a love that's very fine,
           Valara!

2. She's pretty, blonde, and nicely hued;
   I like the way that she attracts.   10
   O God! the thing that I pursued
   You granted exactly as I asked!
       If she is ever denied
       To me, I'll beg and pray
       Until the day I die—   15
           Valara!

3. Lady, in your bailey
   My body and life I've placed.
   By God, please don't assail me!
   Where fine hearts stand with pride effaced,   20
       Mercy and grace
       A man should find
       To bring him solace.
           Valara!

4. Lady, do me a courtesy!   25
   May it please you to impart
   These words for the sake of me:
   My pretty, gentle sweetheart,
       I dare to name you,
       For the love of another   30
       Will never defame you.
           Valara!

141. Thibaut (1201–1253). Acceded to the kingship of Navarre through his uncle in 1234. Led an unsuccessful crusade. Many of his poems believed written for Blanche of Castile. About 60 works survive. The fifth stanza is omitted here. Edited by Kathleen J. Brahney, *Lyrics of Thibaut de Champagne* (Garland, 1989), No. 17.

RUTEBEUF

[142] Empereeur et roi et conte

Emperors and kings and counts
And dukes and princes, who hear recounts
Of diverse tales for your delight
Of men who always seemed to fight
Way back then for the Holy Church,   5
Tell me now the way you'd work
Your way into Paradise.
Those men before paid the price
Through martyrdom and through great pain,
If you listen to the epic strain,   10
That they suffered here as earthly men.
See now the time! God comes again
With outstretched arms, bloodily drenched,
God who for your very sake quenched
The fires of Hell and Purgatory.   15
Well, let's begin a brand-new story!
Serve your God with well-pleased wrath,
For he is now showing you the path
Unto his kingdom and his realm,
Which are now being overwhelmed.   20
Therefore dispose all your affection
On avenging him and on protection
Of the Holy Blessèd Promised Land
Which in great tribulation stands
Almost lost (O God take heed!)   25
Unless to assist it, at once you speed. . . .

142. Rutebeuf (ca. 1230–ca. 1285). North France's moral poet. Left more than fifty pieces, including a play, *The Miracle of Theophilus*, with a Faustian theme. Rather prolix when compared to Marcabrun, whom he resembles. From Champagne, but lived in Paris and elsewhere. This selection from his Complaint for the Crusade omits several lines.

ADAM DE LA HALLE

---

[143] *Amours m'ont si doucement*

1. Love has so gently wounded me
   That I do not feel the pang,
   And so I'll serve in a royal way
   Amours and my sweet *amie*,
   To whom I surrender my person   5
   And make a present of myself;
   Never, despite any torment,
   Will I have it any other way;
   Instead, I want to spend my youth
   In loving her very loyally.   10

2. And so I don't care one bit
   When someone paints me badly,
   Since I pursue my desires
   That lead me often to lie
   Next to her lovely body.   15
   I'm not afraid of gusts or winds
   But it's good to enjoy yourself
   Very quietly and discreetly,
   So that no one can denigrate you
   In front of other people.   20

3. You have wasted too much time
   In begging me for things, my friend (*amis*);
   If you loved me with loyalty,
   I have loved you the very same way
   And even more strongly,   25
   Although at the start a lady
   Should act with reservation;
   For that reason, if she seems aloof,
   Her lover should never falter
   From pursuing her with passion.   30

143. Or Adam le Bossu, "The Cripple, Awkward" (*fl.* 1270–1288). Flourished in Arras, a poetic center north of Paris, although he went to Italy with Charles of Anjou and perhaps died there. Wrote plays such as *Le Jeu de Robin et Marion* and 36 songs with music: *Lyrics and Melodies*, Poem 31 ed. and trans. Deborah H. Nelson; Song 31, ed. Hendrik van der Werf (Garland, 1985); a woman is addressed in line 4 and a man in line 22.

GUILLAUME DE MACHAUT

[144] *De toutes fleurs n'avoit, et de tous fruis*

1. There is no fruit within my bower,
   No flower except for a single rose;
   All the rest have been devoured
   By Fortune, who now fierce opposes
       This sweet flower,   5
   Its scent and color to overpower;
   But if I see it picked or pressed,
   Another one I'll never possess.

2. Ah, Fortune, you're a gulf, a pit,
   Which tries to swallow any man who thinks   10
   He can follow your false law, for it
   Is an ever unsure, deceptive thing.
       Your honor, laugh, and gladness
   Are really nothing but tears and sadness.
   If your deceits wither her rosiness,   15
   Another one I'll never possess.

3. The virtue that my flower encloses
   Does not stem from your fickle ways,
   For Nature it is who makes the roses
   And then donates them straightaway: 20
       I doubt your power
   To kill the worth and value of my flower.
   Let her be mine. But nonetheless—
   Another one I'll never possess.

[145] *Blanche com lys, plus que rose vermeille*

White as a lily, redder than a rose,
More splendid than a ruby oriental,
Your beauty I regard; no equal shows
White as a lily, redder than a rose.

I am so ravished, my heart knows no repose   5
Until I serve you, a lover fine and gentle,
White as a lily, redder than a rose
More splendid than a ruby oriental.

144. Guillaume de Machaut (*ca.* 1295–1377). Master musician. Author of long *dits* or narrative poems that influenced Chaucer. Worked for John of Luxemburg, who was King of Bohemia, as secretary. Buried in the cathedral of Reims, where he served as canon. This poem is a ballade; the other two rondeaux.

[146] *Se par amours n'amiez autrui ne moy*

If for your love you took no one, not me,
My grief that's great would be a lesser thing.
For love creates a sure expectancy
Unless for your love you took no one, not me.

But when I see you love and you desert me,   5
It's worse than death. And so this word I bring:
If for your love you took no one, not me,
My grief that's great would be a lesser thing.

EUSTACHE DESCHAMPS

[147] *O Socrates plains de philosophie*

To Geoffrey Chaucer

O Socrates, full of philosophy,
Anglus in practice, Seneca ethical,
Great Ovid in your poetry,
Lively in speech, wisely rhetorical,
Most high eagle who by your theory   5
Illuminate Aeneas' domain,
The Isle of Giants, Brutus' plain
Sòwn with your flowers and your rosy plants;
You taught those ignorant of romance,
Noble Geoffrey Chaucer, translator grand! . . .   10

[148] *Poux, puces, puor et pourceaux*

Lice and fleas and swine and reeks—
These are Bohemia's native stuff;
Bread and salt-fish, weather gruff,
Pepper, aging cabbage, and leeks,
Meat that's smoked till it's black and tough;   5
Lice and fleas and swine and reeks.

147. Eustache Deschamps (1346–*ca.* 1407). Follower of Machaut, who may have been his uncle. Served Charles VI during the Hundred Years War. Wrote more than 1000 ballades like this Ballade to Chaucer, of which only one of three strophes is presented. Anglus in line 2 is an eponymous hero based on the French word for England, "*Angleterre.*" The sense in line 9 is difficult.
148. Rondeau on Bohemia.

Twenty mouths from two bowls stuffed,
Drinking beer of a bitter brew,
Bedrooms with straw and dung astrew,
Lice and fleas and swine and reeks;   10
These are Bohemia's native stuff,
Bread and salt-fish, weather gruff.

[149] *Quant j'ai la terre et mer avironnee*

To Paris

1. When you've circled earth and sea,
   And been wherever man can be,
   Jerusalem, Egypt, Alexandria,
   Galilee, Damascus, Syria,
   Cairo, Babylonia, Tartary,   5
       And all the ports they have there
   Where sugars and all spices are sold,
   Cloth of silk and drapes of gold,
   Something better the Frenchmen hold—
       For Paris is beyond compare.   10

2. Crowned over other cities she reigns,
   Fountain of sense, center for brains,
   Nicely placed on the River Seine,
   With orchards, woods, and open plains,
   With every good that mankind claims   15
       And more than you can find elsewhere.
   Strangers love her the very first day
   Because she's always lighthearted and gay;
   They'll find no equal when they go away,
       For Paris is beyond compare.   20

149. Ballade to Paris. Third stanza omitted.

CHRISTINE DE PIZAN

[150] *Se souvent vais au moustier*

If I often go to chapel,
It's to see the Maiden who
Is as fresh as the rose that's new.

Why should those others babble?
Is it really some great news   5
If I often go to chapel?

There's no road that I will travel
Unless she will advise me;
They are fools to criticize me
If I often go to chapel.   10

[151] *Ce moys de may tout se resjoye*

1. This month of May all is joy,
   Except for me, who am full of woe;
   For I don't have my long-held boy
   And I weep with a voice that's low.
   I had a love that made me glow,   5
   But now he's staying far from me.
   Alas! come back, come soon, *ami!*

2. In this month when all turns green,
   Let us go sporting in the park
   Or hear the nightingale who preens   10
   Or listen to the warbling lark.
   You know where. If you'll just hark
   To a voice that whispers lovingly,
   "Alas! come back, come soon, *ami!*"

3. For in this month Love's little boy   15
   Gathers in prey and he commands
   Every lover to find some joy,
   Every lady with her man;

150. Christine de Pizan, Pisan (1364–1431?). Native of Venice whose father was chief physician to Charles V of France; he hailed from Pizzano, a little town near Bologna, where he studied and taught medicine. Grew up at the French court. Widowed at age 25 in 1389 she supported herself by writing. Fond of feminist causes; idolized Joan of Arc. Died in a convent. Ed. Kenneth Varty, *Ballades, Rondeaux, and Virelais* (Leicester U., 1965), Nos. 81, 94, 3, 6, 115. No. 151 is a ballade; the rest, rondeaux. For biography, see Charity Willard, *Christine de Pizan* (Persea, 1984).

None should be left to go single-hand,
Night or day, it seems to me.   20
Alas! come back, come soon, *ami!*

4. This heart of mine for your love grieves,
   Alas! come back, come soon, *ami!*

[152] *Je suis vesve, seulete, et noir vestue*

I am a widow, lonely, clad in black,
With a mournful face, dressed with simplicity,
With a manner that's distressed and grieving;
Inside I carry a bitter grief that kills me.

And it's right that I should be downcast,   5
Abounding with tears and short of speech,
For I'm a widow, lonely, clad in black.

Since I've lost that man whose memory
Brings me a grief that always maddens me,
All my bright days and joys have gone away;   10
My destiny has fallen to a lowly state,
For I'm a widow, lonely, clad in black.

[153] *Com turtre suis, sans per, toute seulete*

I'm like a lonely dove without a mate;
Or like a sheep who's left without a shepherd
Because I've been cut off some time by death
From my beloved—which I constantly regret.

It's seven years now since I lost him—woeful me!   5
It would have been better to have been buried then!
I'm like a lonely dove without a mate;

Ever since that time I've languished in grief
And in suffering and in bitter sorrow,
And as long as I live, I have no shred of hope   10
For any comfort that will bring me any joy:
I'm like a lonely dove without a mate.

[154] *Mon chier Seigneur, soyez de ma partie*

My dear lord, please come and take my side!
For they've involved me now in a great war—
Those allies of that *Roman de la Rose*
Because I'm not a convert to their party.

154. Probably addressed to an unknown noble in 1401 or 1402, when she attacked the last
part of the *Romance of the Rose* by Jean de Meun for being antifeminist and immoral.

They've waged such a bitter battle against me   5
That they think they have me surrounded;
My dear lord, please come and take my side!

But I shall never be hampered by their assaults
To abandon my purpose because it's commonly known
That all who dare defend the right are attacked;   10
But if I'm poorly equipped with proper sense,
My dear lord, please come and take my side!

CHARLES D'ORLÉANS

[155] *Dedens mon Livre de Pensee*

Within the Book of My Meditation
I found my heart very busily
Writing Grief's True History
Complete with tearful illuminations,

Blotting out the once pleasant sketch   5
Of much beloved happiness,
Within the Book of My Meditation.

Ah, where did he find this theme?
Heavy drops of sweat now stream
Down from him as he keeps expending   10
Pain on this task that's never ending
Within the Book of My Meditation.

[156] *Alez vous ant, alez, alés*

O go away, away, away!
Melancholy, Grief, and Strife.
Think that you'll rule me all my life
The way you've done in other days?

155. Charles d'Orléans (1394–1465). Son of Louis d'Orléans, the brother of King Charles VI. Captured by the British at Agincourt in 1415 and imprisoned in England for twenty-five years, where most of his poems were written. Married Marie of Clèves and spent his final years at Blois, where he entertained many poets, including Villon. Texts: *Poésies*, ed. Pierre Champion, 2 vols. (Champion, 1924); this rondeau, II, 308–309. See also Nos. 286, 287 here.

156. Rondeau; ed. Champion, II, 320–321.

I promise you: this will not be.   5
Reason will gain the mastery.
Away, away! O go away,
Melancholy, Grief, and Strife!

And if you ever do come back,
I pray that God may send a pox   10
On all your wretched, cursed pack,
And stifle all that gives you life.
O go away, away, away!
Melancholy, Grief, and Strife!

[157*] Le temps a laissié son manteau

Time has laid aside his cape
Of wind and cold and rain,
And puts on vestments once again
All in brilliant sunshine draped.

There is no beast, there is no bird   5
Who does not sing or cry these words:
"Time has laid aside his cape."

Rivers, brooks, and all the springs
Carry in lovely livery
Cuts of silvery jewelry,   10
Each dressed in his brand-new things—
Time has laid aside his cape.

[158] Les fourriers d'Esté sont venus

The furnishing men of Summer have come
To ready up his dwelling place.
They've fastened all his carpets down
With flowers and grass interlaced.

His velvet rugs extended stand   5
In grassy green throughout the land,
The furnishing men of Summer have come.

A heart with sorrow wearisome—
Thank God!—will soon be hale and gay.
Take to the road, O go away,   10
Winter! you can no longer stay,
The furnishing men of Summer have come.

157. Rondeau; ed. Champion, II, 307–308.
*Original text appears in Section IX.
158. Rondeau; ed. Champion, II, 307.

[159] *Les en voulez vous garder*

Would you truly try to prevent
Running rivers from rushing by,
Cranes that circle in the sky
Would you gather into nets?

Just to dream of such a try   5
Causes me astonishment;
Would you truly try to prevent
Running rivers from rushing by?

Let the time go brushing by
At Lady Fortune's commandment;   10
And all those other steady events
You never really can turn awry
Would you truly try to prevent?

[160] *En la forest d'Ennuyeuse Tristesse*

1. In the Forest of Troubled Sadness
   One day as I happened to pass alone,
   I met the Goddess of Loving Gladness,
   Who called to me, saying, "Where are you going?"
   I said that because of Fortune's throws   5
   I'd been exiled long among these trees,
   So that my name now could only be
   The Man Deranged Who Knows Not Where He Goes.

2. She laughed, and with great humbleness
   Replied: "My friend, if I just knew   10
   Why you've fallen into this distress,
   I'd gladly do everything I could for you,
   For I put you on the road a while ago
   Toward Every-Pleasure. Who sent you astray?
   It makes me unhappy now to survey   15
   The Man Deranged Who Knows Not Where He Goes."

3. "Alas!" said I, "my sovereign Princess,
   You know my story; what more can I tell?
   It's Death who did it, making crude redress;
   He took away that thing I loved too well   20
   Who was the source of all my many hopes,
   Leading me ever onward as my guide;
   Nobody called me, with her at my side,
   The Man Deranged Who Knows Not Where He Goes.

159. Rondeau; ed. Champion, II, 372–373.
160. Ballade; ed. Champion, I, 88–89.

4. "I'm blind. The road, the road is—where?   25
   I've wandered tipping, tapping here and there,
   With just a stick, the pathway to disclose;
   What a great pity this is the fate I bear:
   The Man Deranged Who Knows Not Where He Goes."

[161] Quant j'ay ouy le tabourin

Whenever I hear the tambour's cry
That tells me to run after May,
Back in my bed, without dismay,
My head deep in the pillow lies.

I say to myself: "It's early yet.   5
I'll get up later—by and by . . .
Whenever I hear the tambour's cry.

"The young ones can split up the cuts;
I'll be Nonchalance's friend.
He and I can share an end.   10
He's the partner I find most nigh
Whenever I hear the tambour's cry."

[162] Esse tout ce que m'apportez

Tell me, is this all you bring
On this your day, Saint Valentine,
Only the butt of hope, the thing
For which all unconsoled men pine?

Briefly you bring encouraging   5
To be happy on this morning fine.
Tell me, is this all you bring
On this your day, Saint Valentine?

Nothing else except a greeting,
"Happy day" inscribed in Latin,   10
An ancient relic on ancient satin.
Such presents set you chuckling.
Tell me, is this all you bring?

[163] On parle de religion

1. They talk about religion,
   With its strict governing;

161. Rondeau; ed. Champion, II, 311.
162. Rondeau for Valentine Day; ed. Champion, II, 449.
163. Ballade; ed. Champion, I, 158–159.

They talk of great devotion
That causes suffering;
But as far as I can discover,   5
My intentions I will fashion
Where I feel the most compassion:
In the observances of lovers.

2. Always in contemplation
   They hold their hearts ravished in trance,   10
   So that they may pass by gradations
   To the high Paradise of Romance.
   Between hot-cold, thirst-hunger they hover
   Suffering with hope in many a nation;
   Such, you will find, are the observations   15
   In the observances of lovers.

3. Barefooted, they beg dispensations
   From Consolation; from Carefreeness,
   They do not ask for any rations,
   Except for Pity—a small redress   20
   In the sacks where Sustenance lies covered
   For their very simple provisions.
   Are these not holy conditions
   In the observances of lovers?

4. With bigots I want no dealings;   25
   I've no respect for their feelings.
   My affection rests, all else above,
   In the observances of love.

FRANÇOIS VILLON

[164–170] The Last Will (Le Testament)
En l'an de mon trentiesme aage

1. In the thirtieth year of my age
   I have now drunk deeply of shame,
   Not all a fool, not all a sage,
   And not without a little pain,
   Most of which I was forced to meet
   At the hands of Thibault d'Aussigny—
   If he's a bishop blessing the streets,
   Blessings he'll never bestow on me! . . .   8

22. I mourn the slipping days of youth   169
    That more than other men I supped
    For Age kept mum his awful truth,
    Not saying time would soon be up.
    On foot he did not take his fling
    Or horseback. No. How did he go?
    Suddenly—in a burst of wings.
    Not one souvenir did he throw.   176

23. He's gone. And here I sit
    In learning weak, poor in sense,
    Berry-black, sad, out of it,
    Without an income, cash, or rents.
    My lowest relative, I'm sure,
    Steps up to utter he will quit me,
    Forgetting even though I'm poor
    Nature decrees that he admit me. . . .   184

25. It's true that I have loved enough   193
    And willingly I'd love again.
    But a belly that is seldom stuffed
    One-third full and a heart with pain
    Keep me away from those much-trod ways.

164. François Villon (1431–*ca.* 1463). North France's greatest medieval poet. Scholar and thief, imprisoned and condemned for thievery and murder; disappears after banishment in 1463. Wrote *The Last Will* in 1461 when despairing about his health. Reared by Guillaume de Villon, whom he mentions in lines 849 ff. The Pretty Helmress (*Belle Heaulmière* or Seller of Weaponry) was the mistress of Nicholas d'Orgemont, canon of Notre Dame (lines 453 ff). See editions of Barbara N. Sargent-Baur (Appleton-Century-Crofts, 1967) and Jean Rychner-Albert Henry (Droz, 1974). *Le Testament* ends with No. 170. Ballades within the work have separate stanza numbers in parentheses.

Ah well, somebody with bloated pants
Will profit from my absent place.
Out of the belly springs the dance!   200

26. Eh God! if only I'd hit the books
    In the time when my youth ran riot
    And tried to ape a gentleman's looks,
    I'd have a home, soft bed inside it.
    But no! School was a thing I abhorred,
    Running away like a naughty kid;
    Even now as I write these words,
    Heart aches for the dumb things I did. . . .   208

29. Where are the gentlemen debonair   225
    I followed in the days now fled,
    Who sang so sweet, talked so fair,
    Charming in all they did and said?
    Some are stiff, and some are dead,
    And some are almost completely bereft;
    In Paradise may they find a bed,
    And God save all of us who are left!   232

30. Yet some of them have well pursued
    (Mercy God!) lives as lords and profs;
    While others go begging totally nude,
    Eying the butts of bread in shops;
    Still others have entered into cloisters
    To be Celestines or Carthusians,
    Booted and gartered like fishers of oysters.
    Ah, what is man's lot?—diffusion! . . .   240

35. From youth I've known just poverty   273
    Stemming from humble generation;
    My father never lived elegantly;
    Horace was his dad's appellation.
    Poverty follows us, tracks us down.
    On all the tombs of all my tribe
    (May God in Heaven gather them round)
    You'll find no crown or scepter inscribed. . . .   280

38. I'm well aware that I am shoddy: 297
    No angel's son with a diadem,
    Crowned with a star or heavenly body.
    My dad is dead. God quiet him!
    As for his corpse, it's under the stone.
    I've heard that Mother an end will find
    And she's heard it too; the poor thing moans.
    And Sonny—he won't lag far behind.   304

39. I'm positive that the poor and the rich,
    Wise man and fool, the priest and lay,
    Noble, churl, kindheart and bitch,
    Big and little, grisly and gay,
    Women with collars turned up high
    From every heard-of social caste,
    Strikingly hatted as they swirl by—
    Death will snatch to the very last.   312

40. If Paris or Helen faces death
    Or anyone else, he faces pain,
    For that's what makes him lose his breath;
    Poisons pour through every vein;
    And then he sweats; O God, he shudders!
    No doctor can the grief erase;
    And there's no child, sister, or brother
    Who'd volunteer to take his place.   320

41. Death has made him shivery pale.
    His nose is curved; his veins gain height;
    The neck swells out as limp flesh fails;
    Joints and sinews puff out tight.
    Body of woman, now so tender,
    Polished, soft, and nicely leavened,
    Must you to this woe surrender?
    Yes! Or mount up straight to Heaven.   328

[165] Dictes moy ou, n'en quel pays

(1.) Tell me where, in what domain
     Is Archipiades fair of Greece,
     Flora the Roman or that Thaïs
     Who in her looks was their cousin germane,
     Echo who always answered again
     By riverbank or by poolside clear,
     Whose beauty exceeded what was humane—
     But—where are the snows of yesteryear?   336

(2.) Tell me, where is wise Heloise
     For whom Pierre underwent castration?
     Love dealt him this great deprivation;
     He became a monk at St. Denis.
     And where is that queen, O tell me please,
     Who told them to bear old Buridan near
     The Seine in a sack, and then to release—
     But—where are the snows of yesteryear?   344

165. Ballade of the Women of Time Gone By. Pierre in line 338 is Peter Abelard (No. 12).

(3.) Where is Queen Blanche, the lily-white
      Whose siren voice echoed through the palace,
      Big-Footed Bertha, Beatrice, Alice,
      Harembourg, who held the Maine tight,
      Sweet Joan in whom Lorraine took pride;
      In the English fires she disappeared.
      Where, Virgin, where do they all abide?
      But—where are the snows of yesteryear?   352

(4.) Prince, do not ask within this week
      Or in this year when they'll appear;
      The answer this one verse will speak:
      "Where are the snows of yesteryear?"   356

* * * * * * * * * *

46. And so for these poor little tricks   445
      Who now are old without a cent;
      When they see all the young slender chicks
      Taking their places, how they lament
      Inwardly as to God they demand
      Why their time was not to their choosing.
      The Lord is silent. As the matter stands,
      He won't risk answering—and losing.   452

47. It seems to me that I can hear
      The Pretty Helmress, who issued arms,
      Wishing she had those girlish charms
      And speaking like this loud and clear:
      "Ach! Old Age—felon and fierce,
      Why is it me you've so soon pierced?
      What is it—what?—that turns aside
      These blows that would bring me suicide?   460

48. "You've taken away that great franchise
      That Beauty to me one day decreed
      Over merchants, churchmen, and laity,
      For never was man with a pair of eyes
      Who wouldn't have given me his all,
      Though repenting it later in a stall,
      If only I'd give him for a fee
      What beggars now scorn and won't take free.   468

49. "O many a man have I refused—
      And for me it wasn't always smart.
      Instead, I'd expend my finest arts
      On the love of a tender kid with ruses.
      Okay—to others I put on the screws,
      But, on my soul, I loved that one true!
      Yet later he made his crudeness felt
      When I learned he loved me just for my geld.   476

50. "It's true he only knew how to sock
    And kick me around. I loved him more.
    He'd drag my carcass over the floor,
    But I'd forgive all those cruel knocks
    If he'd just ask me for a kiss.
    That glutton, rotten down to his pith,
    Would take me and—O! the devil's name!
    What have I got now? Sin and shame.   484

51. "Now he's dead. Thirty years have gone,
    And here I stand, ancient and gray.
    Christ, when I think of yesterday,
    The thing I was; what I've become!
    When mirrors show my form paraded
    And I see everything desiccated,
    Sick and thin and withered and dry—
    Into a sudden rage I fly!   492

52. "Where is that glance once so merry,
    Those arched eyebrows, that long blonde hair,
    Eyes that sparkled wide-set and fair,
    With which I'd catch even the wary;
    That splendid nose so perfectly shaped,
    Those pretty ears that downward draped,
    The flushed ripe cheeks, the dimpled chin,
    Those beautiful lips of bright vermilion?   500

53. "Cute little shoulders jutting out,
    Those long white arms, lithe fingertips,
    Delicate breasts, high, rounded hips
    Ready for any sudden bout
    Handed down in the lists of love;
    Good wide loins that flared above
    The yoke where thighs sprout muscle-hardened,
    Where pussy lay in her little garden?   508

54. "The brow has linings; the hair is gray;
    Eyebrows have fallen, eyes grown blunt,
    That used to laugh as they made the hunt
    To snatch those devils and make them pay.
    Hooking nose makes me look bossy;
    Ears are drooping—yes, and mossy;
    Complexion's pallid, dull as paste;
    Chin is wrinkled, lips a waste.   516

55. "This is the end to which all beauty slumps.
    Arms get short, and hands get gnarled.
    Shoulders all in humps lie snarled;
    Titties—what? yes, shrunken clumps.
    And haunches fare no better than dugs.

As for that hidden treasure, ugh!
The thighs aren't thighs as vessels burst,
Resembling speckled cuts of wurst. 524

56. "And so for the good old days we call
Among ourselves, old silly twats,
As on our aged haunches we squat,
All hunched up in squalid balls,
Kept warm by little hempen trifles
Whose fire bursts soon, and then is stifled;
Ach, God! I was such a delicate wench
But . . . yes . . . it's happened to many a *Mensch*." 532

[166] *Or y pensez, Belle Gantiere*

(1.) It's time to think, my Pretty Glover,
Who served apprenticeship with me,
About your value as a lover,
And you too, Blanche of the Bootery;
Look to the left and look to the right.
"Spare no man" is my declaration.
Once old, they'll let you feel their spite,
Like surplus coins cried out of circulation. 540

(2.) And you there, little Sausage-Cleaver,
Who at the dance always moved faster,
And you, Guillemette the Carpet-Weaver,
Don't pretend that I'm not your master.
The shop'll soon be bolted and leased
As bloat declares its proclamation:
You're fit now only for an old priest,
Like surplus coins cried out of circulation. 548

(3.) Jeanneton the Bonnet-Bender,
Watch that your lover doesn't cling;
And Katherine the Wallet-Vender,
Don't send your men out pasturing.
Who isn't pretty shouldn't vex,
But cause a constant exultation;
Foul old age must buy its sex
Like surplus coins cried out of circulation. 556

(4.) Girls, will you stop for just one bit
And try to grasp my great frustration?
I'm out of it totally now, I quit—
Like surplus coins cried out of circulation. 560

* * * * * * * * * * *

166. Advice of the Pretty Helmress to the Daughters of Joy, who are prostitutes.

85. CLAUSE NUMBER ONE: This soul entombed   833
    I trust to the Blessed Trinity,
    To the hands of Our Beloved Lady,
    Who chambered God within her womb.
    And now I cry upon the love
    Moved by the nine great orders above
    That they may bear my soul with moan
    Before the precious heavenly throne.   840

86. *Item:* My body I hereby leave
    To our awesome mother, the Earth;
    Because of long famine, there's a dearth
    Of fat, which will cause the worms to grieve.
    And let it be given with great dispatch:
    From Earth it came; to Earth, go back.
    Everything if I've righty learned
    Is always glad to make a return.   848

87. *Item:* To my more than father,
    Master Guillaume, who gave me coddling
    Like a child just risen from swaddling
    In a way as tender as any mother
    (He got me out of many a jam
    Though none was worse than where I am)—
    I beg him on knees to leave the joy
    Of all this mess to his little boy;   856

88. To him I bequeath my library
    With *The Romance of the Devil's Fart,*
    Reproduced by a man with heart,
    Who called himself Guy Tabarie;
    It lies under the table in reams,
    And the matter inside is more than it seems,
    For although it looks like mere porno hack,
    Its ideas will make up for other lacks.   864

89. *Item:* To my poor mother I leave
    This hymn to offer the Mistress in praise
    (She who suffered such bitter days
    For me, God knows, and still will grieve).
    No castle or fortress can I yield
    Where body and soul could find some shield,
    For evil fortune over me rolls—
    You have nothing else, Mother, poor soul!   872

[167] *Dame du ciel, regente terïenne*

(1.) Lady of heaven, regent over Earth,
    High empress of the infernal swampish plain,
    Receive me, a simple person of Christian birth,
    That I may be a part of your select domain,
    Although my life has been one of little gain.
    My goods from you, My Lady and My Mistress,
    Are so great that they dwarf my sinfulness,
    Goods by which the soul wins immortality
    And stays there. O God, don't think that I jest!
    By this faith I want to live and die.   882

(2.) And tell your Son that I'm indeed his woman.
    By him my sins will all be washed away;
    Pardon me, as he did to the Egyptian
    Or the clerk Theophilus, who at last obeyed;
    You freed and quit him after he truly prayed,
    Although the Devil held him in his grasp.
    I pray: keep me from coming to that pass,
    O Virgin who never suffered man's lechery
    And bore the Sacrament we adore in Mass.
    By this faith I want to live and die.   892

(3.) Lady, I'm just a poor and ancient thing;
    One letter I cannot read; I'm completely lewd.
    I see in church where I do my worshipping
    Paradise painted; I hear harps and lutes;
    And Hell—the pot boils over with those brutes.
    One makes me fear, one gives me happiness.
    Give me the joy, O you highest Goddess,
    On whom every sinner finally must rely;
    I'll show my faith, no feints, no laziness,
    For by this faith I want to live and die.   902

(4.) Virgin, you carried, you, my worthy princess,
    Iesus, who'll reign until the earth shall fade,
    Lord Almighty, who took on human weakness,
    Leaving the heavens to come down to our aid,
    Offering to Death his precious youthfulness.
    Now him as Lord I promise to stand by:
    For in his faith I want to live and die.   909

* * * * * * * * * * *

167. Ballade for His Mother to Pray to Our Lady. His name occurs anagrammatically in stanza 4.

[168*] *Se j'ayme et sers la belle de bon het*

(1.) If I love and serve the one debonair   1591
    Will you say I pursue a vile, foolish life?
    She has every good for which I care,
    For her I gird on buckler and knife;
    When visitors come, I run for a pot;
    Scrambling for wine, I keep cool and mute;
    I hand out water, cheese, bread, and fruit,
    And if they pay me, I say, "*Bene stat*;
    Stop in, old fellow, when the load is great
    In this bordello where we hold our estate."   1600

(2.) Ah, then, the venom suddenly erupts
    When Margot climbs in without a sou.
    I can't look at her. I hate her guts.
    I grab dress and panties, girdle too,
    And shout, "I like this loot a lot."
    She handles her flanks: "You damn pariah!"
    She screams; she swears on the dead Messiah
    That she won't take it. A stick I've got
    To inscribe my message on her pate
    In this bordello where we hold our estate.   1610

(3.) Peace we make. A fart she bestows
    Like a puffy beetle on a heap of dung;
    Laughing, she twists her fist on my nose;
    "*Bébé*," she whispers, swats me on the bung;
    Like a log we sleep, drunk, shank to shank;
    We awake to hear her interior toot;
    She climbs on me, will not waste her fruit;
    I groan below, squeezed flat like a plank.
    With steady strokes, my lust she abates
    In this bordello where we hold our estate.   1620

(4.) Come hail or wind or ice, I've baked my bread.
    I'm horny; she has horns upon her head.
    Which one is worse? Well, the man once said:
    "Bad cat, bad rat"—an equal fate we rate.
    Garbage we love; garbage is all we've got.
    We run from honor; honor flees our lot
    In this bordello where we hold our estate.   1627

168. Ballade of Fat Margot. *Bene stat* in line 1598 means "It stands well; all right." Villon's name occurs anagrammatically in stanza 4.
    *Original text appears in Section IX, taken from Sargent-Baur, pp. 93–94.

[169] *Car ou soies porteur de bulles*

(1.) Whether you carry papal bulls,   1692
      Hustle or shoot the dice in crap,
      Make your own money, blow your cool
      Like some neurotic about to snap,
      Are a lying traitor with faith to let,
      Guilty of thievery, rapine, and fraud,
      Where's it all go? Where, will you bet?
      All to the taverns and the broads.   1699

(2.) Rhyme, rail, jangle, or peck the lute
      Like any nutty, nervy clown;
      Act up, work magic, toot the flute,
      Perform in every city and town
      Farces, jests, moralities;
      Win at poker, quilles, and glic—
      Away it goes, just listen to me,
      All to the taverns and the chicks.   1707

(3.) So stay away from this filthy stool;
      Go plow; trim your fields from weeds;
      Feed and groom your horses and mules,
      Even if you never learned how to read.
      If you take it easy, it'll all be okay.
      But if you scutch the hemp into rods,
      The labor won't hold; you'll throw it away
      All to the taverns and the broads.   1715

(4.) Doublets with spangles, even your pants,
      Frilly shorts and robes with furls—
      You could do worse than just to hand
      All to the taverns and the girls.   1719

[170] *Icy se clost le testament*

(1.) Here is closed the final will,   1996
      The end of poor François Villon.
      But his burial's waiting still;
      When you hear the carillon,
      Come in red vermilion dolled
      Because with a lover's death he ended.
      This he swore upon his balls
      As from this world his way he wended.   2003

169. Ballade of Good Advice for Low-Livers. Line 1705 contains the names of three card games.
    170. Ballade to Close the Last Will.

(2.) And I believe he didn't fib
      For he was chased like a lowly peon
      Because of those hateful loves of his
      All the way down to Roussillon.
      There is no bramble, not a gully
      (For so he truthfully contended)
      That did not try to strip him wholly
      As from this world his way he wended.   2011

(3.) That's how he went: violently, so
      That at his death he had just rags;
      He shuddered in those final throes
      Because love gave him spurring jabs;
      He could feel such pricks down under
      That make a buckler's blows seem tender;
      This is the thing that gives us wonder
      As from this world his way he wended.   2019

(4.) Prince, like a merlin straight and fine,
      Know what he did as his parting ended?
      Took a long swig of black, brackish wine
      As from this world his way he wended.   2023

      * * * * * * * *

[171] Je suis François, dont il me poise

I am François—a thing to weigh—
Born in Paris (that's out Pontoise way).
My neck will grasp as the rope descends
How much the ass weighs in the end.

[172] Freres humains qui après nous vivez

1. My fellow brothers, who after us will live,
    Don't let your hearts turn hard against our sins;
    For if you find the pity to forgive,
    Mercy from God the sooner you will win.
    You see us here: five, six, hanging apart;   5
    And flesh, whose care we always have allayed
    Is battered now, devoured and decayed;
    And we, the bones, are of dust and ash composed;
    Yet God forbid you laugh our ills away
    But pray that God salvation on us dispose.   10

171. Quatrain. Ed. A. Longnon, L. Foulet (Champion, 1958), p. 95.
172. Epitaph of Villon. Ed. Sargent-Baur, pp. 132–133.

2. And if we call you brothers, certainly you
   Must not show disdain, though we have been dispensed
   Through Justice. After all, you know it's true
   Not every man has always shown good sense.
   Excuse us, for we have now been sent   15
   To see the Virgin Mary's only son
   And may his grace forever on us run
   And may Hell's thunderbolt not dare come close;
   For we are dead; trouble's no longer fun:
   So pray that God salvation on us dispose.   20

3. Rain's washing we have felt; we have felt the scour;
   The sun has scorched, burned our flesh black and dry;
   Magpies and crows our eyeballs have devoured
   And plucked our beards, the brows above our eyes.
   We have not hanged one hour unagonized: 25
   Now here, now there, restlessly we are carried
   Wherever the constant, shifting winds have harried;
   We are left like pitted thimbles by the carrion crows.
   And so of this company of ours be wary,
   But pray that God salvation on us dispose.   30

4. Prince Jesus, who over us has mastery,
   Watch that Hell never around us close;
   May the Devil never deal with this company.
   Man, there is nothing here of mockery—
   But pray that God salvation on us dispose.   35

Plate 7. Castle Dürnstein on the hill above the town, where Richard the Lion-Hearted, held in captivity by the Austrians, was discovered by his jongleur, the troubadour Blondel de Nesle, who sang Richard's songs up and down the Danube Valley in search of his king until he heard a refrain here. Richard wrote No. 138 before being freed by his mother, Queen Eleanor (see No. 174), the granddaughter of the first troubadour, Duke William IX of Aquitaine (Nos. 43–47). (Courtesy of the Austrian National Tourist Office)

[VI] GERMAN LYRICS

The German lyric tradition follows that of the French. Aside from some anonymous songs, the Middle High German lyric did not really flower until it felt the influence of the Provençal troubadours. Then the tradition of love poetry or *Minnesang* was born in the twelfth century. Previously, in the Old High German period, literature existed, but it was largely composed of lays, riddles, or magic charms—certainly not songs of love. Once it joined the mainstream of European tradition, German poetry adopted many of the conventions that were already established. For example, the notion of *Frauendienst* or "service to women" is a central part of the rhetorical strategy of the *Minnelied* or "love song." There is still much argument over the origin of the word *Minne* ("love"). Most people generally believe that the word is connected with Greco-Roman words for "remember." The learned nature of the term suggests an esoteric import, just as much of the music of the Minnelieder was borrowed from the French.

We must not, however, suggest that the Germans were mere imitators. They adapted the Provençal tradition in a highly realistic way, unlike the poets of Italy. The woman in German songs is almost never an angel. She is a woman and, even more strongly than in her North French counterparts, an object who can be possessed. Love in German poetry is never totally removed from sex. In the most famous of all the Minnesinger poems, Walther von der Vogelweide's *Under der linden* (No. 189), the act of possession is clearly stated. In fact, German poetry, more than that of any other European country, underscores realism almost to the point of naturalism. The nature setting in a North French poem often seems like a window dressing; in a German poem, it is a recurrent reminder of the natural life.

In keeping with this highly objective presentation, the German lyric tradition places strong emphasis upon poetic imagery. The linden tree (or lime tree, for Middle High German *linde* can be translated by either word) becomes a dominant symbol of the force of nature, complemented sometimes by the brooks and the meadows. Yet unlike the nature setting in other countries, the German landscape is frequently focused upon a bird, a flower, a tree, or a star, and does not move upward into another realm.

The realistic nature of German song is also conveyed by the fact that the lyrics frequently have a narrative at their base. Some of the poems that follow are clearly Dawn Songs (*Tagelieder*) or Pastourelles, and others suggest a story line indirectly. As a result, German poetry avoids the danger of too much abstraction.

Furthermore, although much has been said about the so-called courtly-love movement in the poetry, one can see that the works which follow are not encumbered with didactic tropes or motifs, the way some of the works in other countries are. The absence of a metaphysical overtone in much of the verse preserves a certain fresh, folk-sounding quality that prevents the selections gathered here from sounding repetitive or labored; the stifling "court" atmosphere is not at all evident.

German lyrics also have a rather somber, brooding tone that often asserts itself. With this melancholy goes an inclination toward meditation, but the thought is usually secular. See, for example, Walther's famous No. 190. Philosophy to the medieval German poet is frequently not theology, and the poetry itself is the key to the meditation.

Perhaps the major contribution of the Minnesingers was their music, which has been preserved much better than that in many other countries. Those who would like a detailed account of this development, along with a record, should consult B. G. Seagrave and W. Thomas, *The Songs of the Minnesingers* (U. Illinois, 1966).

Three anthologies cited here are *Des Minnesangs Frühling*, ed. H. Moser and H. Tervooren, I (Hirzel, 1977); *Poets of the Minnesang*, ed. Olive Sayce (Oxford, 1967); and the 2-volumed *Die deutsche Literatur: Mittelalter*, ed. H. de Boor (Beck, 1965).

TWO ANONYMOUS SONGS

[173] Dû bist mîn, ich bin dîn

Thou art mine,
I am thine,
And like this we'll always be.
Thou art part
Of my locked heart,   5
And it's true I've lost the key.
So abide
Deep inside
For it's there thou'lt ever be.

[174] Wære diu werlt alliu mîn

If the world were all mine
    From the sea to the Rhine,
        I'd throw it all away
If only the Queen of England lay
    In my arms' entwine.   5

173. Ed. Moser-Tervooren, I, 21.
174. A German song from the *Carmina Burana* (Nos. 23–40). The Queen is undoubtedly Eleanor of Aquitaine, wife of Henry II.

THE KÜRENBERGER

---

[175] *Ich zôch mir einen valken mêre danne ein jâr*

I trained me a falcon for more than a year.
I trained him to heed every wave of my hand;
I bound up his feathers with fetters of gold;
He sprang up and flew to a distant land.

Since then I have seen that falcon flying free   5
With silken jesses dangling from his feet
And feathers shiny with their gold and red:
God grant that all who love each other meet!

[176] *Der tunkel sterne*

Like a dark star
   That wants to hide,
You must, pretty lady,
   Stay from my side,
And always on others   5
   Rest those eyes
So no one discovers
   What between us lies.

[177] *Swenne ich stân aleine in mînem hemede*

When I stand all alone
   In my dressing gown,
And I think about you,
   My knight of renown,
My color rises up in a flush   5
Like a blushing rose on a thorny bush,
And my heart lays claim to a mighty share
   Of desire and despair.

175–177. Der von Kürenberc (*fl. ca.* 1150). Perhaps an aristocrat from Kürnberg Castle near Linz, Austria. Small corpus survives. Texts: Sayce, Nos. 15, 18, 13.

DIETMAR VON AIST

---

[178] Slâfest du, friedel ziere

LADY:
Are you sleeping, tender lover?
They'll be coming to discover—
Ah! there's a bird just now
Striking a tune on the lime-tree bough.

KNIGHT:
I was snuggling in sleep's arms;   5
Now, love, you sound an alarm;
Loving unlabored cannot be;
I do what you order, Milady.

The lady began to moan:
"You ride. You leave me alone.   10
When will you ever come back to me?
God! joy goes with your company. . . ."

[179] Ez stuont ein frouwe alleine

There stood a lady all alone
Waiting upon a moor;
She wanted her own man to come;
She saw a falcon soar.
"O ho! you falcon, how you fly!   5
You go wherever desire flings.
You choose some bough away up high
And there you lower your wings.
Ah me—I share your wanderlust.
I chose a man whom I could trust.   10
I staked him out with my two eyes.
But ladies fair now envy my prize.
O God, when will my lover appear?
I never begrudged another her dear."

178-179. Dietmar von Aist, Eist (*fl.* 1150–1170). Probably an Austrian born near the Aist, a tributary of the Danube. No. 178 is a Dawn Song. Texts: Moser-Tervooren, Nos. 13, 4.

SPERVOGEL (THE SPARROW)

[180] *Swer den wolf ze hirten nimt*

He who asks the wolf to dine
   Is asking for a cause to whine.
No wise man ever overloads his trawler.
This is my wisdom. I am the scholar.
A husband who spends his every thaler   5
To buy rich clothes throughout the year
   Will soon have mighty cause to fear.
Her arrogance will grow and grow
   Till he gets a bastard *quid pro quo.*

[181] *Swa eyn vriunt dem andern vriunde bigestat*

When one friend stands beside another
With firm loyalty through all misfortunes,
His assistance is very fine,
When it is offered willingly;
When two friends support each other   5
Their united strength will grow.
When one friend treasures another,
Their joy is ever abounding.

FRIEDRICH VON HAUSEN

[182] *Mîn herze und mîn lîp die wellent scheiden*

1. My heart and my body would like to part
   Although they've journeyed together a good long time.
   My body wants to go fight against the heathens.
   My heart has chosen its contest in a girl,

180. Spervogel (*fl.* after 1150). Early master of the single-stanza *Spruch* (see Introduction). Text: De Boor, *Mittlelalter* II, 1789.
    181. *Spruch* in Honor of Friendship. For text and music, Seagrave-Thomas, p. 32.
    182. Or Friderich von Hûsen (*ca.* 1155–1190). Rhinelander prominent in the court of Frederick Barbarossa. Served on imperial missions to Italy in 1175 and 1186. Died in 1190, in Syria on the Third Crusade. Ed. Sayce, No. 53. Several melodies in Seagrave-Thomas, pp. 35–50.

The best in the world. It's troubled me a while   5
That the two of them don't get along together.
My eyes have brought me often to great grief.
Only God, I'm afraid, can settle this strife.

2. I thought that I was free from all this turmoil
   When I took up the cross in the Master's name.   10
   It was right for my heart to go along with me,
   But it told me its own steadiness forbade that.
   Right now I could be a rightful-acting man
   If only it would give up its silly will.
   Now I see, though, it doesn't give a damn,   15
   No matter what the end that comes my way.

3. All right, my heart, since I can never stop you
   From wanting to abandon me in distress,
   Then I beg God to guide you to some haven
   Where you will find a welcome without duress.   20
   Alas, poor little thing, what will be your fate?
   How could you dare to enter alone into peril?
   Who will help bring your sorrows to an end
   With all the steady loyalty I have shown?

REINMAR VON HAGENAU, THE OLD

[183] *Ich wil allez gâhen*

1. I will go on the run
   Off to the love I possess.
   Even if a good outcome
   Lies beyond my fondest guess.
   But still I try it every day;   5
   I serve her without her bidding—
      She must soon change the sorrowful to the gay.

2. A twinge went sweeping over me
   When I heard something said:
   They told me she was a lady   10
   And a splendid life she led.

183. Reinmar der Alte (d. *ca.* 1210). Major poet of Austria in the late 1100s, whose death was sung by his successor, Walther von der Vogelweide. Text: Moser-Tervooren, pp. 329–331.

I tested it—and yes, it's fair.
No other woman could pull her down.
    There's no compare—even by the width of a hair.

3. If from any other land   15
   Some loving should ever come to me,
   That all lies within her hands;
   For other women I make no plea.
   She is my shining Easter day
   And fills my heart deep with love: 20
      He knows it's true, the One to whom men pray.

HEINRICH VON VELDEKE

[184] *Tristrant muose sunder danc*

Tristan stood, without giving thanks,
Among Isolde's loyal ranks,
For the magic philter could impel
Stronger even than love's spell.
My Lady then should give me thanks   5
Because that brew I never drank;
And yet my love fares valiantly,
Better than his, if that can be.

    O Lady fair,
    Of falseness bare,   10
    I'll belong to you
    If you will love me true.

184. Heinrich von Veldeke (*fl.* 1170-before 1210). Low German knight from Maastricht region; author of *Eneit*, German version of Vergil's *Aeneid*, based on French sources. Worked for Frederick Barbarossa in 1184. Text: Sayce, No. 40.

HEINRICH VON MORUNGEN

[185] *Ich hôrte ûf der heide*

1. Voices loud and music sweet
   I heard once upon the moor;
   With those sounds I was replete
   With joying and in sorrow poor.
   Her who gave my mind a twang   5
   I found dancing; and she sang.
   Farewell sorrow! I too sprang.

2. There I found her all alone
   With her cheeks bathed in sorrow.
   For my death she made a moan   10
   (She had heard it just that morrow).
   This new upset I could better bear
   Than glib-given love, for as I knelt there
   I watched the ending of her care.

3. I found her walking by the wall-edge   15
   (All alone); I came at her call.
   She would have gladly made the pledge,
   Offering me true love and all.
   I would have burned the land behind,
   Except that she bound up my mind   20
   And left my sense bereft and blind.

[186] *Owê, sol aber mir iemer mê*

MAN:
Will it never again—o woe!—
Gleam for me in the night,
Shining whiter than the snow,
Her body cut just right?
It deceived these eyes of mine: 5
I thought it was the same
As the moon's soft glowing shine—
    And then day came.

WOMAN:
Will he never again—o woe!—
Spend the morning by my side?   10

185. Heinrich von Morungen (*ca.* 1150-1222). Native of Thuringia who died in Leipzig.
Very familiar with Provençal forms, as he shows in his Dawn Song (No. 186). Texts: Moser-
Tervooren, pp. 268–269, 276–277.

Then as night from us will go
We will need no longer cry
"Alas! it's come—the day"—
A lament I heard him shout
When last by me he lay   15
   —Then day broke out.

MAN:
O woe! no one could ever count
The kisses offered me in sleep;
But later on, the tears fell down,
Steeping downward from her cheeks;   20
But as I held her lovingly,
Those tears she put away,
And wholly did she comfort me—
   But then came day.

WOMAN:
O woe! how he repeatedly   25
Devours me with those eyes!
That time when he uncovered me,
He'd let no cover lie
Over this poor naked frame—
Miraculously on and on   30
He never tired of that game—
   But then came dawn.

WOLFRAM VON ESCHENBACH

[187*] Sîne klâwen durh die wolken sint geslagen

WATCHMAN:
1. It has raked its talons downward through the clouds,
   It has risen upward with an awesome might.
   I see the gray of the dawning breaking out;
   I see the end of the night,
   And also that sweet companionship   5
   I fostered when I let him in.
   Now he must make a hurried trip.
   A virtuous man I serve: no prey to sin.

187. Wolfram von Eschenbach (*ca.* 1170–1217). Author of *Parzival* epic. From northern Bavaria of impoverished noble stock. Served the great patron of Minnesinger, Hermann of Thuringia. Only about eight lyrics survive. Here, a brilliant Dawn Song.
   *Original text appears in Section IX, taken from De Boor, *Mittelalter* II, 1673–1674.

LADY:
2. Watchman, my pleasure's fading as you sing.
    You only bring addition to my lament.   10
    Grief is the only thing you ever bring,
    Every morning as the night is spent.
    Please, your total silence keep.
    I order: hold your pledging dear,
    If my true love can share my sleep   15
    I'll slip you something to bring you cheer.

WATCHMAN:
3. He must get out—quick! no delay!
    Give him his leave there, my pretty wife.
    Let him love you later the secret way,
    To keep his name and save his life.   20
    He put himself into my trust
    That I should get him a safe egress.
    Well now, it's day. It's long since dusk
    When kisses lured him from me to your breast.

LADY:
4. Go on singing, Watchman, but leave him here.   25
    He brought me and he got some tender love.
    Your voice is always filling us with fear;
    Even when the dawn-star doesn't twinkle above,
    The man who's come to share my charms
    Is snatched before the night parts: 30
    You grab him quickly from my arms,
    From my white arms—but never from my heart!

POET:
5. As a gleam of daylight struck against the glass
    And as the Watchman warning sang,
    The Lady felt a baleful grasp   35
    And pressed her breast against her man.
    The Rider's courage did not surrender
    (The Watchman's song had failed on that score).
    They took their leave with rewardings tender:
    With kisses and with much, much more.   40

[188] Der helden minne ir klage

1. A lament for a love that can't be shown
    You always sang before the dawn shone,
    Of the sour following the sweet;

---

188. Extraordinary love song that defies the courtly-love tradition by exalting the joy of love from marriage. Text: De Boor, *Mittelalter* II, 1676.

He who love and womanly greetings
In secret adores   5
Must part from both in the end;
This was the warning you did send,
As upward soared
The morning star; O Watcher, be mum!
Of these affairs be ever dumb!   10

2. Whoever swore or ever will say
That he most fondly with his lover lay
Unhidden from all suborning
Should not from the fear of morning
Slink away.   15
No, he may the daylight abide.
No man can ever take him aside
His life to try
If a trusted, tender, open wife
Will give him love for aye and aye.   20

WALTHER VON DER VOGELWEIDE

[189*] *Under der linden*

1. Under the linden
   On the heath
   Where a bed for two was massed,
   There you could see
   Piled up neat   5
   Pluckings of flowers and of grass,
   At the edge of the copse within a vale—
          Tandaradei—
   Sweetly sang the nightingale.

2. I went secretly   10
   To a meadow shady
   Where my sweetheart had gone before.
   He did greet me:

189. Walther von der Vogelweide (*ca.* 1170–*ca.* 1230). Greatest German medieval lyric poet in vast range of genres. Born in Tyrolese section of Austria, but wandered from court to court. Frederick II rewarded him with a small fief near Würzburg.
   *Original text appears in Section IX, reprinted from De Boor, *Mittelalter* II, 1729–1730. For tape: Teldec 8.44015 ZS.

"Pretty lady!"—
Then made me happy forevermore.   15
Did he kiss? Ach, a thousandfold!—
            Tandaradei—
See, my mouth still holds the mold!

3. Heaped up there
   With royal pride   20
   Was a bedstead he formed of flowers.
   A laugh you'd hear
   From deep inside
   If a stranger ventured into our bower.
   From the roses he could tell—   25
               Tandaradei—
   Exactly where my head fell.

4. God forbid
   That our rendezvous
   Be known, for it would bring us shame.   30
   What we did,
   Just we two,
   We've sworn to hide in each other's name.
   O yes—and that little bird—
               Tandaradei—   35
   He said he would keep his word.

[190] *Owê war sint verswunden alliu mîniu jâr?*

1. Alas, where have they vanished, all of my years?
   Was my life a dream, or was it truly real?
   And all I thought truly was, was this not so?
   It seems I've been asleep and never knew it.
   But now I've wakened, and I no longer recognize   5
   Things as common to me before as one of my hands.
   These people, this land where I grew up from a child
   Have become as foreign as if I were never here.
   All of my former playmates are now run-down and old.
   The fields are all dry, the forest has been hacked.   10
   If it wasn't for rivers flowing as they've always flowed,
   I'd really think my misfortune was something great.
   Many now greet me aloofly who knew me once quite well.
   The world in its entirety is devoid of grace.
   And as I review those wonderful days gone by   15
   That have now disappeared like a pebble into the sea,
        Again and again: Alas!

190. Lament that promotes a crusade that Frederick was trying to undertake; often titled "The Elegy." Text: De Boor, *Mittelalter* I, 639–640.

2. Alas, how completely depraved the young people now behave!
  The ones who were once lighthearted have stifled their charm
  And now can only worry; why do they act this way?   20
  Wherever in the world I journey I find no one in joy.
  Dancing, laughing, and singing have all been forced to yield.
  No Christian fellow ever saw such a mournful state!
  Just look at the hats the women now put on their heads!
  And once-proud gentlemen go around dressed like hicks.   25
  Troubling messages are reaching us now from Rome:
  We are only allowed to be glum, never seize our joy.
  This troubles me greatly (after all, we once lived well),
  But now instead of chuckling, I can only choose to whine.
  This lament of mine has quieted even the wild birds.   30
  Is it any wonder that I should feel depressed?
  Yet what am I saying, a fool moved by bitter bile?
  He who seeks worldly pleasures will lose whatever's to come:
      Again and again: Alas!

3. Alas, how all of our sweet things turn into poison!   35
  I see the bitter gall lurking deep in the honey.
  The world is outwardly pretty—white, green, and red;
  But inside the color is dark, as black as is death.
  And yet I'll show a comfort for those who have gone astray—
  With just a little effort they can still absolve their sins.   40
  Just think of it, knights! for this is your kind of thing!
  You're wearing the gleaming helmets, the hardened mail;
  You're carrying the thick shields, the bishop-blessed swords.
  Would to God I were worthy of this victorious crusade!
  For thus I, a needy man, could pile up a handsome hoard.   45
  O no, I don't mean some fiefs or some lordly gold.
  I just want to wear the crown of pure bliss forever;
  This any mercenary can win with just his spear.
  If I could make that yearned-for journey over the sea,
  O God, I'd sing, "Bravo!" and never again, "Alas!"   50
      No, never again, "Alas!"

[191] *Ich saz ûf eime steine*

I sat me down upon a stone
With kneebone crossed on kneebone,
And bent my elbow and my head
And in a palm that I outspread
I rested cheek and chin.   5
And then I pondered deep within
How man should guide his earthly stay,

191. Meditative poem composed during a period of civil strife in 1198. For melody, Seagrave-Thomas, p. 93.

And could not find a single way
That a man could win three things
And keep them all from spoiling: 10
Two are Rich Goods and Good Repute,
Which usually each other refute;
The third is Grace, which comes of God,
To which the others offer laud.
I'd like them all inside a chest.   15
Unfortunately, it's a vain request,
For worldly honor and the goods of men
And the blessing that from God descends
Seldom in a single heart are locked.
The paths and roadways lie all blocked.   20
Deception in ambush is always plotting;
Violence is in the streets marauding;
Peace and Right are sorely beset,
And if these two don't soon get better,
    The other three   25
    Will have no franchise to be free.

[192] Sô die bluomen ûz dem grase dringent

1. As flowers out of the green grass spring
   As if they're laughing at the dazzling Sun,
   On a day in May when the morning is still new,
   And the little birds with skill begin to sing
   In the finest manner known to anyone,   5
   What delight can these ever be compared to?
   It is about one-half of a heaven's *Reich*.
   And if I try to say what it's really like,
   I'll have to speak about that great delight
   That often comes to please my eyes,   10
   And would do so now, if I just had the sight.

2. A noble lady, beautiful and pure,
   In fancy clothes wrapped well about,
   Walks among the people for delectation,
   High-spirited and courteous, not demure,   15
   Glancing on all the faces thereabout,
   Shining like the Sun against constellations:
   Let May bring us all of his many wonders,
   For which of them is something that can plunder,
   Compared to the royal splendor of this lady?   20
   Yes, we should let all of May's blossoms stand
   And stare on every hand at this worthy maid.

3. All right, you say, you prefer the outside world?
   Let us go then to a Maytime festival.

192. Text: De Boor, *Mittelalter* II, 1542.

Let us watch May come with his powers aflame.   25
Look at him! Then cast your eyes on the girls.
Tell me which merits the higher pedestal.
See if I have selected the better game.
O God! If somebody would just let me choose
To treasure one, the other one to lose,   30
My choice would be anything but random!
My dear Herr May, I'd turn you into March
Before my own sweet lady would be abandoned!

NEIDHART VON REUENTAL

[193] *Kint, bereitet iuch der sliten ûf daz îs!*

1. Children, get the sleigh ready for the ice!
   This wearisome winter's cold,
   It's taken all our wondrous blooms away.
   Many a green linden stands there shivering gray,
   On its branches is no song.   5
   This has happened because of old Frost's anger.
   Can't you see how he has done up our meadows?
   It's his fault that all things fall.
   Even the nightingale
   Tells her tale far yonder.   10

2. Truly I need the words of some wise friend
   About a thing that's troubling me:
   That is: where can our children play?
   Megenward has a great big wide room
   And if you all consent,   15
   We'll spend our holiday there with roundelays.
   That is what his daughter wants when we are there.
   Go and tell your friends.
   Engelmar will dance quite ably
   All around the tables.   20

193. Nithart "From Ruing Dale" (*fl.* 1200–before 1246). Lower Bavarian knight who was master of realistic village poetry. Often penniless, though protected by Ludwig I of Bavaria and Frederick II of Austria. Winter Song. A fourth stanza on women's fashions omitted. Text: De Boor, *Mittelalter* II, 1708–1710. Music: Seagrave-Thomas, pp. 110–111. For tape of other works: Teldec 8.44015 ZS.

3. Go tell Kunegunde; that brings us all together!
   She has always loved the dance
   And bitches that we keep leaving her out!
   Gisel, go over to Jiuten and tell them too
   That Ella must join them balling.   25
   There's a promise between us, and it's fast.
   And, child, don't forget our Hedwig there!
   Demand that she come too! . . .

   (*The party begins.*)

5. Eppe's hitting Geppe Gumpen on the hand,
   And hard with his threshing flail.   30
   All is quieted then by the rod of Master Albert.
   This mess was caused when old Ruprecht found an egg
   (Found, hell! the Devil gave him it).
   He kept threatening to toss it over here.
   Eppe got just as burned up as he is bald: 35
   Gruffly he grumbled: "Hold it, man!"
   Ruprecht splattered him on the pate,
   And the yolk streamed down.

6. Friedlieb had to come here with Godelinde—
   Just as Engelmar had dreaded.   40
   I'm not going to tease. I'll tell it to the end.
   Eberhardt the Bailiff had to step in between them,
   And make the two make up.
   If he hadn't, they'd have had each other's heads.
   Like two dumb gawking ganders the whole day long   45
   They eye each other intently.
   And the man who leads our singing
   Is our trusty Frederick.

7. Once upon a time my hair hung splendidly,
   Twirling in locks around my band.   50
   But that's forgotten now I've got a house.
   Salt and grain I'm buying all the year.
   Hell, what did I do to him
   Who shoved stupid me into all these woes?
   My debts to him were small,   55
   But my curses now aren't little
   When I'm there in Reuental
   Without my victuals.

[194] *Der meie der ist rîche*

GIRL:

1. "The May is rich about
   And leads, without a doubt,
   The wood to green again.
   The trees are full of leaves:
   The winter's at an end.   5

2. "Ah, the pleasure from the heath
   As I watch the brightening sweep,
   Yes, it's coming on to meet me,"
   Proclaimed the well-shaped maid.
   "Joyously I'll run to greet it!   10

3. "Mother, no lectures; let me be!
   I'm going to the fields directly.
   I want to leap and dance and spring.
   Ah, it's been a long, long time
   Since I've heard my playmates sing."   15

MOTHER:

4. "No, no, my dearest daughter, no!
   All alone I've watched you grow,
   Suckled you here at this breast.
   O please, please do what I say:
   Relax and let the menfolk rest."   20

GIRL:

5. "I want my lover's name to shine.
   If you just knew him, you'd think him fine!
   I'll rush away to see his face,
   That gentle man from Reuental,
   The man I'm yearning to embrace.   25

6. "Green across the branches is blent,
   And all the trees will soon be bent
   With blossoms down to the earth.
   Ah, listen now, mother of mine,
   I'm going away with that man of worth.   30

7. "Ah, my sweet honored mother—
   He's calling me, my lover.
   Shall I say never to romance?
   He tells me I'm the most beautiful
   Girl from Bavaria into France."   35

194. Spring Song. Text: De Boor, *Mittelalter* II, 1702–1703.

TANNHÄUSER

[195] *Der winter ist zergangen*

1. The winter has thoroughly gone away, / as I can see from the meadow; / and as I was walking out there, / my sight was well rewarded
2. By blossoms nicely arrayed. (5) / Who ever saw such a pretty field? / I gathered some for a garland, / and took them with *joie* (joy) to the ladies dancing. / Whoever wants a good time should rise up now for his *chance!*
3. Violets and clover were growing (10) / and summer-buds and germander, / and crocus highly prized; / I also found some gladioli, lilies, and roses. / Then I wanted to chat with my lady.
4. She gave me the prize (15) / of being her *doux ami* (sweetheart) / with service for this May, / and so for her I'll dance.
5. Nearby there stood a *forêt* (forest) / and there I rushed to go, (20) / and there I heard some birds / greeting me very sweetly. / And greetings to them too!
6. I heard the *chanter* (singing) / as nightingales were piping. (25) / Then I had to *parler* (say) / exactly how I felt: / I didn't have a care in the world!
7. Then I saw a *rivière* (river); / a brook was running through the *forêt* (30) / to a glen across the field. / I meandered along this until I stumbled on a very beautiful *créature* (creature). / She was sitting by the spring, shining and charming in every feature.
8. Her eyes were radiant and nicely set; / she wasn't too forward in her speech; (35) / you could easily tolerate her presence; / her mouth was rosy, her throat white, / her hair light and curly, / resembling silk. / Even if I had to die, I knew I could never leave her. (40)
9. Her two little arms / were as white as an ermine. / Her body was slender / and nicely shaped in every part.
10. She was a little *grande* (big) down there, (45) / but slim everywhere else. / Nothing was forgotten in creating her: / soft thighs, straight legs, well-shaped feet. / I never saw a prettier figure to seize my heart; / in her everything was perfect. (50) / When I saw this lovely, I broke out in *parole* (speech).
11. I was delighted / and I said this: / "My lady, / I am yours; you are mine—(55) / and let all arguments forever cease! / To me you are unsurpassable. / You will please my heart forever. / Whenever men judge women, I shall sound your praise / in beauty and in virtue; (60) / you give every *contrée* (region) a lift with *joie* (joy)."
12. I said to that lovable one: / "Only God and no one else / should ever watch over you!" / Her *parole* (answer) was very sweet. (65)

195. Tannhäuser (*fl.* 1245–1270). From Nuremberg; his "earthy" Pastourelles like this made him a legendary lover whom the goddess Venus herself took to her mountain, the Venusberg, and only reluctantly released later, as Richard Wagner told in his opera *Tannhäuser* (1845), where the Minnesinger becomes a paradigm for the "holy sinner." Palermo in st. 17 is a joke. Text: Paden, *Medieval Pastourelle*, II, No. 130. Sprinkled with many French phrases (in italics), the poem is close to one by Colin Muset (Paden, I, No. 72).

13. Then I bowed to that lovely. / My whole body rejoiced / as I heard her *salutation*. / She asked me to *chanter* (sing) / to her about linden boughs (70) / and the splendor of May.

14. We were very comfortable / on our Round Table, / which was made of leaf and grass; / she knew exactly what to do! (75)

15. There were no servants there / as we lay in the clover. / She listened to me as she should have, / and did exactly what I wanted her to do.

16. I gave her some gentle pain, (80) / and I'd love to do it again. / I liked it when she laughed. / Then we began some funny games, / moved by love and magic things.

17. I spoke to her about *amour* (love); (85) / and she rewarded me *doucement* (sweetly). / She said she'd gladly let me / do to her what they do to women in Palermo.

18. And so it happened, I do recall: / she was my woman and I her man. (90) / What a wonderful outcome! / Whoever sees her's forever blessed, / since everyone agrees that she's the best; / she is so excellent! / We reached an agreement on that field. (95)

19. If anyone can do any better, / without any envy, to him I yield. / She was so ecstatic / that I lost myself too. / May God give her everything good! (100) / Her love impels me so!

20. What is it that she does to me? / I feel everything's fine with the highest spirit / that emanates from her; / I could never forget her. (105)

21. So rise up there, Adelaide, rise up! / You'll be happy by my side! / And up, up there, my Irmengard! / You have to join our dance!

22. Any girl who won't spring must be bearing a child. (110) / Let them all be merry, whoever they are!

23. Over there, I hear some flutes underway; / and here I can hear the pounding of drums. / Anyone who wants to sing / and spring in our round-dancing (115) / will easily succeed / in everything!

24. Where are the youngsters / who haven't joined us?

25. Be happy, my Cunegund! (120) / If I could kiss her a thousand times / on her rosy-colored mouth, / then I'd feel safe and sound, / because she has wounded my heart / down to its depths with love. (125)

26. Yes, it's broken— / hey hey, now, hey!

27. The string on the fiddle / has broken!

MECHTHILD VON MAGDEBURG

[196] Dialogue of the Senses and the Soul from Das fliessende Licht der Gottheit

So speaks the Soul to the Senses, her treasurers:
    I am tired of dancing for a while,   65
    I'm forced to turn and go away to cool myself.
The Senses answer the Soul:
    Lady, if you wish to cool yourself
    In the love-tears
    Of St. Mary Magdalen,
    They may well refresh you.   70
SOUL: Be quiet, sirs; you don't understand at all what I mean.
    Please don't bother me;
    I want to drink the unmixed wine a little longer.
SENSES: Lady, chastity in the maiden   75
    Goes hand in hand with great loving.
SOUL: That may well be,
    But that is not my chief concern.
SENSES: You could also cool yourself
    In the blood of martyrs.   80
SOUL: I've been martyred for so many days
    That I shouldn't go there again.
SENSES: In the advice of the confessors
    Reside pure and joyous sounds.
SOUL: I shall always stand with their advice,   85
    But the doing and the leaving
    I cannot always reconcile.
SENSES: In the wisdom of the Apostles
    One can find great security.
SOUL: I have the wisdom right here,   90
    Ready to make the wisest choice.
SENSES: Lady, the angels are resplendent
    And beautifully colored with love.
    If you cooled yourself there, they would raise you up.
SOUL: The bliss of the angels causes my love pain,   95
    Since I don't see my Bridegroom with his lords.
SENSES: So cool yourself in the secure and holy life
    That good St. John the Baptist has given us.

196. Mechthild (*ca.* 1207–*ca.* 1282). Female mystic from the Lowlands who lived after 1230 among the reforming Beguines in Magdeburg, eastern Germany, and around 1270 among the Cistercians in Helfta. Her *Flowing Light of the Divinity* recounts the passage of a soul to God, here held back by the Senses for a time. Text: De Boor, *Mittelalter* I, 578–580.

SOUL: I'm ready now for the pain,
    But the power of love has won control over all.   100
SENSES: Lady, if you want to cool this love,
    Bend down and accept the Virgin's protection
    Like a little child, and see and taste
    How the angelic joy, through supernatural milk,
    Gives suck from the eternal Maid.   105
SOUL: That's a childish love
    That cradles and suckles little children.
    I'm a fully grown bride
    Who wants her groom.
SENSES: O Lady, if you approach him,   110
    Then we'll surely end up blinded,
    For the Godhead is so fiercely hot
    As you yourself know
    That all the fire and burning heat
    That make the stars and heavenly lights glow   115
    And burn—all of this is an outpouring
    Of the divine breath
    And from its human mouth,
    From the words of the Holy Spirit;
    Who can stand this for even an hour?   120
SOUL: A fish can never drown in water,
    Nor can a bird ever sink in the air.
    Gold will not break up in fire,
    Where it gains a splendor and brilliant color.
    God has willed to all his creatures   125
    That they should be true to their natures.
    How can I then rebel against mine?
    I have to move from all things up to God,
    Who is my father from nature,
    My brother in his humanity,   130
    My Bridegroom in his love,
    And I was his from the beginning.
    When did he will that I should not feel him?
    He can both violently burn and coolly comfort us.
    So don't disturb yourself too greatly.   135
    You may still teach me.
    When I come back from God,
    Then I shall need your lore,
    For if that deceives, it's full of many tricks.

STEINMAR

[197] *Ein kneht der lac verborgen*

1. A farmhand lay all hidden,
   A farm girl by his side.
   The morning rays had smitten:
   A herdsman then outcried—
   "Get up! Let out the herd . . ."   5
   It startled them as they both heard.

2. He had to push the straw away
   And from the farm girl fly.
   He dared to brook no great delay,
   But clasped her closely by.   10
   The hay that around the maiden lay
   Flew away in the sun's bright ray.

3. Ah! how she had to laugh aloud
   As she saw him standing nude.
   Tomorrow morning he'll be allowed   15
   To take his place with her anew
   And play those games again with joy.
   Who ever saw such bliss with so few ploys?

DER WILDE ALEXANDER

[198] *Hie bevorn dô wir kinder wâren*

1. When we were little kids a while ago
   And time was passing so very slow
   That we could run across the meadow
   Frisking endlessly to and fro—
   Then we spent hours   5
   With violet flowers
   That cattle now cud as round they go.

197. Probably Berthold Steinmar (*fl.* 1250–1288). Gifted Swiss parodist who worked for Rudolf von Habsburg. Dawn Song Parody. Ed. Sayce, No. 159.
198. "Wild or Wandering Alexander" (*fl.* 1260–1300). Fond of riddles, hazy allusions, and religious pronouncements. This poem is explicit in its allegorical implications, with last stanza based on Matthew 25.1–13. Text: Sayce, No. 106. Music: Seagrave-Thomas, p. 136.

2. We used to sit, I remember well,
   Among the flowers trying to tell
   Which the prettiest might be.   10
   And our childishness anyone could see
   As around we'd traipse
   Garland-draped.
   And so the time passed merrily.

3. Look! there we go from beech to pine   15
   Trying to pluck a strawberry vine,
   Rushing over the sticks and stones,
   While all the while the Sun shone.
   Then some gamekeeper pops
   Out of the copse   20
   Yelling: "Home, my laddies, home!"

4. How well I remember the spots and scratches
   That we got from those patches—
   Ah, it was such a kiddish skit!
   And yet, how clearly I recall it: 25
   The game preserver's shout
   Ringing out—
   "Kids, up ahead's a snake pit!"

5. One went walking in the deep brush;
   He yelled and screamed and out he rushed: 30
   "Boys, hey boys! it just went in—
   It's bit our pony on the shin,
   And now he won't get well—
   O hell!
   God damn that wiggling thing!"   35

6. The gamesman cries: "Hey, hey! away!
   And if you don't run and obey
   I'll tell you what's in store:
   You'll lose the light, for even more
   Darkness is lurking in those woods;   40
   Maybe for good
   You'll lose the way; the tears will pour.

7. "Don't you kids know the Five Foolish Maids
   Who over the meadows so long strayed
   That the King had the door bolts slipped?   45
   Ah, how they wailed! Their breasts they gripped
   While wardens tore
   The garments they wore,
   And they stood for the world to see: stripped."

DER GUOTÆRE

[199] *Hievor ein werder ritter lac*

1. Once upon a time a worthy knight was lying
   Upon his bed, and they thought he was dying.
   In came a woman of such wondrous sheen
   She was a beauty no man had ever seen;
   Before all the others she did shine: 5
   She seemed a thing that must be divine.
   She stood before him, saying, "Tell
   Me, good rider, do I please you well?
   You've served me freely all of your days;
   I've come at your death your service to pay."   10

2. Her crown was all gold, and around her furled
   A girdle and belt and robe with pearls.
   He answered, "My lady, who might you be?"
   "I am Lady World," then answered she,
   "And now my back demands your eye;   15
   See! this is the great reward I ply."
   Her back was hollow, it lacked its skin;
   And there were worms and toads within;
   It stank like a foul and long-dead hound,
   "Christ! that I served you," was his weeping sound. . . .   20

199. "Good-Honor" (*fl.* 1275–1300). South German writer of didactic verse. The Lady-World Poem tradition is common in German poetry. Three more stanzas omitted. Text: De Boor, *Mittelalter* I, 490.

[VII] LYRICS OF IBERIA

A. ARABIC LYRICS

When the Arabic-speaking Moors of North Africa invaded the Iberian Peninsula under Tarik in 711, they ended the Romanized Visigothic Kingdom of Roderick and introduced Arabic as a new language. Soon the Umayyad dynasty was founded and Córdoba became the capital of the Western Caliphate, which was distinguished for its mosques and palaces like the Alhambra of Granada. In 1086 the rugged Berbers of Morocco established a new dynasty of the Almoravides, and they were replaced by 1174 by the Almohades. But pressure from the Christian North was constant, and in 1212 at Navas de Tolosa, Alfonso VIII of Castile confined the Moors largely to Granada, which fell in 1492 to Ferdinand V of Castile and Isabella I, who laid the foundations for modern Spain.

The Arabs had a literary tradition from the time of Mohammed, their prophet, and it grew with their empire, which stretched to Baghdad over the years. Their poetry was noted for its quantitative meters (like Greek and Latin), varied rhyme schemes, and precise imagery. By the 900s, Hispano-Arabic poets were writing poems in classical Arabic called *muwashshahas*; these originally had short final refrains or envois called *kharjas* (*jarchas*), which were often written in a more colloquial style and spoken by a girl. After the 1100s, poems called *zajals* were composed entirely in the colloquial Arabic of Spain, as well as other forms.

Although some have claimed that the Arabs deserve credit for inspiring the entire secular tradition of European Christianity, this is difficult to prove either in terms of music or rhetoric (for music, consult MHS 1573 and Hispavox HH S 6). Certainly there are many motifs and images that are common with Provençal literature, but the relationship may be archetypal rather than one of direct borrowing.

There is no doubt, however, that the cult of love as treated in Ibn Hazm's *Tauq al-hamāma* (Dove's Neck-Ring) clearly shows a mystique comparable to that of Provençal "courtly love." Yet the Roman poet Ovid in his *Art of Love* and *Amores* had playfully developed such a mystique, and he was known to both cultures. Arabic poetry differs from Romance poetry by being far more sensual and opulent in imagery, and often homosexual in reference to the beloved. All translations in this section are by James T. Monroe, whose *Hispano-Arabic Poetry: A Student Anthology* (U. California, 1974) provides an excellent introduction to this rich and controversial area.

Plate 8. The Patio de los Arrayanes in the Alhambra Palace in Granada, a classic example of Moorish architecture. (Courtesy of the Tourist Office of Spain)

B. HEBREW LYRICS

The Jews arrived in Spain shortly after their dispersal by the Romans in the first century. When the Moors conquered the country in the 700s, the Jews were in an excellent position to serve as middlemen between them and the Christians, since Arabic and Hebrew are both Semitic languages. Hispano-Hebraic culture reached its height along with the Arabic, and then declined as the Moors were first confined and then expelled from the peninsula. When Ferdinand and Isabella finally drove out the Moors, they expelled the Jews with them in that fateful year 1492, when Columbus discovered America.

The Hebrew lyrics translated here by Miriam Billig show clear connections with biblical poetry. All three poets presented had philosophical or theological interests: Gvirol (Gabirol), also known as Avicebron, was called "the Jewish Plato"; Yehuda HaLevi was a rabbi, and Moshe Ben Ezra was a noted scholar. All maintained close cultural connections with Spanish Muslims and Christians.

C. MOZARABIC *KHARJAS*

The *kharjas* are verses written in Hispano-Romance or in Colloquial Hispano-Arabic (or in a mixture of these two languages) which were used as the final strophes of poems—known as *muwashshahas*—composed in Classical Arabic or in Hebrew by Muslim and Jewish poets writing in Muslim Spain (Al-Andalus) from the eleventh to fourteenth century. The Hispano-Romance language used in the *kharjas* is known as Mozarabic, the everyday dialect of Muslims, Christians, and Jews living in Muslim Spain. Since they were first deciphered in 1948—by the British Arabist and Hebraist Samuel M. Stern—the *kharjas*, their interpretation, and their significance have been the subject of spirited and sometimes acrimonious scholarly polemics.

The philological problems embodied in these verses are extremely complex. There are gaps in our knowledge of the extinct Mozarabic dialect; the Arabic and Hebrew alphabets in which the verses were transcribed do not, in many cases, indicate the presence of vowels and a number of letters can easily be confused with one another; the scribes who copied the surviving manuscripts were from areas other than Spain and thus could not have understood the language of the texts they were copying. All the same, a majority of the *kharjas* can be interpreted with relative certainty and the conclusions to be drawn from that interpretation are dramatic and of far-reaching significance. The *kharjas* embody numerous poetic motifs (the abandoned girl; the faithless lover; the mother or sisters as confidantes), similar formulaic diction (the rhetorical question: What shall I do?), and identical prosodic features in common with later forms of Romance traditional lyric poetry: Galician-Portuguese *cantigas de amigo*, Castilian *villancicos*, Old French and Old Provençal *refrains*. In some cases, it is probable that a genetic relationship exists between individual *kharja* texts and lyric songs known from later stages of the Hispanic tradition.

In many instances, the *kharjas* are said to be sung by girls, thus suggesting, as is also the case with other Romance lyric forms, that they reflect a form of traditional women's poetry (Germanic *Frauenlieder*). It seems certain, then, that the Muslim and Jewish poets who composed the *muwashshahas* borrowed verses from songs current in the popular oral tradition of Al-Andalus and used them, as a sort of poetic punch-line, as the final strophes of their poems. (The word *kharja* means "exit," from Arabic *kharaja*, "to go out.") The *kharjas* would then, in some cases at least, give us a sampling of the Hispanic traditional lyric several centuries older than that preserved in any other source. Of course, the material chosen by the Muslim and Jewish poets is undoubtedly influenced by and adapted to the new poetic context in which it is used. Some *kharjas* are probably imitations created by the poets themselves and do not directly reflect the oral tradition. From a thematic point of view, the *kharjas* are also highly selective: The predominant theme is that of the lovelorn girl who has been abandoned by her faithless lover and who seeks the advice of her mother (or sisters) as confidantes. There are few exceptions to this thematic preference: one is the communal song of welcome for a visiting dignitary (No. 219).

There are three indispensable textual sources for the study of the *kharjas*: Klaus Heger, *Die bisher veröffentlichten Ḫarǧas und ihre Deutungen* (Niemeyer, 1960); Josep Maria Sola-Solé, *Corpus de lírica mozárabe* (Hispam, 1973); Emilio García Gómez, *Las jarchas romances de la serie árabe en su marco*, 2d ed. (Seix Barral, 1975). For a bibliography, see Richard Hitchcock, *The Kharjas* (Grant and Cutler, 1977) and S. G. Armistead's update, "A Brief History of *Kharja* Studies," *Hispania*, 70 (1987), 8–15. The present selection, in general, follows Sola-Solé's readings, but in a number of cases prefers García Gómez's interpretation and in one instance (No. 215) rejects both in favor of a reading proposed by Joan Corominas (Heger No. 27).

D. GALICIAN-PORTUGUESE LYRICS

When the Romans brought Latin to Spain, they created the basis for modern Spanish, which evolved largely from the Castilian dialect of north central Spain. But that was not the only Romance language to evolve in the north. In northwestern Galicia and what is now Portugal, there existed the influential dialect of Galician-Portuguese. The second king of Portugal, Sancho I, probably wrote No. 223, and the important Denis I wrote Nos. 234 to 236. Even Alfonso X (the Wise) of Castile wrote some of his major works in this language (Nos. 225, 226).

Early Portuguese lyrics have a folkloric quality that is related to dances. Women are often used as the primary voice, even in poems composed by men, in a genre known as the *cantiga de amigo* (Nos. 223, 229–234), which may have been influenced by the troubadour Raimbaut of Vaqueiras (No. 82). Songs sung by women anxious about their lovers' departures at sea produced the form known as a *marinha*, as in the samples by Martin Codax (Nos. 230–232). Love songs sung by men were called *cantigas de amor* (Nos. 228, 236).

Eventually a strong Provençal influence was felt, as can be seen in King Denis's No. 236. There also evolved local forms of the *sirventes* (satire), which were called *cantigas de maldizer* when directed against an individual

(No. 235) or *cantigas de escarnio* against a group (No. 225). Other forms like the alba also appeared, but not in great numbers. Eventually the language, disappearing from Galicia as Spanish rose in ascendance, became the national language of Portugal. See Frede Jensen, *The Earliest Portuguese Lyrics* (Odense U. Press, 1978).

E. CASTILIAN LYRICS

Although the Castilian dialect became the national language of Spain, its early developments were more noted for narrative and epic works, like *The Cid* and *The Book of Good Love*, a poetic miscellany by Juan Ruiz that presents a mosaic of Spanish culture. One notable indigenous lyric form is the *serrana* or song about a mountain girl, of which two samples are offered here (Nos. 241, 243). Much of the poetry is religious, as No. 237 by Gonzalo de Berceo shows—a poem that is also striking for its anti-Semitism.

F. CATALAN LYRICS

Catalan is a Romance language spoken in an area that extends from the southwestern corner of France to about half way down the Mediterranean coast of what is now Spain. More conservative than Castilian ("Spanish"), it is most closely related to Provençal. The first Latin texts that contain recognizably Catalan forms date from the ninth century and the first documents entirely in Catalan date from the eleventh century. The troubadour culture easily crossed the Pyrenees into the Principality of Catalonia by about 1160.

Some two hundred Provençal poems by Catalan troubadours survive from the twelfth and thirteenth centuries. Though Catalan literary prose, which began with a collection of sermons around 1200, emerged with Ramon Llull into its own linguistic and stylistic independence around 1270, the Catalan lyric did not reach full independence from Provençal models until Ausias March. The great promise of the Catalan Renaissance, phased in from around 1380–1425, was cut off by the political and socio-economic developments that led to the joining of Catalan-Aragonese and Castilian lands under Ferdinand and Isabella.

A. ARABIC LYRICS
(Translated by James T. Monroe)

ASH-SHARĪF AṬ-ṬALĪQ

[200]

1 A branch which sways on a rounded sand dune, and from which my heart gathers [a harvest of] fire,

2 [Is such that] beauty causes a never-waning moon to arise from his face.

3 He charms us with the intensely white and black eyes of a white antelope whose glance is an arrow notched [to be aimed] at my heart;

4 He smiles from a necklace of pearls, so that I thought he wrested it from our necks [to adorn] his mouth.

5 The *lām* described by the hair of his temples flowed down over his cheek as gold flows over silver plate.

6 Thus beauty reached its maximum proportions in him, for a branch becomes beautiful only when it has borne leaves.

7 His waist is so slender that I thought, from the degree of its thinness, that it was madly in love.

8 It is as though the hips had caught [the waist] in love's snares so that the latter had become troubled and anxious over the former.

· · · · · · · · · · · · · · · · · ·

11 Many a cup which dressed the wing of gloom with a tunic of light which shone from its flash,

12 Did I spend the night offering to drink to a young gazelle in whose glance there was a sleepy languour the sight of my eye kept awake.

13 [The cup] hid itself from the eye until I thought that it feared from his glance what was feared [by us].

14 [Then] it shone in a certain pure [receptacle] consisting of the palm of his hand, like the sun's rays as they meet the dawn.

15 It is as though the cup, in his fingers, were a yellow narcissus rising from a silver [vase],

16 Which arose like a sun, his mouth being the West, and the hand of the shy cupbearer, the East,

17 So that when it set in his mouth, it left a [rosy] twilight on his cheek.

· · · · · · · · · · · · · · · · · ·

34 What noble youth is like me in courage and generosity, in word, in deed, and in piety?

200. ash-Sharīf at-Talīq (*ca.* 961–*ca.* 1009). Umayyad prince, imprisoned and freed by the conquering al-Mansur of Córdoba. Text: Monroe, No. 4. The man in line 38 is ʿAbd ar-Rahman III, first Caliph of Córdoba, and in line 40 the chief ancestor of the Umayyads.

35 My nobility is my own soul; my ornaments are my knowledge, and in the encounter my sword is my eloquence,

36 Because, for him who tries it, my tongue is a viper which no spells can avert.

37 My right hand is the good fortune of any destitute seeker after largesse; it joined a praise that had come to be scattered.

38 My grandfather is an-Nāṣir li-d-Dīn, he whose hands dispersed dispersal from him,

39 The noblest of the noble both in himself and in his ancestors when they rival with him in superiority, the loftiest in rank.

40 It is I who am the glory of the descendants of ᶜAbd ash-Shams, while by me the worn-out portion of their glory is renewed.

41 It is I who clothe in splendor the worn-out portion of their illustrious lineage with the ornaments of my resplendent poetry.

IBN ḤAZM

[201]

1 Are you from the world of the angels, or are you a mortal? Explain this to me, for inability [to reach the truth] has made a mockery of my understanding.

2 I see a human shape, yet if I use my mind, then the body is a celestial one.

3 Blessed be He who arranged the manner of being of His creation in such a way that you should be the only beautiful, natural light in it.

4 I have no doubt but that you are that spirit which a resemblance joining one soul to another in close relationship has directed toward us.

5 We lacked any proof that would bear witness to your creation, which we could use in comparison, save only that you are visible.

6 Were it not that our eye contemplates your essence we could only declare that you are the Sublime, True Reason.

[202]

1 I enjoy conversation when, in it, he is mentioned to me and exhales a scent of sweet ambergris for me.

2 If he should speak, among those who sit in my company, I listen only to the words of that marvelous charmer.

3 Even if the Prince of the Faithful should be with me, I would not turn aside from my love for the former.

201. Ibn Hazm al-Andalusī, Abū Muhammad ᶜAlī (994–1064). A native of the thriving capital of Córdoba, he was persecuted for his support of the Umayyad dynasty by the usurping Almoravides. His *Dove's Neck-Ring* resembles Dante's *Vita Nuova* in analyzing love with poetry containing strong Neoplatonic influences.

201–203. Texts: Monroe, 8C, D, F.

4 If I am compelled to leave him, I look back at him constantly and walk like [an animal] wounded in the hoof.

5 My eyes remain fixed firmly upon him though my body has departed, as the drowning man looks at the shore from the fathomless sea.

6 If I recall my distance from him, I choke as though with water, like the man who yawns in the midst of a dust storm and the sun's noonday heat.

7 And if you say: "It is possible to reach the sky," I reply: "Yes, and I know where the stairs may be found."

[203]

1 Men have observed that I am a youth driven desperate by love; that I am brokenhearted, profoundly disturbed. And yet, by whom?

2 When they look at my condition they become certain of it, yet if they inquire into the matter they are left in doubt.

3 I am like a handwriting whose trace is clear, but which, if they seek to interpret it, cannot be explained;

4 I am like the sound of a dove over a woody copse, cooing with its voice in every way,

5 Our ears delight in its melody, while its meaning remains obscure and unexplained.

6 They say: "By God, name the one whose love has driven sweet sleep from you!"

7 Yet I will never name him! Before they obtain what they seek, I will lose all my wits and face all misfortunes.

8 Thus will they ever remain prey to doubts, entertaining suspicion like certitude and certitude like suspicion.

IBN ḤAMDĪS

[204]

1 I remember a certain brook that offered the impiety of drunkenness to the topers sitting along its course, with cups of golden wine,

2 Each silver cup in it filled as though it contained the soul of the sun in the body of the full moon.

3 Whenever a glass reached anyone in our company of topers, he would grasp it gingerly with his ten fingers.

4 Then he drinks out of it a grape-induced intoxication which lulls his very senses without his realizing it.

204. Ibn Ḥamdīs, ʿAbd al-Jabbār ibn Abī Bakr ibn Muhammad al-Azdī (1058–1132). Fled his native Sicily after the Norman conquest, joining the court of al-Muʿtamid in Seville; fled the Almoravid conquest and died in Bougie, North Africa. A rousing Drinking Song; compare No. 27. Text: Monroe, No. 14.

5 He sends [the glass] back in the water, thus returning it to the hands of the cupbearer at whose will it had floated to him.

6 Because of the wine-bibbing we imagined our song to be melodies which the birds sang without verse,

7 While our cupbearer was the water which brought us wine without a hand, and our drink was a fire that shone without embers,

8 And which offered us delights of all kinds, while the only reward [of that cupbearer] for [giving us those delights] was that we offered him to the ocean to drink.

9 It is as if we were cities along the riverbank while the wineladen ships sailed [the stretch] between us,

10 For life is excusable only when we walk along the shores of pleasure and abandon all restraint!

IBN ARFA^c RA'SUH

[205]

1 The lute trills the most wondrous melodies
2 And the watercourses cut through the flower beds of the gardens.
3 The birds sing on the branches of the *bān*,
4 And joy enlivens the lions of the battlefield.
5 Every one of us is an emir and a sultan because of the wine.
6 The lute-strings speak with eloquent charm
7 While the birds respond to them from the myrtle branches.
8 Come, give me wine to drink for the garden exudes fragrance;
9 The Pleiads have set and it is sweet to take the morning drink
10 Offered to me by a lovely gazelle
11 Who is like a tender branch enveloped in a cloak of eglantine,
12 Whose sides are covered in embroidered silks, who almost breaks because he is so tender.

205. Ibn Arfa^c Ra'suh, Abū Bakr Muhammad; poet at the court of al-Ma'mūn ibn Dhī n-Nūn of Toledo (r. 1037–1075); subject of this panegyric *muwashshaha*. Text: Monroe, No. 19.

AL-AʿMÀ AT-TUṬĪLĪ

[206]

1 Laughing out of pearls,   A full moon appears
  Surpassing all Time   Though held in my heart;
2 Alas for my woe!   I pine in distress!
3 I danced to her tune;   A gentle assailant.
4 If I say: "At last,"   "How d'you know?" says she.
5 She sways like a willow   Green, supple, and fresh
  Which is teased by the hands   Of the breeze and the rain.
6 I cannot resist you: Take my heart in abasement.
7 A fresh spring of honey   Puts an end to the patience
8 Which I try to maintain;   My yearning bears witness
9 To the daughter of jugs   And to that sweet mouth.
  What's the face of all Time   To the flush of that wine?
10 All my love I conceal,   Would my efforts could end it!
11 When it starts to arise,   Its horizon's my heart.
12 That beautiful vision   Leaves my passion unhealed.
13 O, why, by my father,   Did a pearly bright star
   Shine forth and reveal   Her excuse and my plea?
14 Is there no way to you?   Must I always despair?
15 I wept not a little;   Tears flowed and I sighed;
16 I thought what to say;   "Perhaps" makes me sad,
17 Since all comes to nought.   Yet am I headstrong;
   I gallop loose reined,   Unbridling restraint.
18 It harms not my blamer   That she keeps avoiding,
19 Yet for the love of a doe   Whose habit's accusing
20 I'm possessed by despair,   While she sings this ditty:
21 "I see that you're pining;   I say, what's with you, man?
   You know Time will pass   And you will forget me."

206. "The Blind Poet of Tudela" (near Saragossa); born there (d. 1126), famous for his resigned melancholy. Text: Monroe, No. 24; *muwashshaha*. See No. 216 here.

WALLĀDA

---

[207] To Ibn Zaidun

(A)

Can't we find some way
to meet again
and speak our love?

In winter with you near
no need for coals—
our passion blazed.

Now—cut off, alone
day darkens deep
the fate I feared

Nights pass. You're still away
Longing chains me
and Patience brings no release

Where morning finds you
may God stream down upon your land
refreshing, fertile rain

(B)

Wait till the darkness is deep;
    be then my guest.
Night knows how to keep
    love's secret best.

The sun if it loved as I do
    would hide its light,
full moon not come into view
    stars not journey by night.

207. Wallāda (early 1000s). Female poet of whom little is known. Trans. by James T. Monroe and Deirdre Lashgari; reprinted from *Women Poets of the World*, ed. J. Bankier, D. Lashgari and D. Earnshaw (Macmillan, 1983), p. 98.

B. HEBREW LYRICS
(Translated by Miriam Billig)

SHLOMO IBN GVIROL (AVICEBRON)

---

[208] *Katav stav bidyo matarav oobiriveevav*

With the ink of his showers and rains,
And with the shining lightning of his pen and cloud's palm,
Autumn wrote a letter upon the garden, in purple and blue.
It was not possible for others to account for his thoughts.
Therefore, with the pen of lovely earth the face of heaven
embroidered as with his stars the fabric of the flower-beds.

YEHUDAH HALEVI

---

[209] *Ofra tichabes et bigdayha bimay*

The pretty maid washes her garments in the water
of my tears and spreads them in the sun of her splendor.
She asks for no spring water with both my eyes
And no sun for her radiant beauty.

[210] *Leebee bamizrach vianochee bisof ma'arav*

My heart is in the east and I am in the far west—
How can I taste what I eat and how can I enjoy it?

    208. Solomon Ben Judah Ibn Gabirol, called Avicebron and "the Jewish Plato" (*ca.* 1021–
ca. 1055). Born in Málaga, but traveled widely. His primary philosophical work, *The Well of
Life*, was written in Arabic, but, translated into Latin as *Fons Vitae*, was an important
Neoplatonic treatise. See *Penguin Book of Hebrew Verse*, ed. T. Carmi (Viking, 1981), p. 310.
    209–210. Judah HaLevi, Halevy (1075?–1140?). Rabbi and philosopher born in Toledo,
but traveled widely; reportedly killed by an Arab horseman outside the gates of Jerusalem.
Famous for his *Ode to Zion*. See also Poems 218–220. Text: *Selected Poems*, ed. H. Brody
(Jewish Pub. Society, 1924), pp. 51, 2.

How will I fulfill my oaths and vows while
Zion is in Edom's snare and I in Arab chains?
To me it appears easy to leave all which is good in Spain,
As prized it would be to behold the dust of the ravaged
Sanctuary.

MOSHE IBN EZRA

[211] *Shte achi vihasheknee aday-chee*

Drink, my brother and toast with me until
My heart defends the cup of lamentation in your hand,
And if I die before your eyes
Revive me quickly like when the minstrel plays.

[212] *Ayey kivarot eesheem maytoo*

Where are the graves of people who have died
On earth since ancient days?
Grave carved over grave,
Slumberer laid over slumberer,
In dusty holes limestones
with precious red stones dwell together.

211. Moshe Ibn Ezra (*ca.* 1055–*ca.* 1138). Native of Granada, wrote poetry in his youth and philosophy later. Called "The Poet of Contrition" for his penitential verses, many of which are still used today. See *Selected Poems* (Jewish Pub. Society, 1945), pp. 42 and 58.

C. MOZARABIC *KHARJAS*
(Translated and edited by Samuel G. Armistead and James J. Wilhelm)

YŌSEF AL-KĀTIB

[213] *Tanto amare, tanto amare*

Tanto amare, tanto amare, / ḥabīb, tanto amare:
¡Enfermeron welyos nidioš / e dolen tan male!

So much loving, so much loving, / my lover, so much loving
Has made bright eyes grow dim / and suffer so much!

MUḤAMMAD IBN ʿUBĀDA AL-QAZZĀZ AL-MĀLAQĪ

[214] *Mio sīdī Ibrāhīm*

Mio sīdī Ibrāhīm, / yā nuemne dolǧe!
Fen-te mib, / de noḥte.
In non, si non keris, / irey-me tib.
Gar-me a ob plegar-te.

My lord Ibrāhīm, / O sweet name!
    Come to me at night!
If not, if you don't want to, / I shall come to you.
    Tell me where can I find you?

213. Joseph the Scribe (first half of the 1000s; Jewish). Panegyric to Abū-Ibrāhīm Šemūel and his brother Isḥāq. Sources: García Gómez 18; Heger 18; Sola-Solé 1.
214. Muḥammad ibn ʿUbāda, the Silk Merchant of Málaga (second half of the 1000s; Muslim). Sources: García Gómez 1; Heger 22; Sola-Solé 11.

[215] *Al sa'amu mio ḥālī*

Al sa'amu mio ḥālī, / porqe ḥālī qad bāre.
¿Ké farey, yā ummī? /¡Fāneq [me] bad lebare!

My condition is death, / because it's so desperate.
What can I do, O mother? / The falcon will carry me off!

ABŪ-L-ᶜABBĀS AL-AᶜMÀ AT-TUṬĪLĪ

[216] *Yā maṭre mia al-raḥīma*

Yā maṭre mia al-raḥīma, / a rayyo de manyana:
¡Bon Abū-l-Ḥağğāğ, / la fağe de matrana!

O my affectionate mother, / in the light of day:
The good Abū-l-Ḥağğāğ, / his face like the dawn!

IBN HĀRŪN AL-AṢBĀḤĪ AL-LĀRIDĪ

[217] *Non dormireyo, mamma*

Non dormireyo, mamma, / a rayo de manyana:
¡Bon Abū-l-Qāsim, / la fağe de matrana!

Mother, I shall not sleep, / in the light of day:
The good Abū-l-Qāsim, / his face like the dawn!

215. The comparison of a lover/beloved with a hawk/dove is frequent in the traditional lyric. There are close counterparts to this *kharja* in Castilian and in Galician-Portuguese. Sources: García Gómez 6; Heger 27; Sola-Solé 13.
216. The Blind Poet of Tudela (d. 1126; Muslim). Panegyric to Abū-l-Ḥajjāj. Sources: García Gómez XIX; Heger 36; Sola-Solé 25A. See No. 206 here.
217. Ibn Hārūn al-Aṣbāḥī of Lérida (before 1155?; Muslim). Note the similarity to No. 216: *kharjas* were sometimes borrowed from earlier compositions and adapted to new contexts. Sources: García Gómez 17; Heger 36; Sola-Solé 25B.

ABŪ-L-ḤASAN YEHŪDĀ
BEN ŠEMŪEL HALEVĪ

[218] Gare ¿šoš debina

Gare ¿šoš debina / e debinaš bi-l-ḥaqq?
Gar-me kánd me bernad / meu ḥabībī Isḥāq.

Tell me, are you a prophetess / and can truly predict?
Tell me when my lover / Isḥāq will come to me.

[219]

Deš kand meu Sidiello bénid, / ¡tan bona al-bišāra!
¡Kom raya de šole éšid / en Wād-al-ḥaǧāra!

When my Cidiello appears, / such good news!
Like a ray of sun he comes forth / in Guadalajara!

[220]

Garid boš, ay yermanellaš, / ¿kóm kontenere meu male?
Sin al-ḥabīb non bibreyo / ed bolarey demandare.

Tell me, O my little sisters, / how can I bear my pain?
I can't live without my lover; / I shall fly away to find him!

218. Yehudah HaLevi (ca. 1075–ca. 1140). The most famous Jewish poet of the period; see Nos. 209 and 210. Panegyric for Abū Ibrāhīm Isḥāq ibn al-Muhājir. Sources: García Gómez 2; Heger 2; Sola-Solé 31.

219. Panegyric for Yōsef ibn Ferrusiel, nicknamed the Little Cid (Lord), an influential Jew in the court of Alfonso VI. This song of welcome is unique among the kharjas; it reflects contemporary medieval practice: the entire populace of a town would go out to greet a visiting dignitary, playing musical instruments and singing songs of praise. Sources: García Gómez 3; Heger 3; Sola-Solé 32.

220. Panegyric for Isḥāq ibn Qrispín. The verses are similar to many Galician-Portuguese lyrics, where a girl speaks to her sisters or friends of her own age. Sources: García Gómez 4; Heger 4; Sola-Solé 33.

ANONYMOUS

[221] *Mamma, ¡ayy ḥabībe!*

Mamma, ¡ayy ḥabībe! / So al-ǧummella šaqrella,
el-quwello albo / e bokella ḥamrella.

O mother, what a lover! / Below his yellow curls,
his white neck / and his little red mouth!

[222] *¡Amānu, yā ḥabībī!*

¡Amānu, yā ḥabībī! / Al-waḥš me no faráš.
Ben, beǧa mia bokella: / awšak tú no iráš.

Mercy, my lover! / I know you won't abandon me.
Come, kiss my little mouth / and you won't soon run away!

D. GALICIAN-PORTUGUESE LYRICS
(Translated by James J. Wilhelm)

KING SANCHO I OF PORTUGAL

[223] *Ai eu coitado*

1. I'm so distressed!
   I live with such great anguish
   For my friend
   Who has gone away!

221. The *kharja* concludes an anonymous Arabic *muwashshaha*. Sources: García Gómez 14; Heger 33; Sola-Solé 51.
222. Anonymous Arabic *muwashshaha*. Sources: García Gómez 23; Heger 39; Sola-Solé 53.
223. Also called Sanchez el Velho, "the Old" (1154–1211). The son of the founding Alfonso Henriques, he proclaimed himself king of Portugal-Algarve in 1185, and held it to his death. This song, not attributed to him in manuscripts, has nevertheless been considered his by many, who say that he wrote it after 1199, when he founded the border town of Guarda, for Maria Paes Ribeira, his favorite mistress. Text in Frede Jensen, *The Earliest Portuguese Lyrics* (Odense U., 1978), p. 17.

He is much too late,   5
That friend of mine in Guarda!

2. I'm so distressed!
I live with such great passion
For my friend
Who's late, whom I don't see!   10
He is much too late,
That friend of mine in Guarda!

NUNO FERNÁNDEZ TORNEOL

---

[224] *Levad', amigo que dormides as manhanas frias*

1. Rise up, my friend, sleeping in the chilly morn;
All the birds of the world once spoke of love.
    I'm going now with joy!

2. Rise up, my friend, asleep in the morning chill;
All the birds of the world have sung of love.   5
    I'm going now with joy!

3. All the birds of the world have spoken of love;
They have kept in mind this love of yours and mine;
    I'm going now with joy!

4. All the birds of this world have sung of love,   10
Have remembered this love of yours and mine.
    I'm going now with joy!

5. Both my love and yours they truly kept in mind—
But you cut all the branches where they sat.
    I'm going now with joy!   15

6. They have sung about this love of yours and mine;
You cut the very branches where they perched.
    I'm going now with joy!

224. Nuno Fernández Torneol (dates unknown). Served a rich patron with whom he visited Galicia. His Dawn Song here, relatively rare in this literature, attacks the lover rather than the dawn and is interesting for its mysterious symbolism. Text: *Antología de la poesía gallego-portuguesa*, ed. Carlos Alvar and Vicente Beltrán (Alhambra, 1985), No. 170.

7. You tore away the branches where they sat;
   You dried up the fountains where they drank;   20
       I'm going now with joy!

8. You tore away the branches where they perched
   And dried up all the fountains where they bathed.
       I'm going now with joy!

ALFONSO X, THE WISE, OF CASTILE AND LEÓN

[225] *O que foi passar a serra*

1. He who passed over the mountains
   And did not want to serve on the plain—
   Is he the one, when war was returned,
       Who's now bragging?
   Since he vacillates so much now,   5
       Let him be damned!

2. He who doled out his money
   Without attracting any good knights—
   Is it because he wasn't first in the fight
       That he's bragging now?   10
   Since he came at us with his rear,
       Let him be damned!

3. He who raised a great soldiery
   But never quite a good cavalry,
   Since he didn't go to Granada, is he   15
       The one who's bragging?
   Whether he's rich or has a strong band,
       Let him be damned!

4. He who loaded up his bags
   With a little gold and a lot of guff,   20
   And never quite entered the town of Vega,
       Is he bragging now?

225. Alfonso el Sabio, "the Wise" (1221–1284), ruled 1252–1284. In 1264 the Moorish King of Granada raised a rebellion, but in 1265 Alfonso forced him to sign a truce at Vega. This *cantiga de escarnio* (Satire) is directed against Spanish traitors who joined the Moors. Ed. Alvar-Beltrán, No. 52.

Since he's more like fat than butter,
  Let him be damned!

[226] From the *Cantigas de Santa Maria:*
Rosa de beldad'e de parecer

1. Rose of beauty and fine appearance
   And flower of happiness and pleasure,
   Lady of most merciful bearing,
   And Lord for relieving all woes and cares;
     Rose of roses and flower of flowers,   5
     Lady of ladies, Lord of lords.

2. Such a Mistress everybody should love,
   For she can ward away any evil
   And she can pardon any sinner
   To create a better savor in this world.   10
     Rose of roses and flower of flowers . . .

3. We should love and serve her loyally,
   For she can guard us from falling;
   She makes us repent the errors
   That we have committed as sinners: 15
     Rose of roses and flower of flowers . . .

4. This Lady whom I acknowledge as my Master
   And whose troubadour I'd gladly be,
   If I could in any way possess her love,
   I'd give up all my other lovers.   20
     Rose of roses and flower of flowers . . .

AIRAS NUNES

[227] *Bailemos nós ja todas tres, ay amigas*

1. Let's all three dance together, dear friends,
   Under these blossoming hazel-trees,

226. Alfonso wrote or organized the *Songs of St. Mary*, a collection of poems in honor of
the Virgin, often longish narratives relating her miracles. One of the most important music
collections in the Middle Ages, the songs were often sung on pilgrimages. Text for this poem
in Alvar-Beltrán, pp. 423–424; music, 441. For a tape of the *Cantigas*, Astrée E7707.

227. Or Ayras Nunez (*fl.* 1284–1289). Served in the court of King Sancho IV of Castile.
Fewer than 20 poems survive, but of high quality, like this rousing Dance Song. Text: Alvar-
Beltrán, No. 165.

And any girl as pretty as we, my lovelies,
    If she loves a friend
Under these blossoming hazel-trees   5
    Will come to dance!

2. Let's all three dance together, dear friends,
Under the branches of these hazels,
And any girl pretty as we, my pretties,
    If she loves a friend   10
Under these blossoming hazel-trees
    Will come to dance!

3. By God, dear friends, let's do only this,
Let's dance beneath this blossoming branch,
And whoever looks as good as we look,   15
    If she loves a friend
Under this branch under which we dance
    Will come to dance!

JOAN ZORRO

[228] *En Lixboa sóbre lo mar*

1. In Lisbon above the sea
I ordered new galleons built—
    Ah, my beautiful lady!

2. In Lisbon above the strand
I ordered new galleons made—   5
    Ah, my beautiful lady!

3. New galleons I ordered built
And then placed on the sea—
    Ah, my beautiful lady!

4. New galleons I ordered made   10
And then launched on their way—
    Ah, my beautiful lady!

228. Jo(h)an Zorro (nothing known of life). Probably from Lisbon, as this Love Song (*cantiga de amor*) suggests. Text in Alvar-Beltrán, No. 159.

[229] *Cabelos, los meus cabelos*

1. "Tresses, my tresses—
   The King has sent for them.
   Mother, what shall I do?"
       "Daughter, give them to the King."

2. "Ringlets, my ringlets—   5
   The King has sent for them.
   Mother, what shall I do?"
       "Daughter, give them to the King."

MARTIN CODAX

[230] *Ondas do mar de Vigo*

1. Waves of the sea of Vigo,
   Have you seen my dear friend?
   O God, if only he'd come soon!

2. Waves of the stormy sea,
   Have you seen my loved one?   5
   O God, if only he'd come soon!

3. Have you seen my friend,
   The man for whom I yearn?
   O God, if only he'd come soon!

4. Have you seen my lover,   10
   For whom I worry so?
   O God, if only he'd come soon!

229. *Cantiga de amigo*, like 11 of Joan's 12 poems. Text in Alvar-Beltrán, No. 162.

230. Or Martim Codax (dates unknown), presumably a Galician with a strange name (Codex?). Wrote only *cantigas de amigo*, often with a marine background (*marinha*), like this and the poem that follows. The only *cantiga de amigo* composer whose music survives: see Alvar-Beltrán, p. 432; text from Jensen, *Earliest Portuguese Lyrics*, p. 65. For music: EMI Electrola C 063-30118 and Hyperion, CDA 66283.

Plate 9. The city and harbor of Vigo, now in Galician Spain. It was immortalized in two *marinhas* by Martin Codax (Nos. 230 and 231). (Courtesy of the Tourist Office of Spain)

[231] *Mia irmana fremosa, treides comigo*

1. My lovely sister, come along with me
   To the Church of Vigo, where the tide is out,
      And let us gaze at the waves.

2. My lovely sister, come very happily
   To the Church of Vigo by the stormy sea,   5
   And let us gaze at the waves.

3. Where the tide is out, by the Vigo Church,
   My dear friend, O mother, will be coming,
      And we shall gaze at the waves.

4. At the Church of Vigo above the stormy sea,   10
   It is there, dear mother, my lover will be,
      And we shall gaze at the waves.

MEENDINHO

[232] *Sedia-m'eu na ermida de San Simion*

1. I was at the sanctuary of San Simón
   As the waves, which were huge, began encircling me,
   Yet I waited for my friend, / I waited for my friend.

2. I was standing at the shrine before the altar
   As the great waves of the sea encircled me.   5
   Yet I waited for my friend, / I waited for my friend.

3. The waves kept circling me, and they were huge,
   And I didn't have a helmsman or an oarsman.
   Yet I waited for my friend, / I waited for my friend.

4. Yes, the waves of the high sea kept circling me,   10
   And I didn't have a helmsman and couldn't row,
   Yet I waited for my friend, / I waited for my friend.

231. The first two stanzas could be spoken by the girl to a friend or by the beloved to the girl. For Vigo, see Plate 9. Music in Alvar-Beltrán (*Mia yrmana fremosa*), p. 433; text from Jensen, p. 64.

232. Meendinho (dates unknown). The Spanish scholar Ramón Menéndez Pidal placed the scene of his only surviving poem as the tiny island of S. Simão in the Vigo River. Ed. Alvar-Beltrán, No. 152.

5. No, I didn't have a helmsman or a rower,
   And I thought I'd die in beauty on the rising sea,
   Yet I waited for my friend, / I waited for my friend.   15

6. I don't have a helmsman, and I can't row,
   And I think I'll die in beauty on the high sea,
   Yet I'm waiting for my friend, / I'm waiting for my friend.

PERO MEOGO

[233] *Digades, filha, mia filha velida*

1. "Tell me, daughter, my pretty daughter,
   Why did you linger by the cool brook?"
   I have a love,

2. "Tell me, daughter, my lovely daughter,
   Why did you linger by the cool stream?"   5
   I have a love.

3. "My mother, I lingered by the cool brook
   Because the stags from the hills muddied the water."
   I have a love.

4. "My mother, I lingered beside the cool stream   10
   As the stags from the hills came there to drink."
   I have a love.

5. "You're lying, my daughter—lying for a friend!
   I never saw any stag muddy the water."
   I have a love.   15

6. "You're lying, my daughter—lying for a lover!
   I never saw any stag muddy the river bank."
   I have a love.

233. "Peter the Monk," although the name Meogo can be familial (sometimes identified with a cleric of the mid-1200s). His 9 *cantigas de amigo* often contain the image of the deer at the fountain, which has been treated as either primitive or biblical (Song of Songs). The refrain here seems internalized in the girl's mind. Text in Jensen, p. 89.

KING DENIS I OF PORTUGAL

[234] *Ai flores, ai flores do verde pino*

1. "O flowers, yes flowers of the green pine,
   Do you have any news about my friend?
   O God, where is he?

2. "O flowers, yes flowers of the green branch,
   Do you have any news about my love?   5
   O God, where is he?

3. "Do you have any news about my friend,
   The one who lied in his words to me?
   O God, where is he?

4. "Do you have any news about my love,   10
   The one who lied in his pledge to me?
   O God, where is he?"

5. "You ask about your boyfriend?
   I can tell you he's well and alive."
   O God, where is he?   15

6. "You ask about your lover?
   I can tell you he's alive and well."
   O God, where is he?

7. "I tell you truly that he's well and alive,
   And will be back with you before the set time."   20
   O God, where is he?

8. "I tell you truly that he's alive and well,
   And will be with you before that date has passed."
   O God, where is he?

[235] *Joan Bol' anda mal desbaratado*

1. John Bolo's acting very broken down
   And aggravated and rightly anguished
   Because he lost everything he had earned
   And everything his mother left him:

234. Or Dom Dinis (b. Oct. 9, 1261; d. Jan. 7, 1325), leader of Portuguese lyric poetry; his 138 poems are exceeded only by Alfonso X. Wrote 52 *cantigas de amigo*; in this one, natural forces speak. Text in Alvar-Beltrán, No. 186.

235. Sample of *cantiga de maldizer*, Satire like the Provençal *sirventes*. John Bolo, criticized by Denis elsewhere, is unknown. Text in Alvar-Beltrán, No. 192.

A young guy who acted as his servant 5
Filched his nag, leaving him his mule.

2. If the mule had been stolen instead
   And the nag left to John Bolo,
   It wouldn't have hurt so much, I think,
   And wouldn't have seemed such a loss; 10
   But the young guy, to cause him pain,
   Filched his nag, leaving him his mule.

3. If that young guy who filched his nag
   Had lifted the mule instead
   Which he left for our John Bolo, 15
   John wouldn't have whimpered the way
   He did in all the streets;
   But the young guy, hoping to cause him pain,
   Filched his nag, leaving him his mule.

[236*] *Quer' eu en maneira de proençal*

1. Now in the Provençal manner
   I'd like to write a song of love.
   And I'd like to praise Milordess,
   Who lacks nothing in nobility, beauty
   Or goodness. I'll tell you more about her: 5
   God created her so beautifully that
   She's worth more than any other worldly woman.

2. God wanted to create Milordess here
   So that when he had finished, he had made
   Her a knower of all virtue and value, 10
   And with all this she is very widely known
   As should be; he gave her good sense
   And this was no small favor,
   So that nobody could surpass her.

3. God put nothing wrong in her, 15
   But a great deal of worth, beauty and praise,
   Along with fine speech and a better smile
   Than any other woman has; and so she
   Is very loyal, and therefore I don't know
   Anyone to whom I can completely describe 20
   Her good qualities, since they exceed all others.

236. Love Song (*cantiga de amor*) in clear imitation of the Provençal *canso*. The word Milordess, *mha senhor* (8), imitates *midons*.
   *Original text appears in Section IX, taken from Frede Jensen, *Earliest Portuguese Lyrics*, p. 47.

E. CASTILIAN LYRICS

GONZALO DE BERCEO

---

[237] From the *Lament of the Virgin:*
Tornaron al sepulchro vestidos de lorigas

(The Jews, sent by Pilate, go to guard the sepulcher of Christ.
The watchmen's song:)

They went back to the tomb wearing their coats of mail,
Mumbling many foul insults with their mouths,
Letting loose songs that were not worth three figs,
Playing their instruments: zithers, harps, and viols.

Those ruffians were singing some rhymed verses   5
That were harsh and cruel against the Mother:
"Let us keep watch, you Jews, let's move carefully;
If we don't, they'll mock and scorn us!"

Song

Eya, keep watch; eya, keep watch; eya, keep watch!

Keep watch, you band of Jews—eya, keep watch!   10
So that nobody can steal the Son of God—eya, keep watch!
For they will try to take him away from you—eya, keep watch!
Andrew and Peter and John—eya, keep watch!
You'll never again get any rest—eya, keep watch!
Or be able to crawl out from under a stone—eya, keep watch!   15
All of them are little thieves—eya, keep watch!
Who keep peeping through any keyhole—eya, keep watch!
Your tongue that's far too talkative—eya, keep watch!
Has carried you on a bad course—eya, keep watch!
They are all a mangy crew—eya, keep watch!   20
Of mongrels thoroughly bastardized—eya, keep watch!
Your tongue, which knows no censure,—eya, keep watch!
Has led you to a bad end—eya, keep watch!
You don't know enough tricks—eya, keep watch!

---

237. Gonzalo de Berceo (*ca.* 1195–after 1246), author of many saints' lives and the *Duelo de la Virgen,* from which these extracts were taken: Ramón Menéndez Pidal, *Crestomatía del español medieval,* rev. ed. (U. Madrid, 1965), I, Nos. 39, 176 ff.

To slip your way out of prison—eya, keep watch! 25
You don't have enough good sense—eya, keep watch!
To escape by this year's end—eya, keep watch!
Both Thomas and Matthew—eya, keep watch!
Are very eager to steal him—eya, keep watch!
One disciple already sold him—eya, keep watch! 30
Without the Master even understanding—eya, keep watch!
Don Philip and Simon Peter and Judas—eya, keep watch!
Are looking for helpers for their theft—eya, keep watch!
If they want to finish the job—eya, keep watch!
This is the day for it to happen—eya, keep watch! 35

Eya, keep watch; eya, keep watch; eya, keep watch!

While they were boasting and cracking villainous jokes,
Uttering disgusting things with massive insults,
The Lord of Heaven grieved over all the nonsense
That they spoke about his Christ and his companions. 40

THREE ANONYMOUS SONGS FROM THE *CANCIONEROS*

[238] *No quiero ser monja, no*

I do not wish to be a nun, no!
Because I'm a girl in love.

Leave me to my pleasure,
to my pleasure and my happiness.
Leave me to my stubborn ways 5
Because I'm a lovesick girl.

[239] *A los baños del amor*

To the baths of lovers
I shall go alone
And bathe myself within them,

So that I may heal this sickness
That misfortune has brought on me, 5

238–240. Selections from *Songbooks* of the 1400s and later, but showing a much earlier folk spirit.

An illness that is so grievous
It is destroying my looks.
To the baths of sadness
I shall go alone
And bathe myself within them.   10

[240] *Tres morillas me enamoran*

Three Moorish girls in Jaén
Have attracted me: Axa, Fátima and Marién.

Three very pretty Moorish girls
Were going to pluck some olives,
But found themselves plucked instead   5
In Jaén: Axa, Fátima and Marién.

Yes, they found themselves plucked
And they returned dismayed,
With their coloring all lost
In Jaén: Axa, Fátima and Marién.   10

Three very lively Moorish women,
Yes three very lively Moorish women
Were going to pick some apples
In Jaén: Axa, Fátima and Marién.

JUAN RUIZ, ARCHPRIEST OF HITA

[241] Serrana from *The Book of Good Love: Cerca la Tablada*

1. By Tablada, / having left the mountains, / I met Alda / at the break of dawn.
2. At the top of the pass / I thought I would die / from the snow and the cold / and the ice / and the terrible frost.
3. On the decline, / I ran downhill; / I met this mountain girl / who was pretty and lively / and had a good hue.
4. I said to her: / "Greetings, beautiful!" / She replied: "You run very nicely, / so don't stop here; / keep right on going!"

241. Juan Ruiz (1283?–1350?), Archpriest of Hita near Guadalajara, imprisoned by the Archbishop of Toledo. From 1330 to 1343 wrote his *Libro de Buen Amor*, a poetic miscellany of 1728 lines with religious and secular verse (trans. R. Mignani and M. A. Di Cesare, SUNY Press, 1970). This *serrana* (Song of the Mountain Girl) was a popular form in Spain. Text: Paden, *Medieval Pastourelle*, II, No. 181.

5. I said to her: "I'm cold; / that's why I've come here / to you, my lovely; / I beg you to give me / lodging out of kindness."

6. The girl replied: / "My friend, / he who shacks up with me / has to marry me / and give me some coins."

7. I said: "That's fine, / but I have a wife / here in Herreros; / but, my darling, / I can still pay you a little something."

8. She answered: "Then come along!" / She took me home / and lighted a nice fire, / as is the custom / up in those snow-capped hills.

9. She also gave me some gritty bread, / which was dark and sooty, / and some low-grade wine / that was bitter and watery, / and some salted meat.

10. And she served me some goat cheese. / "Good sir," said she, / "stretch out your arm / and take a piece of this bread / that I keep stored up."

11. She continued: "Eat, my dear guest, / and drink and feel refreshed; / warm yourself and then you can pay; / and may you forever be safe from harm / until you return.

12. "A man who gives me / all I ask for / will get a good meal / and enjoy a nice bed / and it won't cost a thing."

13. "Well, why don't you / tell me precisely / what you want?" She replied: "Indeed! / Will you be so kind?

14. "Then give me a belt / of dark-tinted red / and a nice-looking shift / of just the right size / with a fancy collar.

15. "And give me a full string / of bright tin beads, / as well as some jewels / that have a real value, / and a fancy fur.

16. "And give me a nice hood / with elegant stripes, / and give me a pair / of good high boots / finely crafted of leather.

17. "With treasures like these, / I can quite assure you / that you'll come out well. / You'll be my husband / and I your wife."

18. "Lady of the Mountains, / it just so happens / I don't have these things with me, / but I'll promise you them / when I return."

19. The ugly thing then replied: / "Where there isn't any cash, / there isn't any deal, / and the day turns sour, / and the credit comes dear.

20. "I don't know any decent merchant / who goes around without some kind of cash; / I'm not at all kind / to those who have nothing, / and I don't put them up!

21. "You can't pay a hostelry bill / with sweet-talking words; / but with a little money / you can get all you want. / That's the way it goes."

DIEGO HURTADO DE MENDOZA

[242] *Aquel árbol que buelbe la foxa*

1. Something has taken hold
   Of that tree that is moving its leaves.

2. Something has taken hold
   Of that tree with the beautiful shape
   That seems to want to bear flowers.   5

3. Something has taken hold
   Of that tree with the beautiful look
   That seems to want to flower.

4. It seems to want to bear flowers—
   And now they're appearing. Come out and look!   10
   Something has taken hold of that tree.

5. It seems to want to flower—
   And now it does. Come out and see!
   Something has taken hold of that tree.

6. Now it's flowering. Come out and look!   15
   Let ladies come to cut away the fruit.
   Something has taken hold of that tree.

242. Diego Hurtado de Mendoza, High Admiral of Castile (*ca.* 1364–1404). Few poems survive besides this *cosante*, Round Dance. Father of the Marqués de Santillana. Text: Menéndez Pidal, II, No. 130.

IÑIGO LÓPEZ DE MENDOZA, MARQUÉS DE SANTILLANA

[243] *Moçuela de Bores*

1. A little lass from Bores / over beyond Lama / made me fall in love.

2. I thought that love / had forgotten me, / like one who long before / has utterly abandoned / that discomfort, / which burns all lovers / worse than any flame.

3. But then I noticed her beauty / with her elegant bearing, / her pleasing face, / as fresh as a rose, / with a complexion / never seen on any lady, / my lords, / or on anyone else.

4. And so I said to her: / "Milady, in all truth / your excellent beauty / will be known from now on / beyond these hills / because it merits the fame / produced by high praise."

5. She replied: "My dear knight, / please take yourself away; / let this cowgirl / go on up the hill, / since two workers from Frama / have asked for my hand— / both of them shepherds."

6. "Milady, I can become / a shepherd if you ask me; / you can order me around / like a common servant. / The bellowings of bulls / will sound sweeter to me / than the calls of nightingales."

7. And so we concluded / our little discussion / without going too far, / and we reached an agreement; / and the flowers / that blanket Espinama / were our gentle cover.

---

243. The Marquis of Santillana (1398–1458). Courtier born near Burgos to Hurtado de Mendoza. Imitated Italian styles, but excelled in the *serrana* or Song of the Mountain Girl as here. Text: Paden, *Medieval Pastourelle*, II, No. 194.

F. CATALAN LYRICS
(Translated by Nathaniel B. Smith)

RAMON LLULL

---

[244] D'esperança

When at daybreak the dawn-star appears
And all the flowers prepare themselves
For the sun to multiply their colors
    With rays of hope,
Happiness dresses me   5
In a sweetness that is the faith
    I have in the Lady of Love;
Then I ask to make confession
And admit my sins to all,
    And may my confessor order   10
Me to repair the great
Harm my sins have done
    Against those who serve
The Queen of Virtue
Whose help I hope to have,   15
    So that in sin
I'll not be trapped
As long as I'm well confessed.

244. Ramon Llull (1233?–1315 or 1316), known in English as Raymond Lully, wrote troubadour-like verse as a young man but after a mystical conversion became a prolific author of religious treatises, lyrics, and novels. His 250 or so surviving books include the *Book of the Lover and the Beloved*. His missionary efforts came to an end when he was stoned to death in Algeria. This selection, "On Hope," from the 6000-line *Medicine for Sin*, written more in Provençal than in Catalan, uses some of the troubadours' favorite images in a didactic and spiritual cause. Text: Joan Triadú, *Anthology of Catalan Lyric Poetry* (Oxford: Dolphin, 1953), p. 5.

THE QUEEN OF MALLORCA

[245] E-z ieu am tal que es bo e bell

1. I love one who's good and handsome;
   I'm as happy as the white bird
   Who, for love, bursts out in song;
   I am a sovereign lady,
   And let him I love make no appeal,   5
   Because I love more than any other woman,
   Since I have chosen him of greatest worth,
   The best in the world; I love him so
   That in my mind I think I see him
           And hold him close;   10
           But this is not true,
   And great despair sweeps over me
           When I realize he's away in France.

2. My longing and the great desire
   I have for you have all but killed me,   15
   My sweet, beloved lord;
   I could easily die ere long
   Because of you whom I love and want so much,
   If I don't see you soon return:
   I'm so impatient for our kisses,   20
           Our intimate talks,
           And all the rest.
   When I think of how you went away
           And haven't come back
           And how far away you are,   25
   My despairing heart barely beats:
           I'm as good as dead
           If I'm not cured fast!

3. Have pity, husband; in pain I endure
   The sufferings you give me: please return!   30
           No treasure
           Is worth a heart
           That dies for you
           With loving thought.

245. The sole extant manuscript attributes this poem to "The Queen of Mallorca," who is traditionally identified as Constance (died 1346), wife of James III, last king of the Catalan-speaking island kingdom of Mallorca. However, the poet is more probably Violant, who married James in 1347. James's business in France included selling his domain of Montpellier to France to finance his unsuccessful attempt to regain possession of Mallorca, where he died in battle. Text: *Ocho siglos de poesía catalana*, ed. J. M. Castellet and Joaquim Molas (Madrid: Alianza, 1969), pp. 65–67.

JORDI DE SANT JORDI

[246] *Jus lo front port vostra bella semblança*

1. Below my brow I bear the image of your beauty,
   Which makes my heart both night and day rejoice;
   For when I gazed upon the beautiful features
   Of your fair face, its print remained on mine
   So that not even death will take it from me,   5
   And when I leave this world behind,
   Those who carry my body to be buried
   Will see your sign emblazoned in my eyes.

2. Just like the child who stares beyond the altar
   To take in the figures of the painting   10
   With his pure heart and cannot be distracted,
   So much the framing gold pleases him,
   So am I, before the loving circle
   Of your body, with so many good things adorned
   That in it I see more than if I saw God,   15
   Such joy I have from the love that invades me.

3. Thus burning love binds me in its prison
   And holds me there as if it were a coffer
   Locked with a key, and in it were my body,
   Which in no way could wriggle its way out;   20
   So greatly do I love you and so firmly
   That no pain can turn my heart aside
   From you, O beautiful one, but rather like a tower
   It stands firm, white dove, in loving you.

4. Matchlessly fair, with nobleness of presence   25
   God made your body, fairer than all others;
   Pleasing, with grace, it shines more than a jewel,
   Full of love, more piercing than a star;
   When I see you among a flock of ladies,
   You put them to shame, as does the glowing garnet   30
   Whose virtues overcome all noble stones:
   You are to them as is the goshawk to the merlin.

246. The Valencian noble Jordi de Sant Jordi (1400?–1425?) fought in Italy and elsewhere for Alfonso III of Catalonia (IV of Aragon). His fate is not known after his capture by
the Milanese. This much admired love poem in blank verse (*rims estramps*) shows traces of
Arnaut Daniel (No. 78) in stanzas 5 and 6 and elsewhere of Petrarch. The Middle Ages
considered Aristotle (line 37) not only as a philosopher but as a man overcome by irrational
love. Penthesilea (line 52) was the Queen of the Amazons. Text: Triadú, pp. 43–44.

5. My love of you has splintered my whole body;
   No man has loved with such a heartfelt passion:
   A love so strong as this which opens my heart wide   35
   Has never been in human soul or body.
   I'm out of my mind more than Aristotle was
   With love that burns me and unravels my five senses;
   As the good monk is never parted from his cell,
   I'll part no more from you than nail from finger.   40

6. Body of grace, unspotted by deception,
   Take pity on me, beautiful lady,
   And don't let me perish for love of you;
   I love you more than others can even claim;
   I pray you, who are the tree of beauty   45
   Which bears good fruit and gives shade to all virtue,
   That in your noble chamber you keep me,
   Since I am yours and all my life will be.

7. My precious ruby, the richest crest is yours
   Among all names in the census of the world,   50
   For you give birth each day to good and worthy things
   And nurture them, more than Penthesilea.

AUSIAS MARCH

[247] *Pren-me'n així com al patró qu'en plaja*

1. I'm like the merchant who holds his great vessel
   Just off the beach and thinks he owns a fortress.
   Observing that the sky is fair and cloudless,
   He is convinced one anchor is enough.
   But suddenly he senses rising up   5
   A time of tempest not to be withstood,
   Changes his mind and thinks, if this lasts long,
   He'd better find a port than linger here.

247. Ausias (Auzias) March (1397–1459) was a member of a poetically gifted noble family from the region of Valencia. His densely imaged poems portray the struggle between mind and body, the refining power of suffering, and other themes indicating the anguish of *vera amor* (true love, line 26). He is the first Catalan poet to write verse virtually free of Provençalisms and the first to evince a post-courtly and individualistic psychology. He is considered the greatest Catalan lyricist until at least the early twentieth century. Text: Triadú, pp. 55–56.

2. Often the gale is so tempestuous
   We can't leave port without a change of wind: 10
   The key that locks us in the closet
   Is not the one that can open the door.
   This is my plight on finding I'm in love
   For the great joy that comes from you, my lady:
   Non-joy leads down the path of not-in-love,   15
   But no single step will I take there.

3. Less likely than for fish to swim through forests
   Or lions in the sea to make their den
   Is it for my love to take a wrong turn,
   As long as I know it gives you pleasure;   20
   I trust that you will know me as I am,
   And truly known, I won't be ill rewarded
   For all the pain that I have felt for you;
   Then you will see the flames of love increase.

4. If I've expressed my love to you unclearly,   25
   Know that it's not because I shun true love;
   More than the sun grows hot in the month of June,
   My weak heart burns though earning paltry thanks.
   Someone else deserves the blame for this;
   Please wish him ill, since I, your humble servant,   30
   From weakness still remain unknown to you;
   It's Love, I swear, who makes your lover guilty.

5. Now my Desire allies itself with Reason;
   They come to an accord to seek out Quality,
   And act in such a way that soon the body   35
   Is diminished by a great part of its flesh.
   Too little sleep thins my body down,
   Doubling my skill at contemplating Love:
   A body that is fat inclines to sleep
   And can't go forward up that rugged slope.   40

6. Full of Wisdom, give me just one crust
   Of your bread to take this bitterness away;
   A great distaste for food has come to me
   Except for that which costs me so much love.

JOAN ROÍÇ DE CORELLA

[248] *Si en lo mal temps la serena bé canta*

If in bad weather the siren sweetly sings,
I too should sing, since I am torn by sadness
To such a point that my mind would welcome
Early death; all else it sees with terror.
But if you permit that underneath your cloak
I die near you, my pains will come to an end:
I'll be the bird that in a perfumed bed
Dies, happy that its life could be so full.

248. Joan Roíç de Corella (*ca.* 1438–1497), Valencian humanist and Master of Theology, wrote, besides poems of love, religious works and translations in prose and verse and a *Triumph of the Ladies*, as well as adapting Ovidian fables in Catalan. Text: R. Miquel i Planas, *Obres de J. Roíç de Corella* (Barcelona: Biblioteca catalana, 1913), p. 427.

Plate 10. The windswept ruins of Castle Tintagel on the coast of Cornwall, facing the Atlantic Ocean. King Arthur was reputed to have been born here. (Courtesy of the British Tourist Authority)

[VIII] LYRICS OF GREAT BRITAIN

The lyric tradition of the British Isles falls into two linguistic classes: the Germanic, which is represented in the two early time phases of the English language; and the Celtic, represented by Irish and Welsh. The Celts had a vital bardic tradition, and their narratives were the predominant vehicles for the early spread of Arthurian material.

The Irish lyric tradition can be dated to the seventh and eighth centuries, but a florescence occurred from 800 to 1000, as our samples indicate. All of these poems are anonymous, but the names of some bards and minstrels are known. Irish verse is notable for its emphasis on nature: brief, imagistic portraits that can be compared with Japanese *haiku*. There is also a characteristic sense of humor, as can be observed in the satiric No. 253 or No. 250, where the life of a cat named Pangur is compared with the poet's life in a way that does not disparage the cat. The world is certainly not condemned or despised. The two editions used by Joseph F. Eska as texts are: Gerard Murphy, *Early Irish Lyrics* (Oxford, 1965), and James Carney, *Medieval Irish Lyrics* (U. California, 1967).

Welsh (or Cymric), the original language of the Britons before the Anglo-Saxon invasions of the 400s, has an equally ancient tradition. A documented poet named Taliesin of the 500s wrote an elegy on the death of Owain (Ywain, Yvain), and a poet named Aneirin may have written a battle poem called *The Gododdin*. For an excellent account of this early literature by John Bollard, see *The Romance of Arthur* (ed. Wilhelm and Gross, Garland, 1984, Chapter II). These works are not included here because of their heroic-narrative qualities. Similarly the Welsh triads have been excluded because they were written in prose—except for 18W, which purports to be a three-line poem written by King Arthur himself:

These are my Three Battle-horsemen:
Menedd, and Lludd of the Breastplate,
and the Pillar of the Welsh, Caradog.

(trans. Bollard, *Romance*, p. 24) The standard edition is *Trioedd Ynys Prydein: The Welsh Triads*, ed. Rachel Bromwich (U. Wales, rev. 1978).

To represent the Welsh tradition, we have chosen the major poet of medieval Wales, Dafydd ap Gwilym (*fl.* 1330–1360). Most of his poems are written in seven-syllable lines of rhymed couplets, with patterned repetitions that include alliteration and internal rhyme. Richard M. Loomis's translations bring out the same humor and love of life and nature that we can observe in the Irish selections. Five samples are taken from Loomis's *Dafydd ap Gwilym: The Poems*, printed with permission of the Medieval and Renaissance Texts and Studies Series of the Center for Medieval and Early Renaissance Studies at the State University of New York, Binghamton, Vol. 9, 1982: Nos. 48, 117, 118, 122, and 124 respectively. These are based on the Welsh edited by Sir Thomas Parry (U. Wales, 3rd ed., 1979).

Looking at the Germanic tradition, we find two major time periods: the Old English or Anglo-Saxon period, which began with the North Germanic invasion of Britain in the fifth century; and the Middle English period, which followed the Norman invasion in 1066. The Old English poetry has been translated into Modern English, but the Middle English work has merely been edited.

The Old English period supplies most of the oldest documents for Germanic languages. Cædmon's Hymn, for example, may be dated as early as 670. This literature is extremely valuable, for it gives us a glimpse of pre-Christian existence among the Teutons that we could not get as thoroughly from any other source. In a poem like *The Wanderer* (No. 264), one is struck by the hard, cheerless conditions of life, where tragedy is always vying with Christian assumption. The mind is drawn back to Norse mythology with its *Ragnarök* or *Götterdämmerung* sensibility.

Two of the most distinctive features of Old English poetry are its alliteration and its use of the rhetorical device called a kenning. The kennings are formulaic, imagistic ways of presenting more common objects: the sea is "swan's road," the sky is "dove's lane," buildings are "the halls of the Tall Folk (or the Giants)" (*Wanderer*, line 86). These devices, along with the interesting compound nouns, provide the poetry with great freshness. Since rhyme is seldom practiced, alliteration becomes the tool that binds the verse together, with a strong caesura in every line. One sound is repeated in each verse, usually three times. In my translations I vary this practice, sometimes using separate alliterations on both sides of the break. The alliteration tends to toughen the sound system, at least for the modern ear, which is accustomed to the more soothing effect of rhyme.

The Old English delighted in paradoxes. The Riddle Poem presented here (No. 265) is just one of a sizable body showing a continuing interest in the puzzles of life. By contrast, Cædmon's Hymn strikes the firm chord of Christian belief, and it is this new-found optimism that provides the joy that underlies much of the lyric tradition that follows.

The poetry of the Middle English period shows an undeniable lilt that suggests its closeness to the pulse of the people. If the Normans conquered and imposed their language, they still did not transform the "folk" in any immediately significant way. The pre-Chaucerian work is remarkably free of the conventions established in Provençal verse. Here only No. 285 and Charles d'Orléans' Nos. 286 and 287 indicate a following of the Continental traditions. Both of these are late, and Charles was a North French man living in captivity in England.

One continuing feature of English composition is a love of ambiguity, which expresses itself in the use of puns. In No. 269, for example, there is a play upon "son" (Sone) and "sun" (Sonne). The supernatural descent of the Son on the Cross is imposed over the natural portrayal of the Sun sinking in the branches of a tree; the effect is striking. In the terse little No. 273 the sinister overtones of the opening lines come to a climax in the word "beste," which can mean either "beast" or "best one." The ambiguity of love is thus presented in as trenchant a way as Sappho's famous coinage "bittersweet." A poem like No. 277 is so elusive and haunting that it escapes any definite classification: is the maiden like Mary or Elvira Madigan or The Lady of the Lake? One cannot be sure.

The spirit of puzzlement is brought to the fore in the ballads, which are much concerned with the mysteries of life and death. We never really know who killed the lord lying in the green field (No. 292) or if the Wife of Usher's Well actually did see her sons. These works manage to capture the tragic spirit without destroying a sense of the fragile beauty of life.

The ballads, in fact, form the best link between the Middle Ages and the modern world. They cannot be accurately dated, and even if many were written down in the eighteenth and nineteenth centuries, they still were in the hearts and on the tongues of the people at a much earlier date. With them questions of time are unimportant, for the dilemmas they present are common to all time. The standard edition, especially for numbering, is still F. J. Child, *English and Scottish Popular Ballads*, 5 vols. (1882–1898).

To assist the general reader, I have italicized those *e*'s and *i*'s that are voiced in Middle English in places where they might not be in Modern English. The selection of some words for voicing over others must necessarily be arbitrary in some cases. The reader is advised to pronounce all final *e*'s at the ends of lines, where I have not italicized them. The spelling has been normalized wherever possible. Standard editions: *English Lyrics of XIIIth Century*, ed. Carleton Brown (Oxford, 1932), and *Secular Lyrics of XIVth and XVth Centuries*, ed. R. H. Robbins (Oxford, 1955). Many songs can be found on RCA Victor LM 6015(3, 4).

A. IRISH LYRICS
(Translated by Joseph F. Eska)

[249] *Is acher in gáith in-nocht*

Fierce is the wind tonight,
tossing the white hair of the sea;
I do not fear that the clear sea
will bring eager warriors from Norway.

[250] *Messe ocus Pangur bán*

I and white Pangur,
each of us at his special art:
his mind is on hunting,
my own mind is on my own special craft.

I love quiet (better than any fame),   5
studiously at my little book;

---

249. (9th century) Text: Carney No. 10. See Introduction to this section.
250. (9th century) Text: Murphy No. 1.

white Pangur is not envious of me:
he loves his own childish art.

Whenever we are (a story that never tires)
in our house, the two of us alone,   10
we have (an endless game)
something to which we may apply our ingenuity.

It is usual, at times, after valorous attacks,
for a mouse to stick in his net;
as for me, into my own net falls   15
a difficult rule of complex sense.

He directs his bright, perfect eye
against an enclosing wall;
I direct my own clear eye,
though it is weak, against keenness of knowledge.   20

He is happy with swift movement
when a mouse sticks in his sharp claw;
when I understand a beloved difficult problem
I myself am happy.

Though we be thus at any time,   25
neither hinders the other:
each of us likes his art;
each one rejoices in his own.

He is master for himself
of the work which he does every day;   30
to understand what is difficult with clarity
is my own work.

[251] *Dom-farcai fidbaidæ fál*

A hedge of trees overlooks me,
a blackbird's song sings to me
(a message not concealed);
above my little book, the lined one,
the birds' trilling sings to me.
A clear-voiced cuckoo sings to me (a fine song)
in a grey cloak from bush fortresses.
God's judgment! The Lord befriends me:
well do I write under the great wood of the forest.

251. (9th century) Text: Murphy No. 2, Carney No. 9.

[252] *Int én bec*

The little bird
has whistled
from the end
of a bright yellow bill;
it sings a note
above Belfast Loch,
a blackbird from
a yellow-heaped branch.

[253] *Ro-cúala*

I have heard
that he does not give horses for poems;
he gives that which is native to him,
a cow.

[254] *Clocán binn*

Little bell of pleasant sound
which is ringing on a windy night;
I would prefer going to a tryst with it
than to a tryst with a wanton woman.

[255] *Scél lem dúib*

I have news for you:
the stag bells,
winter snows,
summer has gone.

The wind is high and cold,
the sun is low,
its course is short,
the sea runs strongly.

Bracken is very red,
its form has been concealed;
the call of the barnacle goose
has become common.

252. (9th century) Text: Murphy No. 5.
253. (9th century) Text: Murphy No. 38.
254. (9th century) Text: Murphy No. 3.
255. (9–10th century) Text: Murphy No. 53, Carney No. 6.

Cold has seized
the wings of birds;
season of ice;
that is my news.

[256] *Fégaid úaib*

Look out
to the northeast;
the excellent sea
abounding with life;
the dwelling place of seals,
playful, glorious;
the tide has reached
its height.

[257] *Cride hé*

He is my heart,
a grove of nuts,
a dear boy is he,
a kiss for him.

[258] *Fil súil nglais*

There is a blue eye
which will look back on Ireland;
never again will it see
the men of Ireland nor its women.

256. (9–10th century) Text: Carney No. 16.
257. (9–10th century) Text: Carney No. 14.
258. (11th century) Text: Murphy No. 29, Carney No. 36.

B. WELSH LYRICS
(Translated by Richard M. Loomis)

DAFYDD AP GWILYM

[259] *Plygu rhag llid yr ydwyf*

I'm doubled over with passion,
A plague on all the girls of the parish!
Because I didn't get (outrage of a broken tryst)
Any one of them ever,
Not a virgin of sweet promise,   5
Not a little girl, not a hag, not a wife.

    What obstacle, what wickedness,
What failure that they don't want me?
What harm for a girl of thin eyebrow,
Getting me in a thick, dark wood?   10
It would be no shame for her
To see me in a bed of leaves.

    At no time did I not love
(No enchantment was so clinging as this,
Passing that of men of Garwy's passion)   15
One or two in a day.
And despite this, I was no nearer
Getting one than the woman who is my enemy.
There was no Sunday in Llanbadarn
That I would not be, though others condemn it,   20
With my face toward the fine girl
And the nape of my neck toward the good God.
And after I had long surveyed
Over my feathers the people of my parish,
Says a bright, fresh sweetheart   25
To another, lively and famous for wit:

    "The pale boy with a coquette's face
And his sister's hair on his head,

259–263. Dafydd ap Gwilym (*fl.* 1330–1360). Greatest poet of medieval Wales. See
Introduction to this section.

Adulterous is the looking
Of him with the crooked glance; he's acquainted
    with evil."   30

    "Is it that pretense he has?"
Is the word of the other beside her.
"He'll get no answer as long as the world lasts;
To the devil with him, mad thing!"

    Rough for me, the shining girl's curse,   35
Small recompense for dazed love.
I'll have to manage to stop
This practice (dreams of horror).
I must go like
A hermit, a wretch's office.   40
From too much looking (grim lesson)
Backwards (the picture of weakness)
It happened that I (friend of strong song)
Bent my head, without one companion.

[260] *Yr wybrwynt helynt hylaw*

Sky-wind of adroit course
That goes there with mighty uproar,
You're a prodigious warrior, rough of sound,
Rash one of the world, without foot, without wing.
It's strange how terribly you were put   5
From the sky's pantry without one foot
And how swiftly you run
Now over the slope above.
There's no need for a swift horse under you,
Nor bridge on an estuary, nor boat.   10
You will not drown, you were alerted,
You won't get stuck, you lack corners.
Of stealing nests, though you winnow leaves,
No one will accuse you; there will not arrest you
Either a swift host or the hand of a sergeant   15
Or a blue blade or flood or rain.
Neither officer nor retinue will catch you
In your day, winnower of treetop plumes.
No mother's son will slay you, false report,
No fire burn you, no deception weaken you.   20
No glance will see you, bare, enormous lair,
A thousand will hear you, great rain's nest;
Cloud-notary swift in nature,
Fine leaper over nine wilderness-lands.

    God's blessing are you along the earth,   25
Roar of the grievous breaking of the oak-top.
Dry-tempered, potent creature,

Trampler of cloud, massive in sojourning.
Shooter of an empty, noisy heap of husks
On the snow regions above.   30
Tell me, faithful bead,
Your course, north-wind of the glen,
Wild tempest on the sea,
Sportive boy on the seashore.
Fluent author, you're a wizard.   35
Sower, you're a leaf-chaser.
Hurler, privileged laugher on the hill,
Of the white-breasted, wild-masted sea.

    You fly the lengths of the world,
Weather of the hillcrest, tonight be aloft,   40
Ah, man, and go to Uwch Aeron,
Bright and handsome, clear of tone.
Do not linger, do not spare,
Do not fear despite Y Bwa Bach
Of accusing complaint, serving poison;   45
Closed is the land and its fostering to me.
Woe for me, when I set pensive love
On Morfudd, my golden girl;
A girl has made me exiled.
Race aloft between where you are and the house
    of her father.   50

    Knock at the door, make it open
Before daybreak to my messenger,
And seek a way to her, if it's to be had,
And grieve the voice of my sigh.
You come from the pure constellations,   55
Say this to my generous truelove:
"As long as I am in the world,
A faithful plaything am I."
Alas for my face without her,
If it be true she's not unfaithful.   60
Go up, you'll see a girl,
Go down, choice one of the sky.
Go to a pale, blonde girl;
Come back in health, you're the sky's bounty.

[261] *Yr wylan deg ar lanw dioer*

Surely, fair gull on the tide,
Of the same color as snow or the white moon,
Your beauty is unspotted,
A fragment like sun, gauntlet of the salt sea.
Light you are on the ocean wave,   5
Swift, proud, fish-eating bird.
There you'd go at anchor,

Hand in hand with me, sea lily.
Fashioned like writing paper shining in nature,
A nun atop the sea-tide are you.   10

    With well-made praise for a girl, you shall
      have praise afar,
Seek the bend of a fort and castle.
Look, seagull, whether you may see
A girl of Eigr's color on the fine fort.
Say my harmonious words.   15
Let her choose me, go to the girl.
She'd be by herself, dare to greet her.
Be adroit with the polished girl
For profit; say that I won't
(A refined, gentle lad) live unless I have her.   20

    I love her, full assurance of joy,
Alas, men, never loved
Healthy Myrddin of flattery's lip
Or Taliesin a prettier girl!
The face of a sought-for girl under copper,   25
Supreme beauty very perfect and right.

    Alas, gull, if you get to see
The cheek of the loveliest girl in Christendom,
Unless I have the tenderest greeting,
The girl will be my death.   30

[262] *Lle digrif y bûm heddiw*

I was in a pleasant place today,
Under mantles of the fine, green hazel trees,
Listening at the start of day
To the skillful cock-thrush
Singing a polished *englyn*,   5
Bright prophecies and lessons.

    A traveler from afar, judicious of nature,
Long was the journey of the gray love-messenger.
He came here from the fine county of Caer,
Because my golden girl commanded him.   10
Wordy, without one password,
There he heads, to the valley of Nentyrch.
Morfudd had sent it,
The metrical song of May's foster son.
About him there was an alb   15
Of flowers of the sweet boughs of May,
And his chasuble (they resembled green mantles)
Was of wings of wind.

By the great God, there was nothing there
But all gold as the altar's roof.   20
I heard in shining language
A long chanting, unfailing,
Reading to the parish, no excess of agitation,
The Gospel distinctly.
He raised there on a height for us   25
A mass-wafer of a good leaf.
And a nightingale, fine, slim, eloquent,
From the corner of the grove beside him,
The valley's poetess, rang for a hundred
A sanctus bell, loud was her whistle.   30
And the elevation of the Host
To the heaven above the thicket;
And devotion to our Lord Father,
And a chalice of passion and love.
I'm content with the music,   35
A birch-grove in the gentle woods fostered it.

[263] *Deuthum i ddinas dethol*

I came to a choice city,
With my handsome squire after me.
Fine, lively spending, a place of abundant complaint,
I took, I was proud from my youth,
A respectable enough common lodging,   5
And I'd have wine.

    I saw a slender, beautiful maiden
In the house, my lovely soul.
I cast my mind entirely (color of the rising sun)
On my slim beatitude.   10
I bought a roast, not for boasting,
And costly wine, for me and the girl there.
Young men like to play—
I called the girl (a shy one) to the bench.
I whispered (I was a bold, insistent man,   15
This is sure) two words of magic;
I made (love was not idle)
An agreement to come to the spirited girl
When the company would go
To sleep; she was a girl of black eyebrow.   20

    After they slept, sad was the expedition,
Everyone but me and the girl,
I tried expertly to gain
The girl's bed; there was a surfeit.
I got, when I made a sound there,   25
A bad fall, there were no good successes;

It was easier to rise (rash sin)
Clumsily than very quickly.
I hit (I didn't leap healthfully)
The shin (and alas for the leg)   30
Against the side (some ostler's work)
Of a loud, stupid stool, above the ankle.
I got (it was a tale of repentance)
Up (Welshmen will love me);
I hit (too much desire is evil)   35
Where I was set without one easy step
(Frequent deception of a foolish effort)
My forehead on the edge of the table,
Where there was a bowl for some time loose
And a talking brass pan.   40
The table fell (very stout arrangement)
And the two trestles, and all the furnishings;
The pan gave a cry
After me, it was heard far off;
The bowl shouted (I was too vain a man),   45
And the dogs barked at me.

    There were beside thick walls
Three Englishmen in a stinking bed,
Troubled about their three packs—
Hickin and Jenkin and Jack.   50
The slave with a mouth of dregs whispered,
An angry speech, to the two:

    "There's a Welshman, the constant stir of trickery,
Roaming too slyly here;
He's a thief, if we allow,   55
Watch out, keep guard against this one."

    The ostler roused up all the crowd,
And it was a monstrous story.
Scowling were they around me,
Searching round me to find me;   60
And I, ugly, unsightly pains,
Keeping silent in the dark.
I prayed, no bold face,
Secretly, like one in fear;
And by the power of true, loving prayer   65
And by the grace of the faithful Jesus,
I gained, a tangle of sleeplessness,
Without wage, my own old bed.
I escaped, good the saints nearby;
I pray to God for pardon.   70

C. OLD ENGLISH LYRICS
(Translated by James J. Wilhelm)

ANONYMOUS

---

[264] *The Wanderer*

"Oft does the lone-liver   endure for some dowry,
Some mercy from the Maker,   although he be angst-filled
And long must he labor   yonder on wave-ways
Stirring with oar-stakes   the ice-speckled sea
On the road of the outtrod.   Fate so unflinching!"   5
So spoke the earth-roamer   mindful of miseries,
Victims of violence,   deaths of the dear-loved.
Sometimes I sounded   in dusk of the dawning
Words of my woefulness;   now there's no man,
None among quick ones   to whom in clear confidence   10
I dare declare me.   In truth I have thought
That a man is most masterly   in all of his manners
Who fixes down fastly   the broils in his breast
And hoards up the heartstrings   (let him think what he will!).
One who is spirit-sore   can't foist off fatings;   15
Nor can the mixed mind   hand over help;
And so great glory-seekers   stash down securely
Dreary-doomed gloom   bound in their breasts.
Thus have I shackled   thoughts in the mind that
Came to me, wretch-racked,   hewn from my homeland,   20
Far from kind kinsmen,   fixed thoughts with fetters
When in years yonder   my belovéd gold-giver
I buried in deep dirt   and thence I went forth
In woe, winter-weary,   over bindings of breakers,
Sore-seeking the grand halls   with outheavers of hoards,   25
Where near or where far   I might perchance happen
On some man in mead-hall   who spoke of my folk
Or could bring me some comfort,   me lorn of my loved ones,
Could enjoin me with joy.   He who has felt it
Knows that sorrow as soul-mate   is so terribly tough   30
To a man who is banished   from friends who defend.
The exile-path gapes there;   no baubles are brandished;

264. Lament of an exile who has lost his lord to death. Some critics consider the religious elements in the poem, especially at the end, additions by another hand. "Wyrd" in line 107 is Fate.

Care is his cargo;   no fruit of the field.
He harks back to buddies,   the troving of treasures,
How him in his young time   some dispenser of doles   35
Feted with feastings.   O fun now how fallen!
He knows, when the need is,   to forgo for a long time
The talk of his teacher,   his sweet master of men,
When sleep and when sorrow   gathered together
To the unlucky loner   bind up the mind.   40
Then he will think that   he is kissing and clipping
His much-loved man-master   as he kneels on his knees,
Hand, head in that lap,   as in days long ago
He yarely yearned for   his due from the dole-stool.
Ah, he awakens,   that friend-bereft fellow,   45
And before him he sees   the black, spume-capped sea
Where brine-birds are bathing,   fanning their feathers,
Where freeze-frost and snow   come slashing with sleet.
How balefully laden   his breast then with bane,
Sorrow for some sweetheart,   sorriness renewed   50
As the images of kinsmen   swim into his mind.
Ah, with glee how he greets them,   eying them eagerly,
Those old fellow-fighters.   But off they go, floating.
These forms that are flitting   can proffer no comfort,
Rouse no lays long sung.   Care is the comer   55
To him who must fetch forth,   his spirit all weary,
Again and again,   out on breakings of brine.
And thus as I'm thinking   thoughts of the world's ways,
The mind's meditation   grows swart in the gloom.
When only the mere line   of men's lives is measured,   60
How suddenly they surrender   their space in the hall,
Those young, trusty thanes.   Mind how this midworld
In day after day   cracks and then crumbles.
Thus no man is master   of wisdom till winning
His winter's deal in world's domain.   Sage is foresuffering, 65
Is never hot-hearted,   not slick in his speaking,
Not weak in his warring,   nor yet vain in valor,
Neither fearless nor 'fraid,   and ne'er money-hungry
Nor brash into boasting   till true wisdom's his.
A warrior knows waiting   once his vow is out,   70
Till brimful of boldness   he clearly can call
Whither his heart-thought   will twist and will turn.
The smart man will gather   how ghastly the passing
When all of the world's wealth   lies there as a waste
As now hither-thither   throughout all the earth's realm   75
Stand walls that were racked   by the wind and the rain,
With hangings of hoarfrost,   dwellings dashed by the storm.
The wine-hall is weakening,   the lordlings are lying
Lorn of their lustihood;   the man-bands lie hacked,
Fallen proud by a wall.   War wore down many,   80
Jolted into last journeys.   Some did the birds bear
Over steepings of sea.   Grim came the gray wolf,

Dealing out death-shares.　Some by one glum-faced
Were dumped into trenches,　heroes left there to hide.
Thus did the Great Shaper　swipe down his setting,　　　85
Till the halls of the Tall Folk　stood idle and still,
And the bruiting of the burghers　was a noise voiced on wind.
He pondered profoundly　the pillage of the place;
He reflected then deeply　on the darkness of days;
Wise in the heart's ways,　he summons to mind　　　90
The crops of the corpses,　and these words he says:
"Where's the hero? the horse?　Where's the gift-giver gone?
Where the seats of the feast-hall?　Where joy and the noise?
O alas, those bright beakers!　Alas, armored man!
Alas, pomp of princes!　How time ticks away,　　　95
Hid under night's hood　as if it ne'er were.
All that's outlasted　is the wall wondrous high,
Cut with snake-carvings;　banished our bands.
The splinter of ash-spear　has hewn down our heroes,
With arms anxious for slaughter,　Fate famous as ere;　　　100
And storms now are striking　the slopings of stone;
A blinding blizzard　is fast binding the earth;
Winter is howling　and blasts black and blear;
Swartens the night-shadow;　sent out of northland
Hailstones are hitting,　a hell now for men.　　　105
The domain of menfolk　is most dour and drear.
Wyrd works the ways　of the world under heaven.
Riches soon run,　and friends fade away;
Man cannot long stand;　the kin spin away;
All earth's establishment　soon will be empty!"　　　110
So spoke the sage one,　sitting in sole pondering.
Good hap to the faith-holder,　not brandishing breast-care,
Keeping grief deep inside,　unless he kens curing
That can comfort with courage.　Good hap to the grace seeker
Humble to Heaven-Father,　Who is our earthly fastness.　　　115

[265] *Hwelc is hæletha thæs horsc*

Who is so seerlike　or crafty and clever
That he can answer　what forces me forth?
For I rise up raging,　wrathful and rueless,
Violent of voice　and cruel in pursuit,
Faring o'er earthfolds,　burning the folks' barns　　　5
Wreaking much ravage.　The smoke rises high,
Black over thatchings.　Ah, the din among dwellings,
The massacre of man　as I fell the forest,
I break the bowers,　I blast out the beams,
Welling with water,　with the high, mighty powers　　　10
Impelling my pillage　over land and o'er sea. . . .
Who am I?

265. Riddle Poem. Answer: a storm. Some terminal lines omitted.

[266] The Wife's Lament

I pour forth this poem   of my life pathetic,
Tracing the self's trip.   This I can say:
How I suffered miseries   once I had grown up,
Some new, some old,   but none more than now.
Fore'er I've experienced   expeditions in exile.   5
First fared my liegelord   hence from his land
Over waves' winnows.   I suffered wan-care,
Wondering where my lord   wandered abroad.
I took then to traveling,   seeking out service,
A winsomeless wanderer   out of woeful need.   10
The kin of my kind one   began to conspire
In soft, secret whispering   to split us apart,
So that sundered completely   I would be cast forth
To a most loathsome life—   ah, indeed how I longed!
Here did my dear lord   command me take dwelling.   15
I had little to love   here in this land,
Very few loyal friends.   And so is my soul sad,
For I found that companion   most fit for my side
Suddenly sad-spirited,   strangely ill-starred,
Mulling over murders,   hiding his mind.   20
Before we were both   blithe in our bearing,
Promising ever   that nothing would part us
Unless it were death.   All went helter-skelter:
And now it's as nothing   . . . . . .
Our loyal love.   Whether far, whether near   25
I must bide the bad cheer   of my cherished one.
A man has commanded: go live in that grove!
Under an oak tree,   deep in a den.
Old is my cave-lodge;   I languish with longing;
Dark are the dales round;   high are the hills;   30
Sharp are the hamlet-hedges   brittle with briars,
A home full of groans.   The going of my good lord
Fills me with grief.   Other lovers are living
Lively on earth,   with leisure in the bedstead;
But I walk at daybreak   alone in the dawning   35
Under the oak tree   or deep in my den.
There I may sit   the whole summer day;
There I may weep   the wreck of my roaming,
Hardships so heavy,   never knowing any rest
From the dark depression   that dogs all my days   40
And seizes my soul now   for the length of my life.
A young man may ever be   melancholy and mourning,
Heavy in his heart,   yet he should e'er show
Blitheness of bearing   despite all his breast-cares,

266. Lament of a woman parted from her husband. Line 24 incomplete. Lines 42–50
slightly emended.

His sufferings endless,   whether all the world's weal   45
He holds in his hands   or even if exiled
Among some far folk—   where my friend is sitting
Under some stone heap,   stung by the storm,
Ever mournful in mind,   wet by the water
In some ruined gloom.   Ah, my lord labors   50
With glumness that's great: too oft he remembers
Our hilarious halls.   Woe is the winning
Of one who's awaiting   a lover with longing.

CÆDMON

[267] *Nu we sculon herian*

Now let's give laudings   to the Lord of the Heaven-realm,
The main of the Master   with his firmness of mind,
The Miracle-Maker,   mighty Father everlasting
Who worked in his wise   every wonder that was.
First did he form   for the offspring of humans   5
Heaven for roofing,   great Creator of all.
Then the Warder of mankind   worked out the world.
The Lord ever-living,   the Master all-mighty,
Fashioned the earth-folds   for the mansion of man.

D. MIDDLE ENGLISH LYRICS

ANONYMOUS

[268] *Sumer is i-comen in*

Sumer is i-comen in,   *Summer has come in*
Loude sing cucku!

267.Cædmon (*fl.* 670). First known English poet. The Venerable Bede tells how this rude shepherd, hearing the voice of God, broke forth with this praise. Lived at Whitby; composed other poems.

268. Spring Song sung in round fashion; music often recorded.

Groweth seed and *bloweth meed*   *meadow blooms*
And springth the *wode nu.*   *woods now*
Sing cucku!   5

Ewe bleteth after lamb,
Loweth after calv*e cu;*   *cow*
Bullock *sterteth;* bucke *ferteth*—   *starts (jumps)/ farts*
Murie sing cucku!   *Merrily*
Cucku, cucku!   10
Well singest thu, cucku.
Ne swik thu never nu.   *Nor be quiet*
(*Repeated in two parts:*)

Sing cucku nu, sing cucku!
Sing cucku nu, sing cucku!   15

[269] *Nu goth Sonne under wode*

Nu goth *Sonn*e under *wode.*   *Sun / wood (Cross)*
Me rueth, Mary, thy faire *rode.*   *I pity/ face*
Nu goth Sonne under tree.
Me rueth, Mary, thy *Son*e and thee.   *Son*

[270] *Say me, wight in the broom*

Say me, *wight* in the *broom:*   *creature/ brush*
Tech*e* me how I shall don
That min hous*e*bonde
Me lov*i*en wolde.

"Hold thine tung*e* stille   5
And have all thine wille."

[271] *When the turf is thy tour*

When the turf is thy *tour*   *tower*
And the *pit* is thy *bour,*   *grave/ bower*
Thy *fel* and thy white throte   *flesh*
Shallen worm*e*s *to note.*   *(have) at need, feed*
What helpeth thee thenne   5
All the worlde *wenne?*   *to win*

[272] *Of oon that is so fayr and bright*

1. Of *oon* that is so fayr and bright,   *one*
   Velut maris stella,   *Like a star of the sea (Latin)*
 Brighter than the day*e*s light,
   Parens et puella;   *Mother and maiden*
 I crye to thee: thou see to me.   5

Lady, pray thy Sone for me,
   Tam pia,   *Thou so devout one*
That I moot*e* come to thee,
   Maria.

2. Of car*e* counsel thou art best,   10
   Felix fecundata.   *Blessed by womb-fruit*
Of all*e* weery thou art rest,
   Mater honorata.   *Honored mother*
Biseech thou him with mild*e* mood
That for us all*e* shed his blood   15
   In cruce   *On Cross*
That we moot*e* come to him
   In luce.   *In light*

3. All this world*e* was forlore
   Eva peccatrice,   *By Eve the sinner* 20
Till our Lord was i-bore
   De te genetrice.   *With you his bearer*
With Av*e* it went away,
Thester night, and cam the day   *The dark*
   Salutis.   *Of health*   25
The well*e* springeth out of thee
   Virtutis.   *Of virtue*

4. Lady, flour of all*e* thing,
   Rosa sine spina,   *Thornless rose*
Thou bar Jesu, heven*e*s King,   30
   Gratia divina.   *By divine grace*
Of all*e* thou berst the *pris,*   *prize*
Lady, Quene of Paradis
   Electa.   *Chosen*
Mayde and mild*e* Moder *es*   *Thou art* (Latin)   35
   Effecta.   *Created*

5. Well he *wot* he is thy Sone   *knows*
   Ventre quem portasti;   *Whom thou borest in womb*
He will not *wern*e thee thy *boone*   *refuse/ prayer*
   Parvum quem lactasti,   *The small one you suckled* 40
So *hend*e and so good he is,   *gentle*
He hath brought us alle to bliss
   Superni,   *Of Heaven*
That hath *i-dut* the foul*e* *put*   *shut/ pit*
   Inferni.   *Of Hell*   45

[273] *Foweles in the frith*

Foweles in the *frith,*   *Fowls (birds)/ forest*
The fish*e*s in the flood,

And I *mon waxe wood*—   *must go mad*
Much sorwe I walk*e* with
For *beste* of bone and blood.   *best, beast*   5

[274] *Bitweene Merch and Aperil*

1. Bitween*e* Merch and Aperil
   When spray biginneth to springe,
   The little fowl*e* hath *hire* will   *their*
   One hir*e lud* to singe.   *tongue*
   I live in love-longinge   5
   For *semlokest* of all*e* thing;   *the prettiest*
   She may me bliss*e* bringe:
   I am in hir *baundoun.*   *power*
        An *hende hap* I have *i-hent,*   *happy fate/ gotten*
        I *wot* from heaven it is me sent;   *know*   10
        From all*e* women my love is *lent*   *taken*
        And light on Alisoun.

2. *On hew* hir heer is fayre enough;   *Of color*
   Hir brow*e* brown, hir eyen black;
   With *lossum cheere* she on me *lough,*   *lovely look/ laughed*   15
   With middel small and well *i-mak.*   *made*
   But she me *wolle* to hire take   *Unless/ will*
   For to been her own *make,*   *mate*
   Long*e* to live I shulle forsake
   And *feye* fallen adoun.   *death-fated*   20
        An hend*e* hap I have i-hent . . .

3. Night*es* when I *wende* and wake,   *turn*
   Forthy min *wonges* waxen wan,   *Because/ cheeks*
   Levedy, all for thine sake   *Lady*
   Longinge *is i-lent* me on.   *has come*   25
   In world is non so *witer* man   *wise a*
   That all hir bountee tellen can:
   Her *swire* is whiter than the swan,   *neck*
   The fayrest mayd in toun.
        An hend*e* hap I have i-hent . . .   30

4. I am for *wowing* all *forwake,*   *wooing/ worn out*
   Weery as water *in wore,*   *in a pond (?)*
   Lest any *reve* me my make   *rob from*
   I have *i-yerned yore.*   *yearned for of old*
   Bettere is *tholien* while sore   *to endure*   35
   Than mournen evermore.
   Gainest under gore,   *Prettiest in gown*
   Herkn*e* to my *roun:*   *speech*
        An hend*e* hap I have i-hent,
        I wot from heven it is me sent: 40
        From all*e* women my love is lent
        And light on Alisoun.

[275] *Lenten is come with love to toune*

1. *Lenten* is come with love to toune,   *Spring*
   With *blosmes* and with briddes *roune,*   *blossoms/ song*
   That all this *blisse* bringeth;
   Daisy*es* in these dales,
   Not*es* sweet of nightengales—   5
   Eech fow*el* song singeth.
   The throstelcock him *threteth oo;*   *chides ever*
   Away is hir*e* winter wo
   When *woderove* springeth.   *woodruff*
   Thise fowles singen *ferly fele*   *wondrous many* 10
   And *wlyten* on hire *wynne wele* *pipe/ joyous wealth*
   That all the wood*e* ringeth.

2. The ros*e raileth* hir *rode.*   *put on/ hue*
   The leav*es* on the light*e* wode
   Waxen all with wille.   15
   The Moon*e mandeth* hir *blee,*   *sends/ ray*
   The lil*y* is *lossum* to see,   *lovely*
   The fennel and the *fille.*   *chervil-flower* (?)
   Wooen thise wild*e* drakes;
   Males merryen hire makes   20
   As streem that *striketh* stille.   *flows*
   Moody meneth, as doth mo; *The spirited one laments, as do others*
   I wot I am oon of tho,
   For love that *liketh ill.*   *pleases poorly*

3. The Moon*e* mandeth hir light;   25
   So doth the seemly Sonn*e* bright
   When bridd*es* singen *breme;*   *loud*
   Dew*es dunken* thise *dounes;*   *dampen/ hills*
   Deer*es* with hire *derne* rounes,   *animals/ secret*
   Domes for to deme.   *tell tales* 30
   Worm*es* wooen under *cloude,*   *clod, earth*
   Women waxen wonder proude,
   So well it will hem seeme.
   If me shall *wante* wille of oon,   *lack the*
   This *wynne wele* I will forgon   *joyous state* 35
   And *wyght* in woode be *fleeme.* *soon/ fleer* (exile)

[276] *All night by the rose, rose*

All night by the ros*e*, rose,
All night by the rose I lay;
Durste I nought the rose *steele*   *steal*
And yet I *bar* the flour away.   *bore*

[277] *Maiden in the moor lay*

1. Maiden in the moor lay—
   In the moor lay—
   Seven-night fulle,
   Seven-night fulle.
   Maiden in the moor lay—   5
   In the moor lay—
   Seven-nights fulle and a day.

2. *Well* was her *mete*.   *Good/ food*
   What was her mete?
   The *primerole* and the—   *primrose*   10
   The primerole and the—
   Well was her mete.
   What was her mete?
   The primerole and the violette.

3. Well was her drinke.   15
   What was her drinke?
   The colde water of the—
   The colde water of the—
   Well was her drinke.
   What was her drinke?   20
   The colde water of the welle-spring.

4. Well was her bour.
   What was her bour?
   The rede rose and the—
   The rede rose and the—   25
   Well was her bour.
   What was her bour?
   The rede rose and the lily-flour.

GEOFFREY CHAUCER

[278] *Madame, ye been of alle beautee shrine*

1. Madame, ye been of alle beautee shrine
   As fer as cercled is the *mapemounde*,   *map of the world*
   For as the crystal glorious ye shine,

278. Geoffrey Chaucer (*ca.* 1343–1400). Greatest medieval English author. Composer of *The Canterbury Tales*. His *Ballade to Rosemounde* mixes formal North French conceits with realistic English detail (pikes, tubs).

And lik*e* ruby been your cheek*e*s rounde.
Therwith ye been so merry and so jocounde   5
That at a revel whan that I see you daunce,
It is an oin*e*ment unto my wounde,
Though ye to me ne *do* no *dalliaunce.*   *offer comfort*

2. For though I weepe of ter*e*s full a *tine,*   *tub*
   Yet may that wo myn hert*e* nat confounde;   10
   Your *semy* vois, that ye so small *out-twine,*   *delicate/ spin out*
   Mak*e*th my thought in joy and bliss abounde.
   So curteisly I go, with lov*e* bounde
   That to myself I say, in my penaunce,
   "Suffiseth me to love you, Rosemounde,   15
   Though ye to me ne do no dalliaunce."

3. Was never *pik walwed in galauntine*   *pike wallowing in sauce*
   As I in love am walwed and ywounde,
   For which full ofte I of myself divine
   That I am tru*e* Tristram the secounde.   20
   My love may not *refreide* nor *affounde;*   *cool down/ go numb*
   I *brenne* ay in an amorous plesaunce.   *burn*
   Do what you list, I will your thrall be founde,
   Though ye to me ne do no dalliaunce.

[279] *Adam scrivain, if ever it thee bifalle*

Adam scrivain, if ever it thee bifalle
Boece or *Troilus* to writen newe,
Under thy long lockes thou moste have the *scalle*   *scab-disease*
But after my making thou writ*e* more true;   *Unless*
So ofte a-day I moot thy werk renewe,   5
It to correcte and eek to rub and scrape;
   And all is *thourgh* thy negligence and *rape.*   *through/ haste*

[280] *Somtime the world was so stedfast and stable*

1. *Somtime* the world was so stedfast and stable   *Once*
   That mann*e*s word was obligacioun;
   And now it is so fals and deceivable
   That word and deed, as in conclusioun,
   Been nothing *lyk,* for turned up-so-doun   *alike*   5
   Is all this world for *mede* and willfulnesse,   *reward*
   That all is lost for lack of stedfastnesse.

2. What maketh this world to be so variable
   But *lust* that folk have in dissensioun?   *pleasure*

---

279. *Words to His Scribe Adam,* who transcribed Chaucer's translation of Boethius'
Consolation of Philosophy and his own *Troilus and Criseyde,* apparently rather sloppily.
   280. *The Lack of Stedfastnesse.*

For among us now a man is *holde* unable   *considered*   10
But if he can by som collusioun
Do his neighbour wrong or oppressioun.
What causeth this but willful wretchednesse,
That all is lost for lack of stedfastnesse?

3. Trouthe is put doun, resoun is holden fable;   15
Vertù hath now no dominacioun;
Pitee exil*e*d; no man is merciable;
Through coveteise is *blent* discrecioun.   *blinded*
The world hath maad a permutacioun
Fro right to wrong, fro trouthe to fickelnesse,   20
That all is lost for lack of stedfastnesse.

Envoi to King Richard II
4. O Prince, desir*e* to been honourable;
Cherish thy folk and hate extorcioun!
Suffer no thing that may be *reprevable*   *reproof-worthy*
To thyn estaat don in thy regioun.   25
Shew forth thy swerd of castigacioun.
Dred God; do law; love trouthe and worthinesse,
And wed thy folk again to stedfastnesse.

[281] *To you, my purs, and to non other wight*

1. To you, my purs, and to non other wight
Complaine I, for ye be my lady deere!
I am so sorry now that ye been light;
For cert*es*, *but* ye maak me hevy cheere,   *unless*
Me were as lief be laid upon my *beere*;   *I'd as soon/ bier*   5
For which unto your mercy thus I crye:
Beeth hevy again, or ell*es* *moot* I dye!   *must*

2. Now *voucheth-sauf* this day, er it be night,   *please grant*
That I of you the blissful sound may heere
Or see your colour lyk the Sonn*e* bright,   10
That of yellownesse hadd*e* never peere.
Ye be my lif, ye be myn hert*es* *steere*,   *steerer*
Queene of comfort and of good companye:
Beeth hevy again, or ell*es* moot I dye!

3. Now purs that been to me my liv*es* light   15
And saviour, as doun in this world here,
Out of this toun help*e* me thourgh your might,
Sin that ye wol not been my tresourere;
For I am shaven as *nie* as any *frere*.   *close/ friar*

281. *Complaint to His Purse.* In the Envoi, Brutus, a Roman, is taken as the legendary
founder of England (Albion).

But yet I pray unto your curteisye: 20
Beeth hevy again, or elles moot I dye!

Envoi to King Henry IV
4. O conquerour of Brutus' Albioun,
Which that by line and free eleccioun
Been *verray* king, this song to you I sende; *true*
And ye, that mowen alle our harmes amende, 25
Have minde upon my supplicacioun!

ANONYMOUS

[282] I have a gentil cock

1. I have a gentil cock,
Croweth me the day;
He doth me risen erly,
My matins for to say.

2. I have a gentil cock; 5
Comen he is of *gret*; *great lineage*
His comb is of red coral,
His *tayil* is of jet. *tail*

3. I have a gentil cock;
Comen he is *of kynde*; *of good kin* 10
His comb is of red coral,
His tayil is of *Inde*. *India*

4. His legges been of *asor*, *azure*
So gentil and so smale;
His *spures* arn of silver-whyt *back-claws* 15
Into the *wortewale*. *root of spur*

5. His eyen arn of crystal,
Looking all in aumber;
And every nyght he percheth him
In myn lady's chaumber. 20

[283] I have a yong syster

1. I have a yong syster
Fer beyonde the see;
Many be the *drueries* *love-tokens*
That she sente me.

2. She sent*e* me the cherry   5
   Withouten any ston;
   And so she did the dove
   Withouten any bon.

3. She sent*e* me the *brere*   *rose-briar*
   Withouten any *rinde*;   *bark* 10
   She bad me love my *lemman*   *lover*
   Withouten longinge.

4. How should any cherry
   Be withouten ston?
   And how should any dove   15
   Be withouten bon?

5. How should any brere
   Be withouten rinde?
   How should I love my lemman
   Withouten longinge?   20

6. Whan the cherry was a flour,
   Than hadde it no ston.
   Whan the dov*e* was an *ey*,   *egg*
   Than hadde it no bon.

7. Whan the brere was *unbred*   *unborn* 25
   Than hadde it no rinde.
   Whan the maid hath that she loveth
   She is without longinge.

[284] *I singe of a Maiden*

1. I singe of a Maiden
   That is *makeless*;   *matchless*
   King of all kinges
   To hir Sone she *ches*.   *chose*

2. He cam all so stille   5
   Ther his Moder was,
   As dew in Aperille
   That falleth on the grass.

3. He cam all so stille
   To his Modres bour,   10
   As dew in Aperille
   That falleth on the flour.

4. He cam all so stille
   Ther his Moder lay,
   As dew in Aperille   15
   That falleth on the spray.

5. Moder and maiden
   Was nevere non but she.
   Well may swich a lady
   Goddes Moder be.   20

[285] *Have all my hert and be in peese*

1. Have all my hert and be in *peese*,   *peace*
   And think I love you fervently;
   For in good faith, it is no *leese*;   *lie*
   I would ye *wist* as well as I.   *knew*
   For now I see, both night and day,   5
   That my love will not ceese.
   Have mercy on me as ye best may—
   Have all my hert and be in peese.

2. Have all my hert wherever I go:
   Hert, body, and all my might.   10
   Me for-thought we parted in two   *It grieved me*
   When I to you had most right.
   Have mercy on me, *mickel* of might,   *muchness*
   For of my love I cannot ceese,
   Tho I be selden in your sight—   15
   Have all my hert and be in peese.

3. It is a thinge that me can *nye*   *bother*
   But if ye hold *that* ye have *hight*;   *Unless/ what/ promised*
   For traitors' tonges: "Evil *moot* they *thee!*"   *may/ thrive*
   I say to you, myn sweete wight.   20
   Therfore I sweere, as moot I dye,
   If I said aught whan ye *bad* peese,   *asked for*
   I will full meekly aske mercye—
   Have all my hert and be in peese.

4. Ye have my hert as I you highte;   25
   I pray God elles that I be dede.
   But I love you with all my mighte
   As he that weers furred hood on hede!
   This song was maad, *withouten drede*,   *doubtlessly*
   For youre love that I first *cheese*;   *chose* 30
   Wher-so-ever I be, *in stall or stede*,   *in any place*
   Have all my hert and be in peese.

CHARLES D'ORLÉANS

[286] *So faire, so freshe, so goodly on to see*

So faire, so freshe, so goodly on to see,
So welle *demeined* in all your governaunce,   *conducted*
That to my hert it is a greete plesaunce
Of your goodness when I remember me;
And trusteth fully, where-that-ever I be,   5
I will abide under your obeissaunce—
So faire, so freshe, so goodly on to see,
So welle demeined in all your governaunce.

For in my thought ther is no *mo* but ye,   *other*
Whom I have serv*e*d without repentaunce;   10
Wherfore I pray you, see to my *grevaunce*   *grief*
And put aside all myn adversitee—
So faire, so freshe, so goodly on to see,
So welle demeined in all your governaunce.

[287] *Madame, as longe as it doth plese yow ay*

Madame, as longe as it doth plese yow ay
To doon me lyve in this paynfulle manere,
Myn hert is redy forto bere it here,
Without *grucchyng*, and shalle *to that y day*;   *grouching/ till I die*
Only in trust yet of a bettir day   5
Endewre y shalle, syn it is yowre plesere,
        Madame, as long as it doth plese yow ay
        To doon me live in this paynfulle manere.
For onys ye woll*e* have pite, dar y say,
When ye have well*e* bithought, yow lady dere,   10
That all*e* is for the love y to yow bere
That wrongfully doth holde me this away,
        Madame, as long as it doth plese yow ay
        To doon me live in this paynfulle manere.

286. See Nos. 155–163. Composed during his English captivity.
287. See *French Chansons of Charles d'Orléans*, ed. Sarah Spence (Garland, 1986), No. 19,
for Charles's own French version.

ANONYMOUS

[288] *In what estaat soevere I be*

1. In what estaat soevere I be,
   Timor mortis conturbat me.   *Fear of death disturbs me*

2. As I went in a myrie morweninge,
   I herde a brid both weepe and singe;
   This was the tenour of hir talkinge: 5
   Timor mortis conturbat me.

3. I axed that brid what she ment.
   "I am a *musket* both faire and gent;   *sparrowhawk*
   For drede of deeth I am all *shent.*   *mortified*
   Timor mortis conturbat me.   10

4. "Whan I shall *deye* I knowe no daye,   *die*
   What contree or place I cannot saye;
   Wherfore this songe sing I may:
   Timor mortis conturbat me.

5. "Jesu Crist, whan he sholde deye,   15
   To his Fader he gan saye,
   'Fader,' saide he, 'in Trinitee,
   Timor mortis conturbat me.'

6. "Alle Cristen peple biholde and see
   This world is but a vanitee   20
   And repleet with necessitee.
   Timor mortis conturbat me.

7. "Wake I or sleepe, ete or drinke,
   Whan I on my laste ende thinke,
   For greete feere my soule doth shrinke—   25
   Timor mortis conturbat me.

8. "God graunt us grace him to serve,
   And be at oure ende whan we *sterve,*   *die*
   And from the Feend he us preserve!
   Timor mortis conturbat me."   30

[289] *I am of Irelond*

I am of Irelond,
And of the holy lond
Of Irelond.

Goode sire, preye I thee
For of Saint Charitee   5
Come and daunce with me
    In Irelond.

[290] *O Western Wind, when wilt thou blow*

O Western Wind, when wilt thou blow:
The small rain down can rain?
Christ! that my love were in my arms—
And I in my bed again!

E. SCOTTISH-ENGLISH BALLADS

[291] *The Wife of Usher's Well*

1. There lived a wife at Usher's Well,
    And a wealthy wife was she;
  She had three stout and stalwart sons,
    And sent them o'er the sea.

2. They hadna been a week from her,   5
    A week but barely *ane*,   *one*
  Whan word came to the *carlin* wife   *peasant*
    That her three sons were gone.

3. They hadna been a week from her,
    A week but barely three,   10
  Whan word came to the carlin wife
    That her sons she'd never see.

4. "I wish the wind may never cease
    Nor *fashes* in the flood,   *troubles*
  Till my three sons come hame to me,   15
    In earthly flesh and blood."

5. It fell about the Martinmass
    When nights are lang and mirk,
  The carlin wife's three sons came hame,
    And their hats were o' the *birk*.   *birch* 20

6. It neither grew in *syke* nor ditch,   *gully*
    Nor yet in any *sheugh*;   *furrow*
  But at the gates of Paradise,
    That birk grew fair eneugh.

291. Child 79. Recording: Argo ZDA 70.

7. "Blow up the fire, my maidens,
    Bring water from the well;
For a' my house shall feast this night
    Since my three sons are well."   25

8. And she has made to them a bed,
    She's made it large and wide,
And she's ta'en her mantle her about,   30
    Sat down at the bedside.

9. Up then crew the red, red cock,
    And up and crew the gray;
The eldest to the youngest said,   35
    "'Tis time we were away."

10. The cock he hadna crawd but once,
    And clappd his wings at a',
When the youngest to the eldest said,
    "Brother, we must awa'.   40

11. "The cock doth craw, the day doth daw,
    The *channerin* worm doth chide;   *devouring*
Gin we be missed out o' our place,   *If*
    A *sair* pain we *maun* bide.   *sore/ must*

12. "Fare ye well, my mother dear!   45
    Farewell to barn and *byre!*   *shed*
And fare ye well, ye bonny lass
    That kindles my mother's fire!"

[292]The Three Ravens

1. There were three ravens sat on a tree,
    Down a down, hay down, hay down.
There were three ravens sat on a tree,
    With a down.
There were three ravens sat on a tree,   5
They were as black as they might be:
    With a down derrie, derrie, derrie, down, down.

2. The one of them said to his mate,
    "Where shall we our breakfast take?"

3. "Down in yonder greene field   10
    There lies a knight slain under his shield.

292. Child 26. Many alternate versions, such as the Scottish *Twa Corbies*. For recording: Argo ZDA 72, which contains many variants, including the strident American *Billy McGee, McGaw*.

4. "His hounds they lie down at his feet,
   So well they can their master keep.

5. "His hawks they fly so eagerly,
   There's no fowl dare come him nie."   15

6. Down there comes a fallow doe,
   As great with young as she might go.

7. She lift up his bloody hed,
   And kist his wounds that were so red.

8. She got him up upon her backe,   20
   And carried him to earthen *lake*.   *pit*

9. She buried him before the prime;
   She was dead herself at evensong time.

10. God send every gentleman
    Such hawks, such hounds, and such a *lemman*.   *beloved one*   25

[293] *The Twa Corbies*

1. As I was walking all *alane*,   *alone*
   I heard *twa corbies* making a *mane;*   *two crows / moan*
   The *tane* unto the t'other say,   *one*
   "Where shall we *gang* and dine today?"   *go*

2. "In behind yon *auld fail dyke*,   *old foul ditch*   5
   I *wot* there lies a new-slain knight;   *know*
   And naebody *kens* that he lies there,   *knows*
   But his hawk, his hound, and lady fair.

3. "His hound is to the hunting gane,
   His hawk to fetch the wild-fowl *hame*,   *home*   10
   His lady's ta'en another mate,
   So we may mak our dinner sweet.

4. "Ye'll sit on his white *hause-bane*,   *neckbone*
   And I'll *pike* out his bonny blue *een;*   *pick / eyes*
   Wi'ae lock o' his *gowden* hair   *with a / golden*   15
   We'll *theek* our nest when it grows bare.   *thatch*

5. "*Mony* a one for him makes mane,   *many*
   But *nane* shall ken where he is gane;   *none*
   O'er his white banes, when they are bare,
   The wind shall *blaw for evermair*."   *blow evermore*   20

[294] *Sir Patrick Spens*

1. The King sits in Dumferling Toun,
   Drinking the blood-red wine:
   "O whar will I get good sailor
   To sail this ship of mine?"

2. Then up and spak an eldern knight,   5
   Sat at the King's right knee:
   "Sir Patrick Spens is the best sailor
   That ever saild the see."

3. The King has written a *braid* letter   *broad*
   And seald it wi' his hand;   10
   He sent it to Sir Patrick Spens
   Was walking on the sand.

4. The first line that Sir Patrick red,
   A loud *lauch* lauched he;   *laugh*
   The next line that Sir Patrick red   15
   The teir blinded his *ee*.   *eye*

5. "O *wha* is this has don this deid,   *who*
   This ill deid don to me,
   To send me out this time o' the yeir
   To sail upon the see!   20

6. "Mak hast, mak hast, my merry men all;
   Our good ship sails the morn."
   "O say na so, my master deir,
   For I feir a dedly storm.

7. "Late, late *yestreen* I saw the new moon   *yester evening* 25
   Wi' the auld moon in her arm;
   And I feir, I feir, my deir master,
   That we will com to harm."

8. O our Scots nobles wer right *laith*   *loath, unwilling*
   To wet their cork-heeld *shoone*;   *shoes* 30
   But lang ere a' the play wer playd,
   Their hats they swam *aboone*.   *above*

9. O lang, lang may their ladies sit
   Wi' their fans into their hand
   Befor they see Sir Patrick Spens   35
   Com sailing to the land.

294. Child 58. Perhaps based on events in 1281 or 1290. For music, consult Argo ZDA 72.

10. O lang, lang may the ladies stand
    Wi' their gold *kems* i' their hair,   *combs*
Waiting for their *ain* deir lords,   *own*
For they'll see them na mair.   40

11. Half *oure*, half oure to Aberdour   *over*
    It's fifty fadom deip.
It's ther lies good Sir Patrick Spens
    Wi' the Scots lords at his feit.

[295] *The Unquiet Grave*

1. "The wind doth blow today, my love,
    And a few small drops of rain;
I never had but one true-love,
    In cold grave she was lain.

2 "I'll do as much for my true-love   5
    As any young man may;
I'll sit and mourn all at her grave
    For a twelvemonth and a day."

3. The twelvemonth and a day being up,
    The dead began to speak: 10
"Oh, who sits weeping on my grave,
    And will not let me sleep?"

4. "Tis I, my love, sits on your grave,
    And will not let you sleep;
For I crave one kiss of your clay-cold lips,   15
    And that is all I seek."

5. "You crave one kiss of my clay-cold lips;
    But my breath smells earthy strong;
If you have one kiss of my clay-cold lips,
    Your time will not be long.   20

6. "Tis down in yonder garden green,
    Love, where we used to walk,
The finest flower that ere was seen
    Is withered to a stalk.

7. "The stalk is withered dry, my love,   25
    So will our hearts decay;
So make yourself content, my love,
    Till God calls you away."

    295. Child 78. Beautifully rendered by Joan Baez on Vanguard VSD-79160, who makes
the dead beloved masculine and sings a modernized version with an additional stanza.

[IX] SELECTED ORIGINAL TEXTS

Original Text for No. 4

O admirabile Veneris idolum,
cuius materiae nihil est frivolum;
archos te protegat, qui stellas et polum
fecit, et maria condidit et solum.
furis ingenio non sentias dolum: 5
Clotho te diligat, quae baiulat colum.

Saluto puerum non per hypothesim,
sed firmo pectore deprecor Lachesim,
sororem Atropos, ne curet haeresim.
Neptunum comitem habeas et Thetim   10
cum vectus fueris per fluvium Athesim.
quo fugis, amabo, cum te dilexerim?
miser quid faciam, cum te non viderim?

Dura materies ex matris ossibus
creavit homines iactis lapidibus: 15
ex quibus unus est iste puerulus,
qui lacrimabiles non curat gemitus.
cum tristis fuero, gaudebit aemulus:
ut cerva rugio, cum fugit hinnulus.

Original Text for No. 7

Phoebi claro	nondum orto iubare,
fert Aurora	lumen terris tenue:
spiculator	pigris clamat 'surgite'.
L'alba part umet mar atra sol	
Poy pasa bigil	*mira clar tenebras.*

(line 5)

En incautos	hostium insidie
torpentesque	gliscunt intercipere
quos suadet	preco clamans surgere.
L'alba part umet mar atra sol	
Poy pasa bigil	*mira clar tenebras.*

(line 10)

Plate 11. Castle Neuschwanstein near Munich. Built in the nineteenth century by Ludwig II (the Mad) of Bavaria under the inspiration of Richard Wagner's operas, it represents a fine link between the medieval and the modern worlds. Various rooms honor Tristan and Isolde, the archetypal lovers, and the poet Tannhäuser (No. 195). (Courtesy of the German Information Center)

Ab Arcturo   disgregatur aquilo
poli suos   condunt astra radios.
orienti   tenditur septentrio.
L'alba part umet mar atra sol
Poy pasa bigil   *mira clar tenebras.*   15

Original Text for No. 20

1. Dies irae, dies illa,
   Solvet saeclum in favilla,
   Teste David cum Sibylla.

2. Quantus tremor est futurus,
   Quando Iudex est venturus,   5
   Cuncta stricte discussurus!

3. Tuba mirum sparget sonum
   Per sepulchra regionum,
   Coget omnes ante thronum.

4. Mors stupebit et Natura,   10
   Cum resurget creatura
   Iudicanti responsura.

5. Liber scriptus proferetur,
   In quo totum continetur.
   Unde mundus iudicetur.   15

6. Iudex ergo cum censebit,
   Quidquid latet, apparebit;
   Nil inultum remanebit.

7. Quid sum miser tunc dicturus,
   Quem patronum rogaturus,   20
   Cum vix iustus sit securus?

8. Rex tremendae maiestatis,
   Qui salvandos salvas gratis,
   Salva me, fons pietatis!

9. Recordare, Iesu pie,   25
   Quod sum causa tuae viae:
   Ne me perdas illa die.

10. Quaerens me sedisti lassus;
    Redemisti crucem passus;
    Tantus labor non sit cassus.   30

11. Iuste Iudex ultionis,
    Donum fac remissionis
    Ante diem rationis.

12. Ingemisco tamquam reus: 35
    Culpa rubet vultus meus;
    Supplicanti parce, Deus.

13. Qui Mariam absolvisti
    Et latronem exaudisti,
    Mihi quoque spem dedisti.

14. Preces meae non sunt dignae,   40
    Sed tu, bonus, fac benigne,
    Ne perenni cremer igne.

15. Inter oves locum praesta
    Et ab haedis me sequestra
    Statuens in parte dextra.   45

16. Confutatis maledictis,
    Flammis acribus addictis,
    Voca me cum benedictis!

17. Oro supplex et acclinis,
    Cor contritum quasi cinis;   50
    Gere curam mei finis!

Original Text for No. 21

1. Stabat mater dolorosa
   Iuxta crucem lacrimosa
       Dum pendebat filius;
   Cuius animam gementem
   Contristantem et dolentem   5
       Pertransivit gladius.

2. O quam tristis et afflicta
   Fuit illa benedicta
       Mater unigeniti
   Quae maerebat, et dolebat,   10
   Et tremebat cum videbat
       Nati poenas incliti.

3. Quis est homo qui non fleret
   Matrem Christi si videret
       In tanto supplicio?   15

Quis non posset contristari
Piam matrem contemplari
    Dolentem cum filio?

4. Pro peccatis suae gentis
  Iesum vidit in tormentis   20
    Et flagellis subditum.
  Vidit suum dulcem natum
  Morientem, desolatum,
    Dum emisit spiritum.

5. Eia, mater! fons amoris,   25
  Me sentire vim doloris
    Fac, ut tecum lugeam;
  Fac ut ardeat cor meum
  In amando Christum Deum,
    Ut sibi complaceam.   30

6. Sancta mater, istud agas,
  Crucifixi fige plagas
    Cordi meo valide;
  Tui nati vulnerati,
  Tam dignati pro me pati,   35
    Poenas mecum divide!

7. Fac me vere tecum flere,
  Crucifixo condolere,
    Donec ego vixero.
  Iuxta crucem tecum stare,   40
  Te libenter sociare
    In planctu desidero.

8. Virgo virginum praeclara
  Mihi iam non sis amara;
    Fac me tecum plangere,   45
  Fac, ut portem Christi mortem,
  Passionis eius sortem
    Et plagas recolere.

9. Fac me plagis vulnerari,
  Cruce hac inebriari   50
    Ob amorem filii;
  Inflammatus et accensus
  Per te, virgo, sim defensus
    In die iudicii.

10. Fac me cruce custodiri,   55
  Morte Christi praemuniri,
    Confoveri gratia;

Quando corpus morietur
Fac ut animae donetur
   Paradisi gloria.   60

Original Text for No. 23

O Fortuna,
velut luna
statu variabilis,
semper crescis
aut decrescis;   5
vita detestabilis
nunc obdurat
et tunc curat
ludo mentis aciem,
egestatem,   10
potestatem
dissolvit ut glaciem.

Sors inmanis
et inanis,
rota tu volubilis,   15
status malus,
vana salus
semper dissolubilis,
obumbratam
et velatam   20
mihi quoque niteris,
nunc per ludum
dorsum nudum
fero tui sceleris.

Sors salutis   25
et virtutis
mihi nunc contraria,
est affectus
et defectus
semper in angaria;   30
hac in hora
sine mora
corde pulsum tangite,
quod per sortem
sternit fortem: 35
mecum omnes plangite.

Original Text for No. 34

1. Iam iam rident prata,
   Iam iam virgines
   Iocundantur, Terre
   Ridet facies.
   Estas nunc apparuit,   5
   Ornatusque florum
       Lete claruit.

2. Nemus revirescit,
   Frondent frutices;
   Hiems seva cessit;   10
   Leti iuvenes,
   Congaudete floribus!
   Amor allicit vos
       Iam virginibus.

3. Ergo militemus   15
   Simul Veneri;
   Tristia vitemus
   Nosque teneri!
   Visus et colloquia,
   Spes amorque trahant   20
       Nos ad gaudia!

Original Text for No. 38

1. Axe Phebus aureo
       Celsiora lustrat
   Et nitore roseo
       Radios illustrat.
   Venustata Cybele   5
       Facie florente
   Florem nato Semele
       Dat Phebo favente.

2. Aurarum suavium
       Gratia iuvante   10
   Sonat nemus avium
       Voce modulante.
   Philomena querule
       Terea retractat,
   Dum canendo merule   15
       Carmina coaptat.

3. Iam Dionea
   Leta chorea
   Sedulo resonat
   Cantibus horum,   20
   Iamque Dione
   Iocis, agone
   Relevat, cruciat
   Corda suorum.

4. Me quoque subtrahit   25
   Illa sopori
   Invigilareque
   Cogit amori.
   Tela Cupidinis
   Aurea gesto,   30
   Igne cremantia
   Corde molesto.

5. Quod michi datur,
       Expaveo,
   Quodque negatur,   35
       Hoc aveo
   Mente severa.
   Que michi cedit,
       Hanc caveo;
   Que non obedit,   40
       Huic faveo
   Sumque re vera:

6. Fidelis, seu peream
   Seu relever per eam.
   Que cupit, hanc fugio,   45
   Que fugit, hanc cupio;
   Plus renuo debitum,
   Plus feror in vetitum;
   Plus licet illibitum;
   Plus libet illicitum.   50

7. O metuenda
   Dione decreta!
   O fugienda
   Venena secreta,
   Fraude verenda   55
   Doloque repleta,
   Docta furoris
   In estu punire,
   Quos dat amoris
   Amara subire,   60
   Plena livoris
   Urentis et ire!

8. Hinc michi metus
    Abundat,
  Hinc ora fletus 65
    Inundat,
  Hinc michi pallor
    In ore
  Est, quia fallor
    Amore. 70

Original Text for No. 40

1. Dira vi amoris teror
  Et Venereo axe feror,
  Igni ferventi suffocatus;
  Deme, pia, cruciatus!

2. Ignis vivi tu scintilla, 5
  Discurrens cordis ad vexilla,
  Igni incumbens non pauxillo
  Conclusi mentis te sigillo.

3. Meret cor, quod gaudebat
  Die, quo te cognoscebat 10
  Singularem et pudicam,
  Te adoptabat in amicam.

4. Profero pectoris singultus
  Et mestitie tumultus,
  Nam amoris tui vigor 15
  Urget me, et illi ligor.

5. Virginale lilium,
  Tuum presta subsidium!
  Missus in exilium
  Querit a te consilium. 20

6. Nescit, quid agat; moritur.
  Amore tui vehitur,
  Telo necatur Veneris,
  Sibi ni subveneris.

7. Iure Veneris orbata, 25
  Castitas redintegrata,
  Vultu decenti perornata,
  Veste Sophie decorata.

8. Tibi soli psallo; noli
   despicere . . . .*   30
   per me, precor, velis coli,
   lucens ut stella poli!

Original Text for No. 42

1. A l'entrada del tens clar, *eya*,
   per joia recomençar, *eya*,
   e per jelos irritar, *eya*,
   vol la regina mostrar
   qu'el' es si amoroza.   5
   A la vi', a la via, jelos,
   laissaz nos, laissaz nos
   ballar entre nos, entre nos.

2. El' a fait per tot mandar, *eya*,   10
   non sia jusqu'a la mar, *eya*,
   piucela ni bachelar, *eya*,
   que tuit non venguan dançar
   en la dansa joioza.

3. Lo reis i ven d'autra part, *eya*,
   per la dansa destorbar, *eya*,   15
   que el es en cremetar, *eya*,
   que om no li voill' emblar
   la regin' avrilloza.

4. Mais per nient lo vol far, *eya*,
   qu'ela n'a sonh de viellart, *eya*,   20
   mais d'un leugier bachelar, *eya*,
   qui ben sapcha solaçar
   la domna savoroza.

5. Qui donc la vezes dançar, *eya*,
   e son gent cors deportar, *eya*,   25
   ben pogra dir de vertat, *eya*,
   qu'el mont non aia sa par
   la regina joioza.
   A la vi', a la via, jelos,
   laissaz nos, laissaz nos
   ballar entre nos, entre nos.

*Schmeller: "Psallo tibi soli;/ despicere me noli."

Original Text for No. 45

1. Ab la dolchor del temps novel
   Foillo li bosc, e li aucel
   Chanton, chascus en lor lati,
   Segon lo vers del novel chan;
   Adonc esta ben c'om s'aisi   5
   D'acho don hom a plus talan.

2. De lai don plus m'es bon e bel
   Non vei mesager ni sagel,
   Per que mos cors non dorm ni ri,
   Ni no m'aus traire adenan,   10
   Tro qe sacha ben de la fi
   S'el' es aissi com eu deman.

3. La nostr' amor vai enaissi
   Com la branca de l'albespi
   Qu'esta sobre l'arbe tremblan,   15
   La nuoit, a la ploja ez al gel,
   Tro l'endeman, que·l sols s'espan
   Per la fueilla verz e·l ramel.

4. Enquer me menbra d'un mati
   Que nos fezem de guerra fi,   20
   E que·m donet un don tan gran,
   Sa drudari'e son anel:
   Enquer me lais Dieus viure tan
   C'aia mas manz soz so mantel!

5. Qu'eu non ai soing d'estraing lati   25
   Que·m parta de mon Bon Vezi,
   Qu'eu sai de paraulas, com van
   Ab un breu sermon que s'espel,
   Que tal se van d'amor gaban,
   Nos n'avem la pessa e·l coutel!   30

Original Text for No. 52

1. A la fontana del vergier
   On l'erb'es vertz josta·l gravier,
   A l'ombra d'un fust domesgier
   En aiziment de blancas flors
   E de novelh chant costumier,   5
   Trobei sola, ses companhier,
   Selha que no vol mon solatz.

2. So fon donzelh'ab son cors belh
   Filha d'un senhor de castelh;
   E quant ieu cugey que l'auzelh   10
   Li fesson joy e la verdors,
   E pel dous termini novelh,
   E quez entendes mon favelh,
   Tost li fon sos afars camjatz.

3. Dels huelhs ploret josta la fon   15
   E del cor sospiret preon.
   "Jhesus," dis elha, "reys del mon,
   Per vos mi creys ma grans dolors,
   Quar vostra anta mi cofon,
   Quar li mellor de tot est mon   20
   Vos van servir, mas a vos platz.

4. "Ab vos s'en vai lo mieus amicx,
   Lo belhs e·l gens e·l pros e·l ricx.
   Sai m'en reman lo grans destricx,
   Lo deziriers, soven e·l plors.   25
   Ay! mala fos reys Lozoicx
   Que fay los mans e los prezicx
   Per que·l dols m'es el cor intratz!"

5. Quant ieu l'auzi desconortar,
   Ves lieys vengui josta·l riu clar: 30
   "Belha," fi·m ieu, "per trop plorar
   Afolha cara e colors;
   E no vos cal dezesperar,
   Que selh qui fai lo bosc fulhar
   Vos pot donar de joy assatz."   35

6. "Senher," dis elha, "ben o crey
   Que Dieus aya de mi mercey
   En l'autre segle per jassey,
   Quon assatz d'autres peccadors;
   Mas say mi tolh aquelha rey   40
   Don joy mi crec; mas pauc mi tey,
   Que trop s'es de mi alonhatz."

Original Text for No. 53

1. Lanqan li jorn son lonc en mai
   m'es bels doutz chans d'auzels de loing,
   e qan me sui partitz de lai,
   remembra·m d'un'amor de loing:
   vau de talan embroncs e clis,   5

si que chans ni flors d'albespis
no·m platz plus que l'iverns gelatz.

2. Ben tenc lo Seignor per verai
   per q'ieu veirai l'amor de loing,
   mas per un ben que m'en eschai   10
   n'ai dos mals, car tant m'es de loing;
   ai! car me fos lai pelleris,
   si que mos fustz e mos tapis
   fos pels sieus bels oills remiratz!

3. Be·m parra jois qan li qerrai,   15
   per amor Dieu, l'alberc de loing;
   e s'a lieis platz, albergarai
   pres de lieis, si be·m sui de loing;
   adoncs parra·l parlamens fis,
   qand drutz loindas er tant vezis   20
   c'ab bels digz jauzira solatz.

4. Iratz e gauzens m'en partrai,
   qan veirai cest'amor de loing;
   mas non sai coras la veirai,
   car trop son nostras terras loing;   25
   assatz hi a portz e camis,
   e per aisso no·n sui devis . . .
   mas tot sia cum a Dieu platz!

5. Ja mais d'amor no·m gauzirai
   si no·m gau d'est'amor de loing,   30
   que gensor ni meillor non sai
   vas nuilla part, ni pres ni loing;
   tant es sos pretz verais e fis
   qe lai el renc dels Sarrazis
   fos eu per lieis chaitius clamatz.   35

6. Dieus qui fetz tot cant ve ni vai,
   e formet cest'amor de loing,
   mi don poder, que·l cor eu n'ai,
   q'en breu veia l'amor de loing,
   veraiamen en locs aizis,   40
   si que la cambra e·l jardis
   mi resembles totz temps palatz.

7. Ver ditz qui m'apella lechai
   ni desiron d'amor de loing,
   car nuills autre jois tant no·m plai   45
   cum gauzimens d'amor de loing;
   mas so q'eu vuoill m'es tan taïs
   q'enaissi·m fadet mos pairis
   q'ieu ames e non fos amatz.

8. Mas so q'ieu vuoill m'es tan taïs: 50
   toz sia mauditz lo pairis
   qe·m fadet q'ieu non fos amatz!

Original Text for No. 55

1. Can vei la lauzeta mover
   De joi sas alas contral rai,
   Que s'oblid'e·s laissa chazer
   Per la doussor c'al cor li vai,
   Ai! tan grans enveya m'en ve   5
   De cui qu'eu veya jauzion,
   Meravilhas ai, car desse
   Lo cor de dezirer no·m fon.

2. Ai, las! tan cuidava saber
   D'amor, e tan petit en sai!   10
   Car eu d'amar no·m posc tener
   Celeis don ja pro non aurai.
   Tout m'a mo cor, e tout m'a me,
   E se mezeis e tot lo mon;
   E can se·m tolc, no·m laisset re   15
   Mas dezirer e cor volon.

3. Anc non agui de me poder
   Ni no fui meus de l'or'en sai
   Que·m laisset en sos olhs vezer
   En un miralh que mout me plai.   20
   Miralhs, pus me mirei en te,
   M'an mort li sospir de preon,
   C'aissi·m perdei com perdet se
   Lo bels Narcisus en la fon.

4. De las domnas me dezesper;   25
   Ja mais en lor no·m fiarai;
   C'aissi com las solh chaptener,
   Enaissi las deschaptenrai.
   Pois vei c'una pro no m'en te
   Vas leis que·m destrui e·m cofon,   30
   Totas las dopt'e las mescre,
   Car be sai c'atretals se son.

5. D'aisso·s fa be femna parer
   Ma domna, per qu'e·lh o retrai,
   Car no vol so c'om deu voler,   35
   E so c'om li deveda, fai.
   Chazutz sui en mala merce,

Et ai be faih co·l fols en pon;
E no sai per que m'esdeve,
Mas car trop puyei contra mon. 40

6. Merces es perduda, per ver,
(Et eu non o saubi anc mai),
Car cilh qui plus en degr'aver,
No·n a ges, et on la querrai?
A! can mal sembla, qui la ve, 45
Qued aquest chaitiu deziron
Que ja ses leis no aura be,
Laisse morir, que no l'aon!

7. Pus ab midons no·m pot valer
Precs ni merces ni·l dreihz qu'eu ai, 50
Ni a leis no ven a plazer
Qu'eu l'am, ja mais no·lh o dirai.
Aissi·m part de leis e·m recre;
Mort m'a, e per mort li respon,
E vau m'en, pus ilh no·m rete, 55
Chaitius, en issilh, no sai on.

8. Tristans, ges no·n auretz de me,
Qu'eu m'en vau, chaitius, no sai on.
De chantar me gic e·m recre,
E de joi e d'amor m'escon. 60

Original Text for No. 65

1. A chantar m'er de so qu'ieu non volria,
tant me rancur de lui cui sui amia,
car eu l'am mais que nuilla ren que sia;
vas lui no.m val merces ni cortesia,
ni ma beltatz, ni mos pretz, ni mos sens, 5
c'atressi·m sui enganad'e trahia
com degr'esser, s'ieu fos desavinens.

2. D'aisso·m conort car anc non fi faillenssa,
amics, vas vos per nuilla captenenssa,
anz vos am mais non fetz Seguis Valenssa; 10
e platz me mout quez eu d'amar vos venssa,
lo mieus amics, car etz lo plus valens;
mi faitz orguoill en digz et en parvenssa,
e si etz francs vas totas autras gens.

3. Meravill me com vostre cors s'enorguoilla, 15
amics, vas me, per qu'ai razon que·m duoilla;

non es ges dreitz c'autr' amors vos mi tuoilla
per nuilla ren que·us diga ni·us acuoilla;
e membre vos cals fo·l comensamens
de nostr'amor. Ja Dompnideus non vuoilla   20
qu'en ma colpa sia·l departimens!

4. Proesa grans qu'el vostre cors s'aizina
e lo rics pretz qu'avetz me·n ataïna,
c'una non sai loindana ni vezina
si vol amar, vas vos non si'aclina;   25
mas vos, amics, etz ben tant conoisens
que ben devetz conoisser la plus fina:
e membre vos de nostres covinens.

5. Valer mi deu mos pretz e mos paratges,
e ma beutatz e plus mos fis coratges,   30
per qu'ieu vos mand lai on es vostr'estatges
esta chansson que me sia messatges:
e voill saber, lo mieus bels amics gens,
per que vos m'etz tant fers ni tant salvatges;
non sai si s'es orguoills o mals talens.   35

6. Mas aitan plus vuoill li digas, messatges,
qu'en trop d'orguoill ant gran dan maintas gens.

Original Text for No. 77

1. En cest sonet coind'e leri,
fauc motz, e capuig e doli,
que serant verai e cert
qan n'aurai passat la lima,
qu'Amors mi deplan'e [marves plan'e] daura   5
mon chantar, que de liei mou
que Pretz manten e governa.

2. Mil messas n'aug e·n proferi,
e n'art lum de cera e d'oli,
que Dieus m'en don bon issert   10
de lieis on no·m val escrima;
e qand remir sa crin saura
e·l cors q'a graile[t] e nou,
mais l'am que qi·m des Luserna.

3. Tant l'am de cor e la queri   15
c'ab trop voler cuig la·m toli
(s'om ren per ben amar pert).

Lo sieus cors sobretracima
lo mieu tot e non s'isaura;
tant a[i] de ver fait renou   20
c'obrador n'a[i] e taverna.

4. Tot jorn meillur et esmeri
car la gensor serv e coli
del mon—so·us dic en apert;
sieus sui del pe tro c'en cima,   25
e si tot venta·ill freid' aura
l'Amors, q'inz el cor mi plou,
mi ten chaut on plus iverna.

5. Ges pel maltraich q'ieu soferi
de ben amar no·m destoli   30
liei (anz dic en descobert) [sitot me ten en
     desert];
car si·m fatz los motz en rima,
pieitz trac aman c'om que laura;
c'anc plus non amet un ou
cel de Moncli N'Audierna.   35

6. Non vuoill de Roma l'emperi
ni c'om mi fassa apostoli,
q'en lieis non aia revert,
per cui m'art lo cors e·m rima;
e s'il maltraich no·m restaura   40
ab un baissar anz d'annou,
mi auci, e si enferna.

7. Ieu sui Arnautz, q'amas l'aura,
e chatz la lebre ab lo bou,
e nadi contra suberna.   45

Original Text for No. 81

1. Kalenda maya
    ni fuelhs de faya
ni chanz d'auzelh   ni flors de glaya
    non es que·m playa,
    pros domna guaya,   5
tro qu'un ysnelh   messatgier aya
del vostre belh   cors, que·m retraya
plazer novelh   qu'amors m'atraya,
     e iaya
     e'm traya   10
  vas vos,   domna veraya;

      e chaya
      de playa
·l gelos,   ans que·m n'estraya.

2. Ma belh'amia,   15
    per Dieu no sia
que ia·l gelos   de mon dan ria;
    que car vendria
    sa gelozia,
si aitals dos   amans partia;   20
qu'ieu ia ioyos   mais no seria,
ni ioys ses vos   pro no·m tenria;
      tal via
      faria,
qu'om ia   mais no·m veiria;   25
      selh dia
      morria,
donna   pros, qu'ie·us perdria.

3. Quom er perduda
    ni m'er renduda   30
dona, s'enans   non l'ai aguda?
    que drutz ni druda
    non es per cuda;
mas quant amans   en drut se muda,
l'onors es grans   que·ylh n'es creguda; 35
e·l belhs semblans   fai far tal bruda;
    que nuda
    tenguda
no·us ai   ni d'als vencuda;
    volguda,   40
    crezuda
vos ai,   ses autr' aiuda.

4. Tart m'esiauzira,
    pus ia·m partira,
Belhs Cavaliers,   de vos ab ira;   45
    qu'alhor no·s vira
    mos cors, ni·m tira
mos deziriers,   qu'als non dezira;
qu'a lauzengiers   sai qu'abelhira,
donna, qu'estiers   non lur garira.   50
    tals vira,
    sentira
mos dans,   qui·ls vos grazira,
    que·us mira,
    consira   55
cuidans,   don cors sospira.

5. Dona grazida,
    quecx lauz' e crida
vostra valor,   qu'es abelhida;
    e qui·us oblida,   60
    pauc li val vida.
per qu'ie·us azor,   don' eyssernida?
quar per gensor   vos ai chauzida,
e per melhor   de pretz complida,
    blandida,   65
    servida
    genses   qu' Erecx Enida.
    bastida
    fenida,
    n'Engles,   ai l'estampida.   70

Original Text for No. 91

Io m'aggio posto in core a Dio servire,
Com'io potesse gire in Paradiso,
Al santo loco, c'aggio audito dire,
O'si mantien sollazzo, gioco e riso.
Sanza mia donna non vi voria gire,   5
Quella c'à blonda testa e claro viso,
Ché sanza lei non poteria gaudire,
Estando da la mia donna diviso.

Ma no lo dico a tale intendimento
Perch'io peccato ci volesse fare,   10
Se non veder lo suo bel portamento
E lo bel viso e 'l morbido sguardare;
Ché lo mi teria in gran consolamento,
Veggendo la mia donna in ghiora stare.

Original Text for No. 103

1. Al cor gentil rempaira sempre amore
    Come l'ausello in selva a la verdura;
        Né fe' amor anti che gentil core,
    Né gentil core anti ch'amor, natura:
        Ch'adesso con' fu 'lsole,   5
    Sì tosto lo splendore fu lucente,
        Né fu davanti 'l sole;

E prende amore in gentilezza loco
Così propiamente
Come calore in clarità di foco.   10

2. Foco d'amore in gentil cor s'aprende
Come vertute in petra preziosa,
    Ché da la stella valor no i discende
Anti che 'l sol la faccia gentil cosa;
      Poi che n'ha tratto fòre   15
Per sua forza lo sol ciò che li è vile,
Stella li dà valore:
Così lo cor ch'è fatto da natura
Asletto, pur, gentile,
Donna, a guisa di stella, lo 'nnamora.   20

3. Amor per tal ragion sta 'n cor gentile
Per qual lo foco in cima del doplero:
    Splendeli al su' diletto, clar, sottile;
No li stari'altra guisa, tant'è fero.
      Così prava natura   25
Recontra amor come fa l'aigua il foco
Caldo, per la freddura.
Amore in gentil cor prende rivera
Per suo consimel loco
Com'adamàs del ferro in la minera.   30

4. Fere lo sol lo fango tutto 'l giorno;
Vile reman, né 'l sol perde calore;
Dis'omo alter: "Gentil per sclatta torno";
Lui sembla al fango, al sol gentil valore:
    Ché non dé dar om fé   35
Che gentilezza sia fòr di coraggio
In degnità di rede,
Sed a vertute non ha gentil core,
Com'aigua porta raggio
E'l ciel riten le stelle e lo splendore.   40

5. Splende 'n la 'ntelligenzia del cielo
Deo criator più che 'n nostr'occhi 'l sole;
    Ella intende suo fattor oltra 'l cielo,
E'l ciel volgiando, a Lui obedir tole;
      E con' segue, al primero,   45
Del giusto Deo beato compimento,
Così dar dovria, al vero,
La bella donna, poi che 'n gli occhi splende
Del suo gentil talento
che mai di lei obedir non si disprende.   50

6. Donna, Deo mi dirà: "Che presomisti?"
Siando l'alma mia a Lui davanti,
    "Lo ciel passasti e 'nfin a Me venisti

E desti in vano amor Me per semblanti,
   Ch'a Me conven le laude   55
E a la reina del regname degno,
Per cui cessa onne fraude."
Dir Li porò, "Tenne d'angel sembianza
Che fosse del Tuo regno;
Non me fu fallo, s'in lei posi amanza."   60

Original Text for No. 106

Chi è questa che vèn, ch'ogn'om la mira,
Che fa tremar di chiaritate l'are
E mena seco Amor, sì che parlare
Null' omo pote, ma ciascun sospira?

O Deo, che sembra quando li occhi gira,   5
Dical' Amor, ch'i' nol savria contare:
Cotanto d'umiltà donna mi pare,
Ch'ogn'altra ver' di lei i' chiam' ira.

Non si poria contar la sua piagenza,
Ch'a le' s'inchin' ogni gentil vertute,   10
E la beltate per sua dea la mostra.

Non fu sì alta già la mente nostra
E non si pose 'n noi tanta salute,
Che propiamente n'aviàn canoscenza.

Original Text for No. 112

1. Donne ch'avete intelletto d'amore,
   I' vo' con voi de la mia donna dire,
   Non perch'io creda sua laude finire,
   Ma ragionar per isfogar la mente.
      Io dico che pensando il suo valore,   5
   Amor sì dolce mi si fa sentire,
   Che s'io allora non perdessi ardire,
   Farei parlando innamorar la gente.
      E io non vo' parlar sì altamente
   Ch'io divenisse per temenza vile;   10
   Ma tratterò del suo stato gentile
   A respetto di lei leggeramente,
   Donne e donzelle amorose, con vui,
   Ché non è cosa da parlarne altrui.

2. Angelo clama in divino intelletto   15
   E dice: "Sire, nel mondo si vede
   Maraviglia ne l'atto che procede
   D'un'anima che 'nfin qua su risplende."
      Lo cielo, che non have altro difetto
   Che d'aver lei, al suo segnor la chiede,   20
   E ciascun santo ne grida merzede.
   Sola Pietà nostra parte difende,
      Che parla Dio, che di madonna intende:
   "Diletti miei, or sofferite in pace
   Che vostra spene sia quanto me piace   25
   Là 'v'è alcun che perder lei s'attende,
   E che dirà ne lo inferno: 'O mal nati,
   Io vidi la speranza de' beati.'"

3. Madonna è disïata in sommo cielo:
   Or vòi di sua virtù farvi savere.   30
   Dico, qual vuol gentil donna parere
   Vada con lei, che quando va per via,
      Gitta nei cor villani Amore un gelo,
   Per che onne lor pensero agghiaccia e pere;
   E qual soffrisse di starla a vedere   35
   Diverria nobil cosa, o si morria.
      E quando trova alcun che degno sia
   Di veder lei, quei prova sua vertute,
   Ché li avvien, ciò che li dona, in salute,
   E sì l'umilia, ch'ogni offesa oblia.   40
   Ancor l'ha Dio per maggior grazia dato
   Che non pò mal finir chi l'ha parlato.

4. Dice di lei Amor: "Cosa mortale
   Come esser pò sì adorna e sì pura?"
   Poi la reguarda, e fra se stesso giura   45
   Che Dio ne 'ntenda di far cosa nova.
      Color di perle ha quasi, in forma quale
   Convene a donna aver, non for misura:
   Ella è quanto de ben pò far natura;
   Per essemplo di lei bieltà si prova.   50
      De li occhi suoi, come ch'ella li mova,
   Escono spirti d'amore inflammati,
   Che feron li occhi a qual che allor la guati,
   E passan sì che 'l cor ciascun retrova:
   Voi le vedete Amor pinto nel viso,   55
   Là 've non pote alcun mirarla fiso.

5. Canzone, io so che tu girai parlando
   A donne assai, quand'io t'avrò avanzata.
   Or t'ammonisco, perch'io t'ho allevata
   Per figliuola d'Amor giovane e piana,   60
      Che là 've giugni tu diche pregando:

"Insegnatemi gir, ch'io son mandata
A quella di cui laude so' adornata."
E se non vuoli andar sì come vana,
   Non restare ove sia gente villana: 65
Ingegnati, se puoi, d'esser palese
Solo con donne o con omo cortese,
Che ti merranno là per via tostana.
Tu troverai Amor con esso lei;
Raccomandami a lui come tu dei.   70

Original Text for No. 129

Or che 'l ciel e la terra e 'l vento tace,
E le fere e gli augelli il sonno affrena,
Notte il carro stellato in giro mena
E nel suo letto il mar senz'onda giace;
Vegghio, penso, ardo, piango; e chi mi sface   5
Sempre m'è inanzi per mia dolce pena;
Guerra è 'l mio stato, d'ira e di duol piena;
E sol di lei pensando ò qualche pace.

Così sol d'una chiara fonte viva
Move 'l dolce e l'amaro ond'io mi pasco;   10
Una man sola mi risana e punge;
E perché 'l mio martir non giunga a riva,
Mille volte il dì moro e mille nasco:
Tanto da la salute mia son lunge!

Original Text for No. 157

Le temps a laissié son manteau
De vent, de froidure et de pluie,
Et s'est vestu de brouderie,
De soleil luyant, cler et beau.

Il n'y a beste, ne oiseau,   5
Qu'en son jargon ne chante ou crie:
"Le temps a laissié son manteau."

Riviere, fontaine, et ruisseau
Portent, en livree jolie,
Gouttes d'argent d'orfaverie,   10
Chascun s'abille de nouveau—
Le temps a laissié son manteau.

Original Text for No. 168

1. Se j'ayme et sers la belle de bon het,
   M'en devez vous tenir ne vil ne sot?
   Elle a en soy des biens a fin souhet.
   Pour son amour seins bouclier et passot;
   Quant viennent gens, je cours et happe ung pot,   5
   Au vin m'en voys, sans demener grant bruyt;
   Je leur tens eaue, frommaige, pain et fruyt.
   S'ilz paient bien, je leur dis: "*Bene stat;*
   Retournez cy quant vous serez en ruyt,
   En ce bordeau ou tenons nostre estat!"   10

2. Mais adoncques il y a grant deshet,
   Quant sans argent s'en vient couchier Margot;
   Voir ne la puis, mon cuer a mort la het.
   Sa robe prens, demy seint et seurcot,
   Sy lui jure qu'il tendra pour l'escot.   15
   Par les costez se prent, "C'est Antecrist!"
   Crye, et jure par la mort Jhesu Crist
   Que non fera. Lors empoingne ung esclat;
   Dessus son nez luy en faiz ung escript,
   En ce bordeau ou tenons nostre estat.   20

3. Puis paix se fait et me fait ung groz pet,
   Plus enffle q'un velimeux escarbot.
   Riant, m'assiet son poing sur mon sommet:
   "Gogo," me dit, et me fiert le jambot.
   Tous deux yvres, dormons comme ung sabot,   25
   Et, au resveil, quant le ventre luy bruyt,
   Monte sur moy, que ne gaste son fruyt.
   Soubz elle geins, plus q'un aiz me fait plat;
   De paillarder tout elle me destruyt
   En ce bordeau ou tenons nostre estat.   30

4. Vente, gresle, gesle, j'ay mon pain cuyt.
   Ie suis paillart, la paillarde me suyt.
   Lequel vault mieulx? Chascun bien s'entresuyt:
   L'un vault l'autre; c'est a mau rat mau chat.
   Ordure aimons, ordure nous assuyt;   35
   Nous deffuyons onneur; il nous deffuyt,
   En ce bordeau ou tenons nostre estat.

Original Text for No. 187

1. "Sîne klâwen   durh die wolken sint geslagen,
   Er stîget ûf mit grôzer kraft.
   Ich sihe in grâwen   tägelîch, als er wil tagen,
   Den tac, der im geselleschaft
   Erwenden wil, dem werden man,   5
   Den ich mit sorgen în verliez.
   Ich bringe in hinnen, ob ich kan.
   Sîn vil manegiu tugent michz leisten hiez."

2. "Wahter, du singest,   daz mir manege fröude nimt
   Unde mêret mîne klage.   10
   Mære du bringest   der mich leider niht gezimt,
   Immer morgens gegen dem tage.
   Diu solt du mir verswîgen gar;
   Daz gebiute ich den triuwen dîn.
   Des lône ich dir, als ich getar: 15
   Sô belîbet hie der geselle mîn."

3. "Er muoz et hinnen   balde und âne sûmen sich:
   Nu gib im urloup, süezez wîp.
   Lâz in minnen   her nâch sô verholne dich,
   Daz er behalt êre und den lîp.   20
   Er gab sich mîner triuwe alsô,
   Daz ich in bræhte ouch wider dan.
   Ez ist nû tac; naht was ez dô:
   Mit drucke an brust dîn kus mirn an gewan."

4. "Swaz dir gevalle,   wahter, sinc, und lâ den hie,   25
   Der minne brâhte und minne enphienc.
   Von dînem schalle   ist er und ich erschrocken ie,
   Sô ninder der morgensterne ûf gienc
   Ûf in, der her nâch minne ist komen,
   Noch ninder lûhte tages lieht.   30
   Du hâst in dicke mir benomen
   Von blanken armen, und ûz herzen nieht."

5. Von den blicken,   die der tac tet durh diu glas,
   Und dô der wahter warnen sanc,
   Si muose erschricken   durch den, der dâ bî ir was.   35
   Ir brüstelîn an brust si dwanc.
   Der rîter ellens niht vergaz;
   Des wolde in wenden wahters dôn:
   Urloup nâh und nâher baz
   Mit kusse und anders gab in minne lôn.   40

Original Text for No. 189

1. Under der linden
   An der heide,
   Dâ unser zweier bette was,
   Dâ mugt ir vinden
   Schône beide   5
   Gebrochen bluomen unde gras.
   Vor dem walde in einem tal,
         Tandaradei!
   Schône sanc diu nahtegal.

2. Ich kam gegangen   10
   Zuo der ouwe:
   Dô was mîn friedel komen ê.
   Dâ wart ich enpfangen,
   Hêre frouwe,
   Daz ich bin sælic iemer mê.   15
   Kust er mich? wol tûsentstunt:
         Tandaradei!
   Seht, wie rôt mir ist der munt.

3. Dô het er gemachet
   Alsô rîche   20
   Von bluomen eine bettestat.
   Des wirt noch gelachet
   Inneclîche,
   Kumt iemen an daz selbe pfat.
   Bî den rôsen er wol mac,   25
         Tandaradei!
   Merken, wâ mirz houbet lac.

4. Daz er bî mir læge,
   Wessez iemen
   —Nu enwelle got!—sô schamt ich mich.   30
   Wes er mit mir pflæge,
   Niemer niemen
   Bevinde daz wan er unt ich
   Und ein kleinez vogellîn:
         Tandaradei!   35
   Daz mac wol getriuwe sîn.

Original Text for No. 236

1. Quer' eu en maneira de proençal
   fazer agora un cantar d'amor
   e querrei muit' i loar mha senhor,
   a que prez nen fremusura non fal,
   nen bondade, e mais vos direi en: 5
   tanto a fez Deus comprida de ben
   que mais que todas las do mundo val.

2. Ca mha senhor quiso Deus fazer tal
   quando a fez, que a fez sabedor
   de todo ben e de mui gran valor   10
   e con tod(o) est'é mui comunal,
   ali u deve; er deu-lhi bon sen
   e des i non lhi fez pouco de ben,
   quando non quis que lh'outra foss' igual.

3. Ca en mha senhor nonca Deus pôs mal,   15
   mais pôs i prez e beldad' e loor
   e falar mui ben e riir melhor
   que outra molher; des i é leal
   muit', e por esto non sei oj' eu quen
   possa compridamente no seu ben   20
   falar, ca non á, tra-lo seu ben, al.

[X] INDICES

A. AUTHORS

(All references are to poem numbers, not pages. Asterisks indicate a woman writer.)

B. TITLES AND FIRST LINES OF ORIGINALS

(All references are to poem numbers, not pages.)

Yr wybrwynt helynt hylaw   260
Yr wylan deg ar lanw dioer   261

C. SELECTED GENRES

(All references are to poem numbers, not pages.)

Alba, Aubade: See *Dawn Song*
Ballads: 291–295
Begging Poem: 2, 281
Chanson de toile: See *Spinning Song*
Cantiga de amigo: 82, 223, 229–234
Cantiga de amor: 228, 236
Complaint (Lament): Latin 1, 10, 11, 15; Prov. 52, 86; Ital. 94; N.F. 138, 142, 160–
    162; Ger. 190; Iber. 237; Eng. 264, 266
Confessional Poem: 3, 24, 164
Conflict, Contrasto: See *Debate Poem*
Crusade Song: Prov. 50; Ital. 94; N.F. 142; Ger. 182, 190
Dance Song: 42, 81, 227, 234, 242, 268, 289
Dawn Song: Latin 7; Prov. 41, 67, 80, 83; Ger. 178, 186, 187, 197 (Parody); Iber.
    224, 244
Death Song: (for self) 25, 47, 109, 172, 288; (for others) 20, 73, 87, 130, 133, 264
Debate Poem: 10, 19, 63, 92, 194, 196 See also *Satire (Sirventes)* and *Dramatic Poem*
Dramatic Poem (Dialogue): Latin 6, 10; Prov. 63, 67; Ital. 92, 96, 117; Ger. 178, 186,
    187, 194–196; Iber. 233–234, 237 See also *Pastourelle*
Drinking Song: 27, 31, 169, 204, 211
Estramps: 246
Fable Poem: 85, 198
Fabliau: 43
Gambling Song: 26
Hymns: (General) 1, 12, 22, 90, 125, 267; (to Virgin Mary) 8, 17, 21 (Parody 28,
    30), 96, 167, 226, 237, 244, 269, 272, 284; (to Fortune) 23; (to Nature) 18; (to
    Sleep) 39
Ill-Married Song: 118, 137, 207
Marinha: 230–232
Panegyrics: 213, 216, 218–220
Pastourelle, Pastoreta: Latin 14; Prov. 51, 52, 89; Ital. 104; N.F. 134, 160; Ger. 195;
    Iber. 241, 243
Pilgrim Song: 5
Planctus, Planh: See *Death Song*
Pleasure Song (Plazer): 69, 71, 79, 120–122
Riddle Poem (Devinalh): Prov. 44, 46, 54, 61, 62; Ger. 198; Eng. 265, 270, 273,
    276, 277, 282, 283
Rondeau: 145–146, 148, 150, 152–159, 161–162
Satire (Sirventes, Tenzone, Spruch): Prov. 49, 68, 70, 84–87; Ital. 97, 100, 115, 116,
    117, 119; Ger. 180, 181, 191; Iber. 225, 235; Brit. 253, 263, 279
Serrana: 241, 243

The Garland Library
of Medieval Literature

General Editors: James J. Wilhelm
Lowry Nelson, Jr.

Series A (Texts and Translations); Series B (Translations Only)

1. Chrétien de Troyes: *Lancelot, or The Knight of the Cart.* Edited and translated by William W. Kibler. Series A.
2. Brunetto Latini: *Il Tesoretto (The Little Treasure).* Edited and translated by Julia Bolton Holloway. Series A.
3. *The Poetry of Arnaut Daniel.* Edited and translated by James J. Wilhelm. Series A.
4. *The Poetry of William VII, Count of Poitiers, IX Duke of Aquitaine.* Edited and translated by Gerald A. Bond; music edited by Hendrik van der Werf. Series A.
5. *The Poetry of Cercamon and Jaufre Rudel.* Edited and translated by George Wolf and Roy Rosenstein; music edited by Hendrik van der Werf. Series A.
6. *The Vidas of the Troubadours.* Translated by Margarita Egan. Series B.
7. *Medieval Latin Poems of Male Love and Friendship.* Translated by Thomas Stehling. Series A.
8. *Barthar Saga.* Edited and translated by Jon Skaptason and Phillip Pulsiano. Series A.
9. Guillaume de Machaut: *Judgment of the King of Bohemia (Le Jugement dou Roy de Behaingne).* Edited and translated by R. Barton Palmer. Series A.
10. *Three Lives of the Last Englishmen.* Translated by Michael Swanton. Series B.
11. Giovanni Boccaccio: *Eclogues.* Edited and translated by Janet Smarr. Series A.
12. Hartmann von Aue: *Erec.* Translated by Thomas L. Keller. Series B.
13. *Waltharius* and *Ruodlieb.* Edited and translated by Dennis M. Kratz. Series A.
14. *The Writings of Medieval Women.* Translated by Marcelle Thiébaux. Series B.
15. *The Rise of Gawain, Nephew of Arthur (De ortu Waluuanii Nepotis Arturi).* Edited and translated by Mildred Leake Day. Series A.
16, 17. *The French Fabliau: B.N. 837.* Edited and translated by Raymond Eichmann and John DuVal. Series A.
18. *The Poetry of Guido Cavalcanti.* Edited and translated by Lowry Nelson, Jr. Series A.
19. Hartmann von Aue: *Iwein.* Edited and translated by Patrick M. McConeghy. Series A.
20. *Seven Medieval Latin Comedies.* Translated by Alison Goddard Elliott. Series B.
21. Christine de Pizan: *The Epistle of the Prison of Human Life.* Edited and translated by Josette A. Wisman. Series A.
22. *The Poetry of the Sicilian School.* Edited and translated by Frede Jensen. Series A.
23. *The Poetry of Cino da Pistoia.* Edited and translated by Christopher Kleinhenz. Series A.
24. *The Lyrics and Melodies of Adam de la Halle.* Lyrics edited and translated by Deborah Hubbard Nelson; music edited by Hendrik van der Werf. Series A.
25. Chrétien de Troyes: *Erec and Enide.* Edited and translated by Carleton W. Carroll. Series A.
26. *Three Ovidian Tales of Love.* Edited and translated by Raymond J. Cormier. Series A.
27. *The Poetry of Guido Guinizelli.* Edited and translated by Robert Edwards. Series A.
28. Wernher der Gartenaere: *Helmbrecht.* Edited by Ulrich Seelbach; introduced and translated by Linda B. Parshall. Series A.

29. *Five Middle English Arthurian Romances.* Translated by Valerie Krishna. Series B.
30. *Les Cent nouvelles nouvelles.* Translated by Judith Bruskin Diner. Series B.
31. Gerald of Wales (Giraldus Cambrensis): *The Life of St. Hugh of Avalon.* Edited and translated by Richard M. Loomis. Series A.
32. *L'Art d'Amours (The Art of Love).* Translated by Lawrence Blonquist. Series B.
33. Giovanni Boccaccio: *L'Ameto.* Translated by Judith Serafini-Sauli. Series B.
34, 35. *The Medieval Pastourelle.* Selected, translated, and edited in part by William D. Paden, Jr. Series A.
36. Béroul: *The Romance of Tristran.* Edited and translated by Norris J. Lacy. Series A.
37. *Graelent* and *Guingamor*: Two Breton Lays. Edited and translated by Russell Weingartner. Series A.
38. Heinrich von Veldeke: *Eneit.* Translated by J. Welsey Thomas. Series B.
39. *The Lyrics and Melodies of Grace Brulé.* Edited and translated by Samuel Rosenberg and Samuel Danon; music edited by Hendrik van der Werf. Series A.
40. Giovanni Boccaccio: *Life of Dante (Trattatello in Laude di Dante).* Translated by Vincenzo Bollettino. Series B.
41. *The Lyrics of Thibaut de Champagne.* Edited and translated by Kathleen J. Brahney. Series A.
42. *The Poetry of Sordello.* Edited and translated by James J. Wilhelm. Series A.
43. Giovanni Boccaccio: *Il Filocolo.* Translated by Donald S. Cheney with the collaboration of Thomas G. Bergin. Series B.
44. *Le Roman de Thèbes (The Story of Thebes).* Translated by John Smartt Coley. Series B.
45. Guillaume de Machaut: *The Judgment of the King of Navarre (Le Jugement dou Roy de Navarre).* Translated and edited by R. Barton Palmer. Series A.
46. *The French Chansons of Charles D'Orléans.* With the Corresponding Middle English Chansons. Edited and translated by Sarah Spence. Series A.
47. *The Pilgrimage of Charlemagne* and *Aucassin and Nicolette.* Edited and translated by Glyn S. Burgess and Anne Elizabeth Cobby. Series A.
48. Chrétien de Troyes: *The Knight with the Lion,* or *Yvain.* Edited and translated by William W. Kibler. Series A.
49. *Carmina Burana: Love Songs.* Translated by Edward D. Blodgett and Roy Arthur Swanson. Series B.
50. *The Story of Meriadoc, King of Cambria (Historia Meriadoci, Regis Cambriae).* Edited and translated by Mildred Leake Day. Series A.
51. *The Plays of Hrotsvit of Gandersheim.* Translated by Katharina Wilson. Series B.
52. *Medieval Debate Poetry: Vernacular Works.* Edited and translated by Michel-André Bossy. Series A.
53. Giovanni Boccaccio: *Il Filostrato.* Translated by Robert apRoberts and Anna Bruni Seldis; Italian text by Vincenzo Pernicone. Series A.
54. Guillaume de Machaut: *La Fonteinne amoureuse.* Edited and translated by R. Barton Palmer. Series A.
55. *The Knight of the Parrot (Le Chevalier du Papegau).* Translated by Thomas E. Vesce. Series A.
56. *The Saga of Thidrek of Bern (Thidrekssaga af Bern).* Translated by Edward R. Haymes. Series B.
57. Wolfram von Eschenbach: *Titurel* and the *Songs.* Edited and translated by Sidney M. Johnson and Marion Gibbs. Series A.
58. Der Stricker: *Daniel of the Blossoming Valley.* Translated by Michael Resler. Series B.
59. *The Byelorussian Tristan.* Translated by Zora Kipel. Series B.
60. *The Marvels of Rigomer.* Translated by Thomas E. Vesce. Series B.
61. *The Song of Aspremont (La Chanson d'Aspremont).* Translated by Michael A. Newth. Series B.
62. Chrétien de Troyes: *The Story of the Grail (Li Contes del Graal)* or *Perceval.* Edited by Rupert T. Pickens and translated by William W. Kibler. Series A.